ESL/EFL TEACHING

Principles for Success

Yvonne S. Freeman

David E. Freeman

HEINEMANN
PORTSMOUTH, NH

Heinemann
A division of Reed Elsevier Inc.
361 Hanover Street
Portsmouth, NH 03801-3921
http://www.heinemann.com

Offices and agents throughout the world

The authors and publisher thank those who generously gave permission to reprint borrowed material.

Library of Congress Cataloging-in-Publication Data
Freeman, Yvonne S.
    ESL/EFL teaching: principles for success / Yvonne S. Freeman, David E. Freeman.
       p.   cm.
     Rev. ed. of : Whole language for second language learners. 1992.
     Includes bibliographical references (p. 277) and index.
     ISBN 0–325–00079–4 (alk. paper)
     1. Language and languages–Study and teaching. 2. Second language acquisition. 3. English language–Study and teaching–Foreign speakers.
I. Freeman, David E. II. Freeman, Yvonne S. Whole language for second language learners. III. Title.
P53.F73   1998
418'.007–dc21   98-26757
                                     CIP

Editor: Lois Bridges
Cover design: Jenny Jensen Greenleaf
Manufacturing: Louise Richardson

Printed in the United States of America on acid-free paper
02 01   RRD   5

To all the teachers of English language learners
and especially to our daughter Mary and our son-in-law Francisco,
who teach bilingual students, and our daughter Ann,
who is completing doctoral studies in bilingual education.

Contents

$\cdot\blacklozenge\cdot$

Preface

•◆•

When we wrote the first edition of this book, *Whole Language for Second Language Learners*, whole language was gaining widespread popular appeal among educators. Despite some confusion over what whole language involved, who it was for, and how to implement it, there was great enthusiasm for this educational philosophy.

Just a few years later, as we write this second edition, we still hear a great deal about whole language. By now, whole language is not a new philosophy. It has moved from the edges of the educational arena to center stage. Because public education in general seems to be under attack, it comes as no surprise that whole language is the target for much of the negative criticism directed toward the schools.

In the first edition, our goal was to present our understanding of whole language. We defined it by contrasting seven commonsense assumptions about education with a set of seven whole language principles. We saw our role as interpreters of this exciting philosophy. We gave many examples of whole language in action as we discussed each of the seven principles. Our examples were taken from classrooms where teachers worked with students for whom English was a second or third language. We feel that whole language is particularly good for such students, and with the help of the outstanding teachers we were working with, we were able to show how whole language theory could be translated into classroom practice for students learning English as another language.

As we revised *Whole Language for Second Language Learners* we worked in a very different sociopolitical context than when we wrote the first edition. Whole language is viewed by some parents, administrators, and teachers as the cause of every difficulty. Rather than being embraced as a solution, this philosophy of whole language, or at least some classroom practices associated with it, are being rejected. In this context, we see an even greater need than before for a clear explanation of what whole language is, who it is for, and how it can be implemented. As the number of Limited English Proficient (LEP) students continues to grow, so there is an increased need for an explanation of how to put whole language into practice with linguistically and ethnically diverse students learning English. Further, English is increasingly being recognized internationally as the most important language to learn for economic and political purposes, so there is an increasing demand worldwide for classes in English as a foreign language.

Originally, we wrote this book to define whole language practice and theory and connect it to methods of teaching a second or foreign language. Many teachers now have a good understanding of whole language. However, other teachers have inaccurate or incomplete information about whole language. As a result, some teachers and districts are not open to anything labeled whole language. However, they do recognize the value of following certain teaching practices based on whole language principles. All along, our focus has been on the principles underlying the successful practice many whole language teachers follow. Therefore, we decided to replace the term *Whole Language* with the phrase *Principles for Success* in this revision. This change helps us focus on certain key principles. These principles are based on solid research in teaching, learning, language, and curriculum as well as on research in second language acquisition, second and foreign language teaching, and bilingual education. What we referred to earlier as whole language forms the basis for the principles for success that we describe here.

In the first edition, we also used the term *second language learners*. Problems always result when we attach a label to such a diverse group as those learning English. One of the problems is that second language often refers to students learning English in the United States. In this edition, we expand our focus to include settings where English is a foreign language. Therefore, the new title ESL/EFL *Teaching* is more accurate.

As we revised, we attempted to keep the examples and explanations from the first edition that teachers said were helpful. At the same time, we added a great number of new examples and updated many of the references.

We retained the basic organization of the first edition, which devoted a chapter to each principle. However, because so much new research is available in the area of bilingual education, we have two chapters to discuss the importance of developing and valuing students' first languages and cultures. This expanded discussion of bilingual education reflects our recognition of the important role that a strong first language base plays in developing a second language.

Another major change in this revision: is that we describe the most widely-known methods used to teach a second or foreign language in one chapter, instead of discussing one or two methods in each chapter. This allows us to place each method within a particular orientation toward teaching and learning. Our hope is that this change makes it easier to review how second or foreign languages have been taught. We end this review of methods by suggesting that the most effective methods are those that teach language through academic content. Then we add a chapter in which we expand on the idea of teaching language through content, because this is an approach that is consistent with all of the principles for success.

We appreciated the feedback to the first edition from both students and colleagues. We hope that you will find this revision helpful as you teach. We offer these ideas on ESL/EFL teaching realizing that many factors contribute to student achievement. Our hope is that the principles we present will lead to increased success for both students and teachers here and abroad.

Acknowledgments

◆

This book was written because we have had the privilege of learning about ESL and EFL teaching from creative, concerned, and dedicated teachers. In this book you will read the stories of teachers and English language learners at many different grade levels and in many different teaching contexts. Although each story is unique, all of these teachers have the common goal of making a difference in the lives of their students. Many thanks to the following talented educators: Nancy Akhavan, Catherine Alba, Michelle Angus, Kay Armijo, Shiloh Bachelor, Steve Bell, Jason Cain, Carolina delaluz Cervantes, JoAnne Campbell, Julie Craig, Lorna Cube, Gina Daniels, Lonna Deeter, Steve Demeter, Rose Marie Dixon, Ann Freeman, Mary Freeman Soto, Linda Gage, Elaine Heune, Marilyn Hutchins, Charlene Klassen, Arnie Kriegbaum, Mike Lebsock, René Lebsock, Pa Houa Lee, Miriam Marquardt, George Mason, Linda Medel, Irene Muñoz, Sam Nofziger, Connie Patton, Teresa Calderón Parker, Michael Roberts, Zilda Rocha, Susan Rodriguez, Bunny Rogers, Kelly Rosales, Sonia Ruan, Andrea Smith, Francisco Soto, Mary Ellen Stuart, Diane Tew, Rhoda Toews, Nancy Triguerio, Katie Bausch-Ude, Vince Workmon, Denette Zaninovich.

We also wish to thank Marisela Serra, Esteban Cresta, and María Stanham and the teachers at her school, all of whom provided valuable insights into applying the principles for success in EFL contexts.

The principles we offer here owe much to the continued influence and inspiration we receive from Kenneth and Yetta Goodman. These dedicated educators serve as models for our work.

Finally, we offer a special thanks to our editor, Lois Bridges, who helped us conceptualize this second edition and whose support, encouragement, and critical comments helped shape this book.

Introduction

◆

*Children learn language easily and naturally, but adults find it hard
to learn a new language.*

For me, learning a language would be hard because I don't have an ear for those sounds.

If I learn a new language, I might lose the language I speak now.

*Learning English is easy for students who live in a country where English is spoken all
the time, but in the EFL setting, teaching and learning are different.*

We keep hearing statements like these. Are they true, or are they just myths? Is it easier for children to learn language than for adults? Do some people have a predisposition for language learning while others really can't learn? Does a new language replace the one you speak now, or can it be added? Are teaching and learning different for ESL and EFL students?

These are legitimate questions, and there are no easy answers. Yet, these questions are important because many teachers have students who need to learn English. Some of these teachers work in English-speaking settings. They may have many students who need to learn English or just a few. The teachers may also be trying to teach other things besides English—subjects like science, social studies, or math. Other teachers work in settings where English is a foreign language. Their students may be children or adults who want to learn English for a variety of purposes. These teachers are often charged with teaching English, and they are not expected to teach anything else.

This book is aimed at helping teachers who are teaching English language learners in both ESL (English as a second language) and EFL (English as a foreign language) contexts. Since students' ages and goals vary and because the teaching contexts, including the available teaching materials, are so different in different contexts, we can't offer a simple recipe to follow. Rather, we present a series of principles based on the practices of successful teachers we have worked with.

Many methods for teaching English language learners ~~are~~ *have* been based on commonsense assumptions about how a new language is learned. The principles we offer contrast with the commonsense assumptions, but as we worked with teachers, they recognized that the principles all make sense, too. Often, teachers commented that the principles reflect what they know works best in their own classrooms. They appreciate the principles because now these teachers can explain better why they follow the practices they do.

Over the last ten years, we worked with teachers in our graduate classes in Fresno, in classrooms, and at workshops around the United States, and in Mexico and South America. They provided us with many wonderful examples of how they put the principles for success into use in their own classrooms. We incorporate many of the practices these teachers shared with us into this book. We chose examples that reflect a wide range of classroom contexts. Some of the teachers work with young children, others with middle or high school students, and still others with adults. Some of the teachers work in settings where English is the common language outside school. Others work in settings where the only place students hear English is in their classroom. Despite this variation, all of these teachers found that they can apply the principles successfully in their classes.

A Note on Labels

One problem we faced in writing this book is how to refer to the students. We decided to use the term English language learners. We recognize that any label can be problematic, but this term focuses on one thing a diverse group of students has in common—they are all learning the English language. This term seems to fit quite well for both children and adults and for those learning in an English-speaking setting and those learning in a setting where English is not widely used.

There are other labels for these students. In settings such as the United States, they might be called language minority, bilingual, or limited English proficient. Each of the labels has its problems. For example, in many communities the language minority students are in the numerical majority. Many of these students are on their way to becoming bilingual, but in the early grades they don't understand, speak, read, and write two languages. A term such as *limited English proficient* focuses on the negative, on what students can't yet do, rather than on their strengths. Even the term *second language* does not accurately describe a student for whom English is a third or fourth language. Many students are linguistically and ethnically diverse. They are often multilingual with multicultural backgrounds. In fact, to avoid the misnomer of second language learners, some national organizations refer to these students as ENL (English as a new language) learners (Lessow-Hurley 1996).

Although we chose to use the term "English language learners," we realize that even native speakers are continuing to learn English as they go through school. One could say that any student in a country like the United States is an English language learner. However, students who enter school speaking a language other than English have as their special additional challenge the task of learning English. Using the term "English language learners" allows us to discuss students learning English in both an English-speaking context and those learning English as a foreign language in non-English contexts. Although at times we refer to students as linguistically diverse, limited English proficient, bilingual, or second language learners for stylistic purposes to avoid over using the term "English language learners," we want our readers to know that we, the writers of this text, are aware that labels are often inaccurate.

The Need for Principles for Successful Practice for English Language Learners

Teaching practices based on sound principles are essential for English language learners. The instruction that many English language learners received in schools was, for the most part, fragmented and dis-empowering (Valdés 1996; Cummins 1996; Miramontes 1997; Brisk 1998, Flores 1982). Teachers and administrators want to do what is best for all students. However, in settings such as the United States, teachers are frequently unprepared for students who come from different cultural and linguistic backgrounds and do not speak English.

Traditional methods have not worked well for English language learners. For example, in the United States, even among those who complete high school, only a small number go on to four-year colleges. In many foreign settings, students study English for years but never progress beyond a basic knowledge of English grammar. To reverse this trend of failure, a new approach is required. For many teachers, the answer is to base their practices on a new set of principles.

Commonsense Assumptions About Teaching English Language Learners and Principles for Success

All teachers make educational decisions based on their beliefs about teaching and learning. Because many educators have limited information about how to work with English language learners, instruction in their classes is based on a set of commonsense assumptions. We believe these assumptions limit students' potential (Freeman and Freeman 1989) In the following list, we contrast these commonsense assumptions with a set of principles for success. We believe that teachers who follow these principles will expand their students' potential for success.

Commonsense Assumptions	*Principles for Success*
Learning proceeds from part to whole.	Learning proceeds from whole to part so teachers organize curriculum around big questions.
Lessons should be teacher centered because learning is the transfer of knowledge from the teacher to the student.	Lessons should be learner centered because learning is the active construction of knowledge by the learner so teachers base lessons on learners' needs and interests.
Lessons should prepare students to function in society after schooling.	Lessons should have meaning and purpose now so teachers draw on student background knowledge and interests and give students choices as they involve them in authentic reading and writing experiences.
Learning takes place as individuals practice skills and form habits.	Learning takes place as students engage in meaningful social interaction so teachers give students opportunities to work collaboratively.
In a second or foreign language, oral language acquisition precedes the development of literacy.	In a second or foreign language, oral and written language are acquired simultaneously so teachers have students read and write as well as speak and listen during their learning experiences.
Lessons should take place in English to facilitate the acquisition of English.	Lessons should support students' first languages and cultures so teachers can draw on and develop students' strengths.

The learning potential of bilingual students is limited.	Learning potential is expanded through faith in the learner so teachers involve students in activities that build their self-esteem and provide them with opportunities to succeed.

As we worked with teachers who have English language learners in their classrooms, we found that when they follow these principles rather than basing their teaching on commonsense assumptions, they helped all of their students succeed. A brief look at each principle provides an overview for the chapters that follow.

1 Learning Proceeds from Whole to Part

Students need the big picture first. They develop concepts and the language to understand and express those concepts by beginning with general ideas and then filling in the specific details. Organizing curriculum around themes based on big questions helps teachers move from whole to part. English language learners need to know where they are going as they learn their new language. For this reason, preview and review in the primary language is especially helpful.

2 Lessons Should Be Learner-Centered

Lessons begin with what students know, and activities build on student interests. Teachers create contexts in which students can construct knowledge because they know that learning is not simply the transmission of information.

3 Lessons Should Have Meaning and Purpose for Students Now

Students learn things that they see as meeting a present need. Students are given choices in what they study. They reflect upon what they are learning and apply what they learn to their life inside and outside of school. In this process, teachers involve students in authentic reading and writing experiences.

4 Lessons Should Engage Students in Social Interaction

When students share their ideas in social settings, individual inventions are shaped by social conventions. Working in groups, students also learn the important life skill of collaboration. English language learners develop cognitive, academic, and language proficiency more easily in classrooms where teachers organize for collaborative learning.

Lessons Should Develop Both Oral and Written Language

Especially for English language learners, the traditional view has been that the development of oral language must precede the development of literacy. However, involvement in reading and writing from the start is essential for developing academic competence. Both written and oral language can be developed simultaneously.

Lessons Should Support Students' First Languages and Cultures

When students come to school speaking a language other than English, teachers can build on strengths by helping the student develop concepts in the first language. Full development of the primary language facilitates the acquisition of English; recognition of the first language and culture, even in foreign language settings, builds self-esteem.

Lessons Should Show Faith in the Learner to Expand Students' Potential

Teachers who believe in their students, including their English language learners, plan activities that show their faith in the learner. All students can learn if they are engaged in meaningful activities that move from whole to part, build on students' interests and backgrounds, serve their needs, provide opportunities for social interaction, develop their skills in both oral and written language and support their first languages and cultures.

Overview

In Chapter One we consider the different contexts for teaching English language learners. Teachers may be working in a setting where English is used as the wider language of communication or in a setting where English is a foreign language. The students may be almost any age, from preschool through adult. We consider the effects these contexts have on how teachers can apply the principles for success.

Then we review orientations to second or foreign language teaching. For each orientation, we describe well-known language-teaching methods. We conclude this review by presenting the orientation we feel is most consistent with the principles for success. Teachers taking this orientation teach language through academic subject area content. Chapter Two expands the idea of teaching language through content. We provide a number of examples from teachers working in different contexts who successfully apply the principles by teaching language through content that is appropriate to their students.

The remaining chapters examine each of the seven principles in detail. We look at how each one applies to English language learners. For each principle we describe specific activities in different contexts that could be used with all students but are particularly appropriate for English learners. Throughout, we emphasize the benefits of teaching language through academic content.

These principles are not a panacea. Following them won't cure all the problems that English language learners and their teachers face. In some settings, these principles may be difficult to implement, and there will be resistance to some of them. Nevertheless, we are convinced that teachers who replace the seven commonsense assumptions with the principles we have listed will provide all of their students with a better chance for school success.

ONE

Contexts and
Orientations

◆

Wood Land • Farm Land
Wet Land • Dry Land
Rough Land • Smooth Land
Low Land • High Land

The above contrasts are found on the first eight pages of the beautifully illustrated book, *America: My Land, Your Land, Our Land*. (Nikola-Lisa 1997). Fourteen artists, representing the rich ethnic diversity of America, illustrate the pages of this powerful book. It offers a wealth of opportunities for teachers working with English language learners in the United States and abroad to develop language and concepts through meaningful content. It can be used in different contexts with learners who have little background with English, as well as with those learners who have studied English for some time.

We begin this chapter with ideas for a lesson organized around powerful contrasts, concepts, and content (Freeman and Mason 1991). Materials such as the Nikola-Lisa book are particularly useful for teaching language through content because they can be adapted for use with students of different ages and at different levels of English proficiency.

Teachers always need to adapt lessons to fit their context and their orientation. In this chapter, we consider the contexts in which teachers of English language learners work and the orientations they take toward teaching second or foreign languages. "Contexts" refers to the different settings and different groups of students a teacher might be working with. "Orientations" refers to a teacher's assumptions about learning and teaching languages. Here are some possible adaptations and expansions of a lesson based on this wonderful book.

Teachers can show the pictures to the students and ask them to brainstorm what they see. For example, beginning students looking at the pages "Wood Land" and "Farm Land" might list *trees, leaves, green, animals, grapes, farmers, woman, basket, house.* The teacher writes these words on the board. Then the teacher asks the students to describe the pictures, using the words they generated. The teacher writes the sentences on chart paper. As she does so, she arranges the sentences so that contrasting features are made parallel:

The wood land has green trees. The farm land has grapes.

Then the teacher reads the sentences with the students. For homework, the students bring in pictures of farms or wooded places they have lived in or visited, then they talk and write about them.

More advanced students might describe the pictures orally or in writing and reflect on a place they know or an experience they have had. Upon seeing the workers picking grapes in the field, two fourth graders who were migrant children in California wrote the following poignant reflections (see Figures 1–1 and 1–2).

Teachers could capitalize on the contrasts in the book to have students discuss and write about social studies concepts. For example, they might reflect on the competing interests and needs of farm workers and farm owners, the need for water for city dwellers or for farm land irrigation, or the conflict between land developers and farmers. These topics might encourage further reading, collecting newspaper and magazine articles, and then presenting a program about what was learned.

Because each page of *America* is illustrated by a different artist, the book offers many art options. The beautiful artwork offers opportunities for discussion in comparison and contrast. For example, the "Wood Land" and "Farm Land" pages are in vivid color with realistic figures while the next two pages, "Wet Land" and "Dry Land" are done in pastel colors with people and animals drawn as caricatures. "Rough Land" and "Smooth Land" has colorful cut-and-paste art to depict people and landscape. Contrasts help develop language and concepts and offer teachers a way to begin to organize their classes in a way that draws on students' interests, uses their many strengths, and moves away from more traditional approaches to second language teaching. Students might want to write and illustrate their own books of contrasts about their native countries (or the United States) following one of the art styles. Teachers who follow the principles for success, listed in the Introduction, use materials such as *America: My Land, Your Land, Our Land* creatively to fit their classroom context.

Fields

I always used to ask my dad for money.

he told me one day I'll take you to work so you

could get your own money, I said "Yes I want to go work."

I woke up early the next day and mom was making

tacas to × take to work. now I know how hard is

it to get a dollar so now I don't ask for money
he told me one day I'll take you to work so you

could get your own money, I said "Yes I want to go work."

I woke up early the next day and mom was making

tacas to × take to work. now I know how hard is

it to get a dollar so now I don't ask for money

anymore because it's so hard to get a dollar but

my dad works his best so I could get a good education.

Figure 1–1   *Fields*

If I worked in the felleds, I can't Drink water
and use the Bathroom And my Back And feet And hand
will Be heartin Like ceSar chauez he was
a good man he worked in the felleds
for the Sumner.

Figure 1–2   *Works in Fields*

The following sections discuss the contexts teachers may work in and the orientations they may take toward teaching a second or foreign language. Each orientation is consistent with one or more of the methods used to teach English language learners. We provide a brief explanation of each method. Then, in subsequent chapters we offer additional examples of lessons that reflect an orientation consistent with principles for successful practice.

Contexts for Teaching English Language Learners

To a large extent, the teaching context determines the methods that a teacher uses. We focus on the principles that successful teachers follow as they plan their lessons because teachers must always adapt their practice to their setting and to their student population. Even though teachers work in a variety of contexts, they can teach effectively if they follow sound principles that apply generally to teaching and learning.

What are some key variables that determine context? Two of these are the role of English in the immediate setting and the age and goals of the students. One typical role for English is that it serves as the primary language for most people living in the country. Students will hear English when they leave the classroom whether they are on the playground, in a store, or in front of their television. This is the role of English in countries like the United States, Canada, England, or Australia. In this setting, teachers of English language learners are often referred to as teaching English as a second language (ESL), even though for some students, English is a third or fourth language.

Teaching in an English-speaking country is quite different from teaching in a country where English is not the primary language of most people. When students leave the classroom they do not hear much English, although they may be exposed to English on television, in popular songs, or at the movies. English does not serve these students on the playground or in a store. For that reason, English teachers in France or Venezuela teach English as a foreign language (EFL).

The distinction between ESL and EFL is not clear-cut in countries such as India, or in parts of Africa. In these countries, English may be the official language of government and education, but the native language is used for everyday activities. Even in countries where English has no official status, students may be motivated to learn English so they can attend a U.S. university. Increasingly, English is a dominant world language. Nevertheless, the ESL/EFL distinction is useful because of the difference in the total amount of exposure to English for students in the two settings.

	English is the primary language	English is the official language but not the primary language	English is a foreign language
Children K-12 multilingual			
Children K-12 bilingual			
College-age students			
Adult learners			

Figure 1–3   *Contexts for Language Teaching*

The second variable that affects the teaching context is the age and the goals of the students. Adult learners may need English for basic communication or for vocational applications. International students in universities need English for academic purposes. Children in public schools will receive most of their formal education in English and need English both for everyday communication and for schoolwork.

Even among school-age children, there is a difference between those in multilingual settings and those in bilingual settings. If a school has children who come from a variety of language backgrounds, then English language learners will probably be placed in ESL programs. However, if the school population is split between two language groups, such as English and Spanish, then English learners may receive ESL as part of a bilingual education program that includes instruction in their native language, Spanish.

Figure 1–3 represents the different contexts we have described. We recognize that teachers may find themselves working in any one or more than one of these arenas, and we tried to provide examples from each of them. Any method must be adjusted to fit the context, but the principles that guide successful teaching should apply to all the possible contexts.

Orientations Toward Teaching English Language Learners

Whatever the context, any teacher will enter the classroom with a set of assumptions, or an orientation, about teaching and learning generally and about teaching and learning languages more specifically. An orientation may be the result of the teacher's own language learning experiences, the teacher's formal coursework, or the teacher's past experiences in the classroom. In many settings, the available materials may also determine, to a large extent, the way someone teaches, and a teacher may simply adopt the orientation of the textbook writer.

At times, teachers just do their best without really thinking through the assumptions that underlie their orientation. Nevertheless, these assumptions still guide teachers' practices. They influence the kinds of materials and activities the teacher chooses. When we look at the history of foreign or second language teaching, we can identify different orientations that have guided the practice of many teachers over time.

Beliefs about how people learn and beliefs about language shape each of the orientations. In the sections that follow, we discuss these orientations by examining the assumptions about language and about learning and teaching that form the basis for each one. Also, we briefly describe the methods associated with each orientation. For more complete descriptions and for examples of these methods in EFL settings, see Larsen-Freeman (1986).

Early methods of language teaching took on either a grammar-based orientation or a communicative orientation. We begin by examining these two orientations and the methods associated with them. Even though we refer to these as early methods, they are still widely used today.

Grammar-Based Orientation

Underlying a grammar-based orientation is a belief in faculty psychology, which holds that different kinds of knowledge are located in separate sections of the brain. Mathematics, for example, might be located in one area, art in another area, and language in a third area. Students need to exercise each of these parts of the brain by studying different subjects. Thus, even if conjugating verbs in Latin does not serve a practical purpose, it might provide good mental exercise.

Traditional grammar forms the basis of this orientation. This is the grammar many of us studied in school. We divided sentences up into subjects and predicates and labeled words as nouns and verbs. We also studied different tenses and moods and learned to make subjects and verbs agree.

A set of assumptions about language and learning forms the basis for each orientation. The following assumptions characterize the grammar-based orientation.

> Learning a language means learning the grammar and the vocabulary.
>
> Learning a language expands one's intellect.
>
> Learning a foreign language enables one to translate great works of literature.

6

Learning the grammar of a foreign language helps one learn the grammar of one's native language (Diller 1978, p. 10).

In this orientation, study of a foreign language involves learning the grammar and the vocabulary of the language. This study is intended to expand the intellect. For example, students don't expect to communicate in Latin or Greek, but studying those languages is thought to be good mental discipline. The goal is to be able to translate great works from the classical languages into English.

Grammar-Translation Method

The method most commonly associated with the grammar-based orientation is the grammar-translation method. If you studied Latin or Greek in high school or college, this is probably the method that was used. Even though grammar-translation is not widely practiced in ESL contexts where young children are learning the language of their new country, it continues to dominate in many EFL settings for students of all ages. Native English speaking students studying modern languages, such as French or Spanish, may not be taught with a pure form of grammar-translation, but, especially at the high school and university levels, students usually experience some aspects of the method.

A typical grammar-translation book begins each lesson with a short reading, often about some place or hero from a country where the target language is spoken. This reading is followed by a list of vocabulary words taken from the reading. Students spend a great deal of time memorizing the vocabulary. Following the reading and vocabulary lists, there are often questions about the reading to be answered orally or in writing.

The next section of the lesson is a grammar point to be learned in the lesson. Grammar study involves learning the parts of speech, learning verb tenses, learning the difference between singular and plural forms, learning about agreement between subjects and verbs, or learning about the use of the subjunctive. Following the grammar explanation there are exercises for students to practice the grammar points translating from the native language to the target language and vice versa.

In a grammar-translation class, students study the grammar and the vocabulary. The goal is to develop the ability to translate between the target language and the students' primary language. For native English speakers learning Latin, for example, the goal is to translate Latin texts into English. Students also learn to translate English into Latin. This proves to be a more difficult (and less useful) exercise, but it is considered to be good mental exercise.

During a grammar-translation class, the teacher and students all speak in their primary language. English speakers learning Latin would speak entirely in English except to occasionally read passages aloud from short readings or works of literature. The focus of grammar-translation lessons is almost entirely on the written language. Students can eventually translate works from or into the target language. They are evaluated with tests of grammar and vocabulary as well as with passages they are required to translate. However, no real attention is paid to oral language development for communicative purposes.

Communicative Orientation

A second early orientation to language learning focuses on communication with native speakers rather than on translating classical literature. This orientation, dating back to the 1800s, was built on the work of Gouin who observed children learning language in a natural setting. In the United States, Sauveur opened a language school in Boston in the late 1860s using his Natural Method (Richards and Rodgers 1986). In these classes, lessons use intensive oral interaction in the target language. The communicative orientation is based on the following premises:

> The native language should not be used in the classroom.
>
> Students should make direct associations between the target language and the meaning.
>
> Language is primarily speech, but reading and writing should also be taught from the beginning.
>
> The purpose of language learning is communication.
>
> Learning a language involves learning about the culture.

In classes using this early communicative orientation, the native language is excluded. The teacher and students speak only in the target language in order for students to learn to communicate in the language they are studying. Teachers want students to associate words in the new language with their meanings instead of translating terms into their native language. The emphasis in these classes is on oral language, but students are also given exercises that involve written language. Readings and discussion often center on the popular culture of the country or countries where the target language is spoken. Thus, a student studying French from a communicative orientation might read and discuss French geography or history.

A method consistent with this early communicative orientation is the Direct Method, which is exemplified in the EFL setting by the Berlitz Method.

Direct Method

The Direct Method gets its name from the fact that students are encouraged to make direct associations between objects or concepts and the corresponding words in the target language. This method dates back to 1884 when the German scholar and psychologist F. Frankle provided a theoretical justification for the method by writing about the direct association between forms and meanings in the target language (Richards and Rodgers 1986). All instruction in the Direct Method is given in the target language, even at the beginning. No translation is allowed. Instead, new target language words or phrases are introduced through realia, pictures, or pantomime. Teachers demonstrate rather than translating to answer questions. A goal of the method is to get students to think in the target language.

Direct Method lessons are organized around topics, such as body parts, food, and clothing. As students become more proficient, the topics include many of the cultural aspects of the countries where the target language is spoken. Students learn about the geography, history, and customs of the target culture. In this process, vocabulary is emphasized, and grammar is only taught inductively. The students and teacher work together. Teachers ask students questions and students ask one another questions. Teachers work on pronunciation and standard grammatical form, but they help students to self-correct rather than correcting directly. Some natural conversation is included in the lessons, but students are asked to use full sentences to improve vocabulary and sentence structure.

The focus of lessons is on the spoken language. However, even though speaking and listening skills are emphasized, reading and writing are taught from the beginning. Teachers create situations in which students can communicate for real purposes using common, everyday speech in the target language. Students are evaluated through actual use of the target language with activities such as oral interviews and assigned written paragraphs.

The most widely known application of the Direct Method is in the Berlitz language schools located throughout the world. Though the founder, Maximilian Berlitz, referred to the method as the Berlitz Method, the principles applied have been, and continue to be, those of the Direct Method. Berlitz classes are generally for highly-motivated adults needing language for business purposes. Although many techniques developed for the Direct Method have also been used in other methods, applying the Direct Method in noncommercial schools fell out of favor as early as 1920 (Richards and Rodgers 1986). Reading and grammar-translation methods dominated public and university language teaching in the United States until World War II.

Empiricist Orientation

The entry of the United States into World War II brought significant changes to language teaching methodology because it soon became clear that grammar-translation methodology did not produce people who could use languages for real purposes. Ph.D.s in foreign languages could not serve as code assistants, translators, or, especially, spies! The U.S. government asked universities to develop foreign language programs in which students would develop conversational proficiency. This renewed emphasis on communication at the university level brought about the development of several new communicative methods.

Changes in beliefs about how people learn and insights into language led to the empiricist orientation to language teaching. This orientation is based on behaviorist psychology and structural linguistics. Psychologists at this time viewed all learning as a process of forming stimulus-response bonds (Skinner 1957). Meanwhile, linguists began to view language as consisting of certain structural patterns (Fries 1945). These insights from psychology and linguistics led to the following set of premises:

Language is speech, not writing.

A language is a set of habits.

Teach the language, not about the language.

A language is what its native speakers say, not what someone thinks they ought to say.

Languages are different (Diller 1978, p. 19).

Grammar-translation focuses primarily on written language, the Direct Method includes both oral and written language, but methods based on an empiricist orientation emphasize oral language because structural linguists held that oral language was primary and written language was a secondary representation. Communicative methods that come from this empiricist orientation follow the natural order of children learning a first language. Thus, students first listen, then speak, and only later read and write.

Behaviorists claim that learning involves forming habits, so they consider a language as a set of habits. Students in grammar-translation classes often failed to learn Latin or Greek. Instead, they learned *about* these languages. For that reason, those who hold an empiricist orientation insist that students should actually learn to use the language. This means that students should be actively involved in drills and exercises in the target language.

Structural linguists attempt to describe languages by recording what native speakers say. Often, textbooks or teachers prescribe a set of rules for students to master. For English learners, a rule might be "Don't use double negatives." Rather than have students memorize such prescriptive rules, teachers following an empiricist orientation might have students learn dialogues that include natural, colloquial speech based on current descriptions of language use.

During this post-World War II period, linguists used a method called contrastive analysis to apply insights from structural analysis to a variety of languages. These linguists realized that languages differed in significant ways (Fries 1945). It followed logically that when someone taught English to a Spanish speaker, for example, the teacher should be aware of the language contrasts and teach the parts that differed. Thus, contrastive analysis could be used to decide on what lessons to teach.

Two communicative methods that follow an empiricist orientation are the audiolingual method (ALM) and Suggestopedia. ALM is probably the most widely used method for teaching second and foreign languages. Suggestopedia is a somewhat exotic method that attracted attention in academic circles. We also include in this section a brief description of the notional-functional approach. Notional-functional is not really a method. We see this communicative approach as essentially a variation on ALM with a different grammatical base. We include it because many textbook series for both ESL and EFL teaching reflect a notional-functional approach.

Audiolingual method (ALM)

The audiolingual method was developed in response to the psychological and linguistic advances described above. In a typical ALM lesson, students begin with a dialogue designed to include a particular structural pattern. The exercises and drills that follow are all based on the dialogue. They give students more practice with the structure being studied.

In an ALM class, the emphasis is on development of the oral language. Accordingly, most of the class time is spent repeating the dialogue or doing drills. ALM teachers act like drill sergeants or cheerleaders as they lead the whole class, groups within the class, or individual students. A number of kinds of drills have been developed. For example, in a single slot substitution drill, the teacher might hold up a pencil while saying, "This is a pencil." Then the teacher would cue the class with the word *pen*, and students then chorus, "This is a pen." A more complicated drill would require filling two slots. After hearing the sentence "Bob is a teacher." and the cues "Betty, dentist." the students would be expected to produce "Betty is a dentist." One problem with such drills is that students may repeat the phrase without understanding it. However, the emphasis in ALM is on the syntactic patterns rather than on meaning. A good deal of attention is also paid to correct pronunciation.

Based on behaviorist psychology, ALM lessons are designed to give students intense practice with the language in order to form good habits in the target language. The theory holds that, with sufficient practice, the language structure will be internalized and come automatically. Errors are corrected immediately to avoid the formation of bad habits. Lessons are based on the structures of the target language and on the contrasts between the native and target languages. Thus, a Spanish speaker learning English would work on sounds in words like *girl* that are present in English but lacking in Spanish.

ALM was touted as a scientific approach to language teaching. It was developed by linguists and psychologists. Textbook publishers were quick to produce a number of ALM series, especially for languages commonly taught in high school and college. Although successful in intensive language institutes with highly motivated students, the audiolingual method has generally not produced fluent communicators. A frequently told joke about the method goes like this:

> A student who studied four years of Spanish using audiolingual materials took a trip to Mexico. Upon her return, she was asked how she did speaking Spanish. Her reply was, "Not very well. I kept waiting to speak Spanish, but no one ever gave me the first line of a dialogue!"

The story is perhaps an exaggeration, but the point is clear. Even though the efficacy of ALM has been brought into question, this method continues to be used widely in both ESL and EFL settings.

Notional-Functional Approach

ALM is based on the patterns of structural linguistics. More recently, a number of linguists looked at how languages express different notions, such as time or space, and different functions, such as greetings or apologies (Wilkins 1976). This new perspective on grammar has led to the publication of a number of texts that in some ways resemble ALM texts but differ in that they reflect this changed perspective on grammar. A typical lesson includes practicing dialogues and doing exercises based on portions of the dialogue. In this respect, a notional functional lesson is very similar to an ALM lesson. The difference would be that in the ALM lesson, the dialogue might be written to help students practice the present continuous tense, and in the notional functional lesson, the dialogue would be written to give students practice with time expressions.

A typical notional-functional lesson for high school and adult learners might include a dialogue containing introductions. Students would listen to the dialogue, repeat it, and then try out the forms in class by going up to classmates and saying, "Nice to meet you." The correct response, "Nice to meet you, too." would come back even if the two students knew one another before the practice with introductions. Later students might be asked to perform introductions for the rest of the class using forms such as, "Tony, this is Maria." Notional-functional lessons often include brief writing activities, such as completing a registration form or creating an advertisement.

Notional-functional texts are widely used in both ESL and EFL settings, especially with adult learners. Lessons focus on practical use of both oral and written language. The content of the lessons is different from the content of ALM lessons, but the beliefs about how people learn language are essentially the same as the beliefs that underlie ALM.

Suggestopedia

Suggestopedia was developed by Bulgarian psychiatrist-educator Lozanov (1982), who wanted to eliminate the psychological barriers that people have to learning. Stevick (1976) summarizes Lozanov's view of learning into three principles: (1) People are able to learn at rates many times greater than what is commonly assumed; (2) learning is a "global" event and involves the entire person; and (3) learners respond to various influences, many of them nonrational and nonconscious. Suggestopedia uses drama, art, physical exercise, and desuggestive-suggestive communicative psychotherapy as well as the traditional modes of listening, speaking, reading, and writing to teach a second language. The influence of the science of Suggestology is clear in this method that calls class meetings "sessions." In these sessions, instruction is made pleasant and students' aesthetic interests are aroused. Lozanov's (1982) goal is that "new material to be learned will be assimilated and become automatic and creatively processed without strain and fatigue" (p. 157).

Several characteristics of Suggestopedia distinguish it from other second language teaching methods. First, the physical setting is extremely important. Classes are small and students sit in comfortable armchairs in a semicircle. On the walls of the room hang posters from countries where the target language is spoken as well as posters with grammatical information such as verb conjugations.

Lessons begin with the teacher speaking in the students' first language. The teacher tells the students about the successful and enjoyable experience they are going to have. Students are told they will choose a new identity and a new name in the language they are learning. Baroque music is played as students close their eyes and do yoga breathing exercises to relax. The students and teacher then read the lesson to the beat of the music. Then students listen to the lesson and music with their eyes closed. In subsequent lessons, students role-play, sing songs, play different games, and make up skits to work with the material in the lessons. Lozanov (1982) claims that Suggestopedia has great success because students can assimilate a great deal of vocabulary. They can put the vocabulary to use, they can read, they can communicate, and they are not afraid to use their new language. Lozanov attributes the success of Suggestopedia to the use of many modalities. Besides listening, speaking, reading, and writing, students listen to music, relax using techniques based on yoga, and engage in role-plays.

In Suggestopedia the teacher decides which material to present, leads all activities, and is the center of instruction. In some respects, Suggestopedia could be seen as an enhanced version of ALM. There are still dialogues, but they are presented artistically by teachers specially trained in presentation skills. Students still do drill-like exercises, but they are seated in comfortable chairs. Unlike ALM, in Suggestopedia classes teachers take into account the physical and emotional needs of students so they can learn more efficiently. Despite these advances over ALM, Suggestopedia has not been widely adopted in the West. It is impractical for large language classes with limited resources. In addition, it would be difficult, in most places, to find textbooks or other materials designed for Suggestopedia or to find teachers trained in its specialized techniques.

Rationalist Orientation

New insights in psychology and linguistics prompted a shift from the empiricist orientation to a rationalist orientation. Chomsky (1959) argued convincingly that behaviorist psychology could not account for language learning. Meanwhile, behaviorism, which emphasized the influence of external stimuli on the learner, was being replaced by cognitive psychology, which stresses the importance of the activity of the learner. It's how the learner acts on the environment, not how the environment acts on the learner that really matters. In addition, it is assumed that people have many innate abilities that need to be developed. They are not simply blank slates or empty vessels waiting to be filled.

Chomsky also developed a new approach to linguistics called transformational-generative grammar. Structural linguists had described patterns in oral language. Chomsky argued that an analysis of what people say or write was not adequate. Instead, he showed that underlying the large number of patterns found in speech or writing (which he called the surface structure of language) was a smaller number of patterns at a more abstract or deep level.

Chomsky also argued that language ability is innate. Humans are born with a knowledge of those aspects of grammar common to all languages, and so learning a language consists of deciding on which parts of the Universal Grammar show up in the particular language people around us speak. This process is carried out subconsciously.

Learning a language is a natural process and involves developing deep structures and also developing the ability to transform them into the different surface structures. Thus, for Chomsky, questions and statements follow the same pattern at a deep level. For example, learning English involves acquiring this pattern and also being able to transform the deep structure pattern into different surface structures that serve as questions. This would not be directly taught but would come from authentic language use.

These new insights into how people learn and how linguistics works led to a new set of assumptions that shaped the rationalist orientation:

> A living language is characterized by rule-governed creativity.
>
> The rules of grammar are psychologically real.
>
> People are especially equipped to learn language.
>
> A living language is a language in which we can think (Diller 1978, p. 21).

When linguists say that languages are "rule-governed," they refer to an innate ability, the knowledge that a sentence sounds right rather than the knowledge of the kinds of grammar rules taught in school. Thus, native English speakers know that "big red balloon" sounds right, but "red big balloon" is somehow wrong. Even though they can't explain rules like this, the rules are psychologically real and speakers can use them to create new sentences or words. They don't imitate or repeat what they have heard. Instead, they use the rules they have internalized to create new sentences. Humans can do this because much of this ability is innate. We are born with an ability to learn language. That's why all humans, unless they are born with severe brain dysfunction or put in some highly restrictive environment, develop language proficiency. On the other hand, not all of us learn other things, like math, science or social studies. Finally, when we acquire a language, we can use that language for thinking. We have not simply memorized words or phrases that we are repeating.

Chomsky and others were attempting to account for the development of a person's primary language. Methods based on a rationalist orientation apply these insights to learning or acquiring additional languages. Four commonly used methods that are consistent with the rationalist orientation are the Silent Way, Community Language Learning, Total Physical Response, the Natural Approach, and CALLA.

The Silent Way

The Silent Way, developed by Gattegno, makes students responsible for their own learning and encourages learners to become independent of the teacher. The method gets its name from the fact that the teacher is silent much of the time. During Silent Way lessons, teachers model an expression only once, and then students are responsible for working together to try to reproduce what the teacher modeled. Gattegno believes that teachers should give students only what is absolutely necessary to promote learning and that students will develop their own internal understanding of the language they are studying as they work together with classmates.

Beginners are initially taught the sounds of their new language from color-coded sound charts. Next, teachers focus on language structures, sometimes using colored, plastic rods to visually represent parts of words and sentences. For example, for a noun plural, such as *boys*, a long white rod could represent the base, *boy*, and a short blue rod could represent the inflectional affix *s*. As students begin to understand more of the language, they are taught stories using the rods as props. For example, in a story about a little girl walking her dog near a park bench, the teacher might use a red rod to represent the little girl, a green rod for her dog, and a yellow rod for the park bench. At all stages of the method, the teacher models as little as possible, and students try to repeat after careful listening with help from each other. The teacher leads them toward correct responses by nods or negative head shakes.

Silent Way has been used successfully, especially with adult learners. It is a fairly complex method that requires students to learn the system of teaching (the charts and rods, for example) as well as the target language. This can cause problems in an adult education setting where students do not attend consistently or where new students enter at various times during the year. This method is also difficult for teachers who are used to talking as they direct class activities. It is hard for most teachers to remain silent most of the time. The idea of shifting responsibility for learning to the student is a good one, but some students may become confused and frustrated by the complex system and the silent teacher.

Community Language Learning

Community Language Learning is a method for teaching a second language that was developed by psychologist Charles Curran, who based his method on Rogers' (1951) principles of humanistic psychology. Rogers saw learners as a group in need of counseling and a kind of positive therapy. In Community Language Learning (CLL) teachers serve as counselors charged with facilitating learning. They join together with students to form a learning community characterized by an accepting atmosphere. The goal is to lower students' defenses and encourage open communication.

In a typical CLL lesson, students who have previously come to know each other sit in a small circle. The teacher/facilitator stands behind one of the students. This student makes a statement or asks a question in his or her native language. In a gentle, supportive voice the teacher translates what the student said from the student's native language to the language being learned. The student repeats what the teacher says until he or she is comfortable enough to record the new phrase or sentence on a tape recorder. This procedure is repeated with others in the circle until a short conversation has been recorded. Then students listen to their conversation, and the teacher writes it on the board. The textbook actually becomes what the students say in their recorded conversation. Students often copy the written conversation from the board to take home and study. As time goes on, students use more complex language and eventually come to need the teacher/facilitator less and less.

What is done with the language once it is written down is important. Often, this language is analyzed for vocabulary or grammar study. For example, if students use the verb *to be* in an early lesson, the teacher might isolate this verb for the students to conjugate and then compare it with a regular verb such as *walk*. In other words, once the conversation is completed, it may become the basis for direct instruction in grammar.

The curriculum in a CLL class comes from the students, but the curriculum is restricted by the fact that it *only* comes from the students. Lessons could be expanded on by the availability of a wide variety of resources, including the teacher, books, magazines, realia, and media. Students in CLL classes learn how to say in a new language what they already know, but do not extend their content knowledge. Another limitation of CLL is that there must be a low student-teacher ratio. In large classes, students would not get many opportunities to participate actively.

Total Physical Response (TPR)

Total Physical Response (TPR) is a method that was developed by Asher (1979) whose research suggests that we learn better when our muscles are involved as well as our minds. In TPR, students listen and respond to a series of commands. At the beginning, students are given simple commands such as "Raise your right hand." Students then indicate their comprehension by raising their hands. As students progress through TPR lessons, the commands become more complex. For example, "If you are wearing a blue shirt, scratch your nose." might be one combination command. Eventually, students begin giving the commands to their teachers and classmates. In some adaptations of TPR, students write the commands or follow commands that are written. However, the sequence that is generally followed is first listen and then speak, with reading and writing coming after students have developed oral language proficiency.

Commands are used as the basis of TPR for two reasons. In the first place, reliance on commands ensures the active involvement of students. Second, in English, the verb forms used for commands are in simple form. Students don't have to consider tense changes or more complex verb forms so long as they are responding to or giving commands.

One popular adaptation of TPR has been developed by Segal. Her book, *Teaching English Through Action* (1983), emphasizes the development of oral language. In her rationale for the book, Segal explains that reading and writing, "Come easily and naturally after considerable exposure to listening and practice in speaking." (p. 1). Although Segal does provide some context for commands by organizing them in a series around different topics to develop semantically-related vocabulary, she doesn't specify exactly what constitutes "considerable exposure." In fact, in her book of 102 lessons, there is no reading or writing at all.

Another popular adaptation of TPR, developed by Romijn and Seely (1979), also presents contextualized series of commands. Their book, *Live Action English*, includes reading and writing much earlier in the process than Segal's version of TPR. The following is a typical sequence taken from *Live Action English*:

Candle

1. Put the candle in the candleholder.
2. Take out your matches.
3. Tear out a match.
4. Light the match.
5. Light the candle.
6. Blow out the match.
7. Throw it away.
8. Put the matches away.
9. Look at the candle.
10. Smell it.
11. Blow it out.

A *Live Action English* lesson begins with the teacher setting out the props, perhaps talking about them while doing so. Then the teacher goes through the steps in the sequence, acting each one out and repeating the words as the students watch and listen. Once students are familiar with the sequence, they perform the actions along with the teacher, but they are still silent. Then the students are shown a written version of the sequence and may be asked to copy it. In the next step, the teacher performs the actions without speaking, and the students provide the dialogue. The teacher may stop at any point to work on students' pronunciation. Once students are able to repeat the sequence, they read the commands and the teacher performs the actions. Finally, students go through the sequence in pairs, one student reading the commands and the other student acting them out.

In their more recent book, TPR Is More Than Commands At All Levels (1995) Seely and Romjin expand the uses of TPR to include dialogues, role play, and storytelling. They provide a number of examples to show how teachers with students at different levels can use these extensions of TPR to provide comprehensible input. They include specific ideas on teaching verb tenses, grammatical features (such as count and noncount nouns), and idioms. One benefit of TPR is that it allows students time to develop an understanding of the target language before they are asked to speak it. Students also enjoy the game-like atmosphere involved in acting out commands. However, for most teachers, TPR is used as one technique with beginning students rather than as a complete method.

The Natural Approach

One of the most widely-used methods of teaching a second or foreign language is The Natural Approach, developed by Krashen and Terrell (1983). The method puts into practice the theory of second language acquisition Krashen (1982) developed. A central tenet of his theory is that we acquire rather than learn a second language. Acquisition occurs in a natural order when students receive comprehensible input, messages they understand.

In the original version of The Natural Approach, the emphasis was on making oral input comprehensible. In recent years, Krashen has written extensively about the value of free voluntary reading, which provides even greater amounts of input than oral language does. The written input from reading is also important because students can begin to acquire the academic language of texts.

Students are able to acquire written or oral language when they are motivated and not nervous. Krashen argues that the rules we consciously learn play only a small part in the development of language proficiency, but these rules can be used to monitor or check the spoken or written language we produce.

The Natural Approach has been adopted by many teachers. It is not an exotic method like Silent Way or Suggestopedia. The teacher's main responsibility is to make instruction comprehensible. This method is helpful to teachers because Krashen and Terrell outline the stages learners typically pass through and the kinds of instruction that are appropriate for each stage.

Early lessons in Krashen and Terrell's (1983) Natural Approach are similar to or actually incorporate strategies from TPR. In The Natural Approach, students move through four stages, which the authors explain are consistent with the stages children go through as they learn a first language. Lessons are designed to provide large quantities of comprehensible input and to keep the anxiety level low.

The following scenarios come from a promotional booklet for *The Rainbow Collection*, The Natural Approach materials produced to be used in elementary school. Each scenario in the booklet is presented in cartoon form to show how a teacher would conduct a typical lesson and how students would be expected to respond in that stage of The Natural Approach.

Scenario One: Preproduction—First Stage In this first scenario for the preproduction stage, the teacher is talking about the color of her eyes as she points to them. She also talks about the color of the students' eyes and has the students point to their eyes as well as other body parts. Students are then asked to point to one of the other students who has brown eyes or to name students who are pointing to different body parts. Finally, the teacher asks some yes/no questions about body parts, such as, "Is this my nose?" In *preproduction*, students do not have to talk except to name other students or answer "yes" and "no". They are encouraged to communicate with gestures and actions. Lessons focus on listening comprehension and build receptive vocabulary. TPR is often used as a strategy during the preproduction stage.

Scenario Two: Early Production—About a Month Later In the pictures for the second stage, or *early production*, the teacher is holding a plant and talking about the flowers and leaves. When she asks, "Do any of you like to smell flowers?" students answer with responses such as, "I do." and "Yes." As the lesson continues, students answer questions about the color of the leaves (*green*) and what we use our noses for (*to smell*). In this stage, students use one or two words or short phrases. Often teachers use either/or questions such as, "Is the plant green or brown?" The vocabulary required to answer the question is contained in the question. The lessons at this stage expand the learners' receptive vocabulary. Activities are designed to motivate students to produce vocabulary they already understand.

Scenario Three: Speech Emergence—Some Time Later

In the example for the third stage, *speech emergence*, the teacher is holding a picture of a boy smelling a flower. When she asks what the boy is doing, students answer, "Smells flower." and "He smelling flower." As the lesson continues, the teacher explores the students' understanding of their senses by asking, "What do our eyes and hands tell us about the flower in the picture?" Students answer, "It's white and yellow." "Leaves are green." "It feel smooth." The teacher may model correct structures in her response by saying, for example, "Yes, it feels smooth." However, the teacher responds to the message and does not overtly correct the grammar. In the speech emergence stage, students are speaking in longer phrases and complete sentences. Lessons continue to expand students' receptive vocabulary. The activities are designed to develop higher levels of language use.

Scenario Four: Intermediate Fluency—Still Later

In the fourth stage, *intermediate fluency*, the teacher is shown discussing several pictures that are related to the senses. When the teacher asks, "How do our senses help us?" one student answers, "We can know if something is hot or cold." When asked how our senses could tell us about the orange in a picture she is holding, students explain "I smell it." "I can see it. It's round and orange." and "You could taste it." At the end of the discussion, the students and teacher write a story together about their senses. At this stage, students engage in conversation and produce connected narrative. They continue to expand their receptive vocabulary. The activities are designed to develop higher levels of language use in content areas, and reading and writing activities are incorporated.

Although The Natural Approach follows the traditional sequence of listen, speak, read, and write, there is some recognition of the value of reading and writing. The authors state that "with adults . . . both reading and writing can be profitably begun during the prespeaking and early production stages" (Krashen and Terrell 1983, p. 88). However, the writing generally consists of copying commands into a notebook, and the reading is limited to recognizing key words written on the board. The authors warn of the danger of "supplying written input too soon" (p. 88). However, Krashen now recognizes an increased role for written language. He has conducted extensive research into the benefits of reading as a form of comprehensible input (Krashen 1993). He now advocates much more reading much earlier than is evident in the original description of

The Natural Approach. He also encourages writing for cognitive development, to help students become better thinkers (Krashen 1982).

It should be noted that methods such as The Natural Approach were developed to counter the emphasis that traditional methods, such as ALM, put on early production. In many second language classes, students were expected to produce the target language (by repeating words or phrases) from the very first day. By delaying production, methods such as The Natural Approach lower what Krashen calls the affective filter by allowing students to relax and understand what they are hearing, before being forced to produce the new language. The list on page 23 summarizes the Natural Approach stages as presented in *The Rainbow Collection*.

CALLA

The Cognitive Academic Language Learning Approach (CALLA) was developed to teach content to second language learners. It is an "instructional system designed to develop academic language skills in English for students in upper elementary and secondary schools" (Chamot and O'Malley 1989, p. 111). The rationale is that "learning a language has more in common with learning complex cognitive skills than it does with learning facts, isolated pieces of information, or even meaningful texts" (p. 112). The idea is that second language students will learn English through an organized approach to the content area materials they need to study in the regular classroom.

Three components comprise CALLA: grade-appropriate content, academic language development, and instruction in learning strategies. With CALLA, students first study content materials in science and mathematics because these subjects are least language dependent. In science, students receive comprehensible input through hands-on activities. Mathematics has an international sign system and somewhat restricted vocabulary. Later, students begin to work in social studies and literature, which involve more language. However, students are given a number of ways to use context for the content.

As students explore various content areas, they also develop the academic language they need. Because much of the academic language used in the content areas is context-reduced, particularly the language of textbooks and lectures, the input is made comprehensible through the use of maps, models, manipulatives, demonstrations, written responses, and discussions. As students become actively involved in the content, they learn the academic language they need.

The third component of CALLA, learning strategy instruction, helps students consciously develop techniques for working with content area materials. In the CALLA model, teachers first find out what learning

Natural Approach

Preproduction

- Teachers ask students to communicate with gestures, actions, yes/no answers, and names.
- Lessons focus on listening comprehension.
- Lessons build receptive vocabulary.
  (Reading and writing are incorporated.)

Early Production

- Teachers ask students to respond to *either/or* questions.
- Students respond with one or two word phrases.
- Lessons expand receptive vocabulary.
- Activities encourage students to produce vocabulary they already understand.
  (Reading and writing are incorporated.)

Speech Emergence

- Students respond in longer phrases or sentences.
- Teachers model correct language forms.
- Lessons continue to develop receptive vocabulary.
  (Reading and writing are incorporated.)

Intermediate Fluency

- Students engage in conversation and produce connected narrative.
- Teachers model correct language forms.
- Reading and writing are incorporated.

strategies students already use by interviewing them and having them "think aloud" as they do a task. Once strategies are identified, teachers provide students opportunities to practice them. Chamot and O'Malley have identified three major types of strategies, and they have developed activities for each type. *Metacognitive strategies* include advance organization, selective attention, and self-evaluation. These strategies help students plan, monitor, and evaluate their own learning. *Cognitive strategies* such as grouping, note taking, imagery, and inferencing, encourage students to manipulate content material in different ways. *Social-affective strategies* such as cooperative learning give students a chance to interact in order to ask questions and clarify the content.

A CALLA lesson is organized into five parts: preparation, presentation, practice, evaluation, and expansion. In the *preparation* phase, the teacher discovers what students already know about the content to ascertain the gaps in students' prior knowledge and to build on what students already know. In the *presentation* stage, new material is presented using different techniques to make it comprehensible. The *practice* phase allows students to engage in hands-on activities in cooperative groups as they go over the content. *Evaluation* may be individual, cooperative, or teacher-directed. However, the emphasis is on helping students to self-evaluate. In the final stage, *expansion*, students are encouraged to go beyond the materials to explore the content in other ways. For example, students might decide to interview family or community members about a topic discussed during a social studies lesson.

In a CALLA lesson, the goal is to provide students with different ways to practice language and learn content at the same time. Through the practice of different strategies, students are shown how to approach content in more than one way. The authors of CALLA have developed textbooks for secondary content area classrooms that follow the model. Many teachers find both the model and the materials extremely helpful as they work to teach content to second language learners. In many ways, CALLA is consistent with the final orientation we describe in the next section and with the content-based language instruction we advocate.

Sociopsycholinguistic Orientation

The final orientation is one we have labeled sociopsycholinguistic. We use this term because it includes both the social and individual psychological aspects of language learning. A number of different researchers have contributed to the formation of this orientation.

The view of learning is influenced by Piaget (1955), Vygotsky (1962, 1978), and Rosenblatt (1978). Each of them contributes something valuable to our understanding of how people learn generally and how they learn language more specifically. Piaget, for example, showed how learners pass through a series of developmental stages as they come to understand the world. These stages may be partly determined by biological maturation and partly formed as the result of the learner's experiences. According to Piaget, we develop concepts through a process of assimilation and accommodation. That is, we take in new ideas, and we change our concepts to include the new information.

Piaget focused on the individual psychological development that occurs as people act on and interact with the environment. Vygotsky, on the other hand, considered the role that other people play in learning. His is a more social theory of learning. In particular, he claimed that learning occurs when we are helped to perform a task by an adult or a more capable peer. What we can first do with someone's help we can later do alone. He also pointed out that we learn new things when we receive help with tasks that are just beyond our ability to carry out alone. What Vygotsky called the "Zone of Proximal Development" consists of the range of activities between what we can do alone and what we can do with the help of an adult or more capable peer. Teaching, he argued, should be targeted toward this Zone of Proximal Development.

A third researcher whose insights help shape the sociopsycholinguistic orientation is Rosenblatt. She explained that learning consists of transactions between a reader and a text. Meaning is not found in the reader or in the text, but rather in the transactions that occur as one reads. Both the mental text the reader creates and the reader are changed in the process of reading. As we read more, we have more experiences to bring to a new text, and those experiences shape how we understand the text at the same time that the text is shaping our understanding of the world. What Rosenblatt described for reading seems to hold equally well for oral language.

Piaget, Vygotsky, and Rosenblatt all offer valuable insights into the learning process. What about language learning? Chomsky argues that language is innate. We are born with the ability to learn languages easily, and we only need experiences with particular languages to learn them. Chomsky's view of language learning is similar, in some ways, to Piaget's view of learning more generally. Humans learn language with little conscious effort. In this respect, learning a language is quite different from learning most school subjects such as mathematics or history.

Chomsky's (1965) theories of linguistics help shape the sociopsycholinguistic orientation. These theories account for the individual psychological aspect of learning. Within a sociopsycholinguistic orientation, however, we must also consider the social aspects of language learning. For that reason, Halliday's (1977) theory of functional grammar is useful. Halliday is interested in the relationship between the different aspects of language and the social functions that different language structures fulfill. In this respect, Halliday's linguistic theory is more similar to the learning theories of Vygotsky and Rosenblatt. These researchers focus on social aspects of learning and on how language is a tool for learning and communicating with others.

The sociopsycholinguistic orientation is shaped by all of these researchers as well as by the miscue research of Goodman (1967), which provides insights into how learners use cues from three linguistic systems—graphophonic, syntactic, and semantic—to construct meaning from written texts. Goodman's writing (1986) also shows how his research and the research of the others whose work helps shape the sociopsycholinguistic orientation can be put into classroom practice.

We based the principles that guide successful practice on this research. These principles, which we listed in the introduction, form the premises of the sociopsycholinguistic orientation for language teaching.

Learning goes from whole to part.

Lessons should be learner-centered because learning is the active construction of knowledge.

Lessons should have meaning and purpose for students now.

Learning occurs in social interaction.

Reading, writing, speaking, and listening all develop together.

Lessons should support students' first languages and cultures.

Faith in the learner expands learning potential.

In subsequent chapters, we discuss each of these principles in detail. Two methods that are consistent with a sociopsycholinguistic orientation are *problem posing* and *content-based language teaching*.

Problem Posing

Problem Posing (Wallerstein 1987) was developed by Paulo Freire (Freire 1970) to help teach literacy to adults. In this method, the teacher first listens to the students and assesses their situation to help them determine the things that truly concern them. The teacher then chooses a code (a picture, a story, a song, etc.) to present to students to help them take an objective look at their personal experiences and concerns, the problems they have posed. For example, the teacher might show students a snapshot that depicts the substandard housing in the neighborhood where they live. The students meet in small groups that Freire calls culture circles to discuss the picture. In the process, they identify or "pose" what they perceive as a problem. Through their collective dialogue in the culture circles, they plan for social action to improve their situation.

In discussing their situation and planning social action, students learning a second language can use the target language to solve a real problem. Younger students might deal with a problem such as lack of playground space. High school or college students might tackle the problems presented by drug dealers on campus. Adult students could consider the effects welfare programs have on members of their community.

Problem Posing is consistent with the principles that underlie successful practice. The following list shows how aspects of Problem Posing correspond to the principles.

Principles for Success	Problem Posing
Learning goes from whole to part	The code is a whole story, picture, or film.
Classes should be learner-centered.	The code is based on the learners' lives.
Learning should be meaningful and purposeful.	Learners identify and solve real-life problems.
Learning takes place in social interaction.	Learners work collaboratively to solve community problems.
Reading, writing, speaking, and listening all develop together.	Students move from talking to reading and writing about problems.
Lessons should support students' first languages and cultures.	Lessons build on the cultural and linguistic backgrounds of the learners.
Faith in the learner expands learning potential.	The goal is to empower learners—to develop their faith in themselves.

Problem Posing provides appropriate social content for adult learners. In this respect, students in a Problem Posing class learn language through content. Creative teachers use problem posing even with beginners, but less guidance is available for this method than for other methods. In a later chapter, we provide an extended example of a lesson based on Problem Posing.

Content-Based Language Teaching

In a sense, any method of teaching a language could be called content-based. The difference between other methods we have described and what we are calling content-based instruction is that the content studied in traditional methods is really the target language itself. This is clearly the case with grammar translation. Students study the grammar and the vocabulary of the target language. In the Direct Method, the content includes the culture of the people who speak the target language, but no academic content. The content for ALM, Silent Way, and the other methods is also limited to the culture of speakers of the language, but the language itself is really the content of the class.

The Natural Approach has been used more recently to teach content even though, originally, most applications focused on developing vocabulary. CALLA is also designed for teaching language through content. Most materials developed for CALLA have one or two sample chapters that show how to teach each content area. For example, there might be a chapter on biology and another on social studies. Teachers can use the CALLA principles and lesson format to create additional lessons for the content area they teach.

Content-based language teaching is a dual approach in which teachers teach language through content. To do this, they must be aware of both the academic and language needs of their students. If a teacher is teaching math or science to English language learners, depending on the students' English proficiency and their academic preparation, the teacher will focus more on either language or the academic subject. But, in every situation, the teacher must be aware that he or she is teaching both academic content and language.

For adult learners, the content for their classes may be primarily social. This is the case with Problem Posing where students investigate social problems that affect them directly. Other adult learners may study English for specific purposes, such as English for engineering or for medical studies. Classes for business people learning English in an EFL setting might use aspects of business as the content.

Conclusion

We began this chapter by considering the different contexts that teachers of English language learners may encounter. The context for language teaching includes a number of factors. Two that we highlighted were the role of English in the setting and the ages and goals of the students. There is a clear difference between teaching English in a setting where English is the language most commonly used outside the school and a setting where students hear little or no English once they leave the language class. Similarly, teachers have to take their students' ages and goals into account when planning lessons.

We also reviewed different orientations toward language teaching. We consider an orientation to be a set of assumptions about teaching and learning generally and about teaching and learning languages more specifically. For each orientation, we listed and explained the basic assumptions. Then we described traditional methods consistent with each orientation. The following list displays in chart form the methods associated with each orientation.

Orientation	Methods
Grammar-Based	Grammar Translation
Communicative	Direct Method
Empiricist	Notational-Functional Approach
	Audiolingual Method
	Suggestopedia
Rationalist	Silent Way
	Community Language Learning
	Total Physical Response
	Natural Approach
	CALLA
Sociopsycholinguistic	Problem Posing
	Content-Based Language Teaching

Our focus in this book is on content-based language teaching from a sociopsycholinguistic orientation. In the next chapter, we review the development of the idea of teaching language through content, and we give examples of content-based language lessons. Then, in subsequent chapters, we provide additional examples of lessons in which teachers working in different contexts teach language through content. Each of these chapters focuses on one of the principles for successful practice.

TWO

Teaching Language Through Content

◆

"How many of you eat tamales?" Juan Carlos asked the intermediate level students in his adult EFL class in Medellín, Colombia. Most of his students were business people who studied English grammar in secondary school and were trying to improve their English for the workplace. They came to his class two evenings a week, and although they arrived tired, they were always interested and eager to use their second language.

In answer to his question, most of his students nodded or raised their hands. "Now, the important question is, 'What kind of tamales do you like?'" asked Juan Carlos. "Tamales *antioqueños*," shouted some. "No, profesor, tamales *tolimenses*," called out others. Two smaller groups protested that their favorites were "tamales *santanderianos*" and "tamales *santafereños*." The different types of tamales represent different regions of Colombia, so Juan Carlos asked students to form groups according to the type of tamale they chose and to write in English a description of the tamale. As students discussed, they wrote down ingredients, preparation, and words such as "delicious" and "spicy."

Then, students from each group read their descriptions. Next, Juan Carlos drew four columns on the board and wrote the name one of kind of tamale on the top of each column. "Now, let's compare and contrast the different tamales." Students got involved as they began to compare ingredients, size, and taste. When they finished the comparison, which included many good-natured claims about which tamale was the most delicious, Juan Carlos changed the topic by asking the students, "What other dishes are typical of this country and served on special occasions?" He wrote as students called out different dishes and foods including, *arepas* (a kind of thick tortilla), *empanadas* (a meat or sweet turnover), *sanchocho* (a popular soup), and *sudado* (a thick stew). This activity motivated students to talk naturally about which of these dishes, or ingredients in the dishes, they liked and which they disliked. So Juan Carlos gave the students an assignment, "For tomorrow, I want you each to bring me a list of ten foods or dishes that you like and ten that you dislike."

The following day students were divided into pairs. They interviewed each other about the foods they liked and disliked, asking, "What food do you like?" or "What food don't you like?" Then, Juan Carlos asked students to go to the blackboard and write down two foods or dishes they liked under "Likes" and two they disliked under "Dislikes." The class examined the list, noting several students disliked carrots and *chicharrón* and most liked chicken and *arepas*.

Next, Juan Carlos changed the direction of the lesson by taking out a world map and saying, "We have been looking at food typical of Colombia, now let's look at food that is not typical of Colombia, but may be typical of some ethnic groups living in our country. What different countries do we have restaurants for in our city?" The class brainstormed a list that included Japan, China, Italy, Germany, and France. As each country was mentioned, one student found it on the world map, and the class talked about whether the country was north or south, east or west of Colombia. For homework, Juan Carlos asked students to find or draw a picture of a food sold in Colombia that is typical of another country.

For the next class, students brought in pictures of French bread and French pastry, Italian pasta dishes and pizza, a Chinese rice dish, and even German sauerkraut. The students told about their pictures and named some of the ingredients. At the end of class, Juan Carlos gave the students a related assignment, "For tomorrow look around your house or in a supermarket and find one food product that has a label with writing in English. Bring that next week, and we will discuss it."

Over the next few weeks students brought in an extended collection of labels and other kinds of environmental print in English. They discussed not only the ingredients on labels, but the types of products that had labels in English, and eventually got into a discussion of the influence of U.S. economics and U.S. culture on Colombia. This led to reading articles from magazines such as *Time* and *Newsweek*. Students examined the U.S. political positions, including its position on intervention in other countries.

The contexts for second language teaching may vary, but from a sociopsycholinguistic orientation, the best way to teach language in any context is through content. Juan Carlos took what could have been a traditional vocabulary lesson on foods and drew his students into a series of related lessons on food traditions in their country and other countries. He continued the lesson with discussion of commercialism and politics. Juan Carlos was teaching English to his EFL students through content that was relevant and interesting to them.

Why Teach Language Through Content?

Halliday (1984) argues that children learn language, they learn through language, and they learn about language. All three aspects develop simultaneously in classes where language is taught through academic content. It is this idea of learning language through meaningful language use that is the basis for content-based instructional methods for English language learners. Because people learn language as they use it, it is logical to have them learn English as they study meaningful content, rather than to have them study the English language as a separate subject apart from meaningful content. Arnie, a foreign language teacher who studied language acquisition from a principled perspective, discovered that one of the main problems with his foreign language curriculum was that he really had no content to teach! Arnie realized that instead of having his students study the grammar of the foreign language, they should learn the language by studying topics related to social studies, science, or math. In other words, he could teach them language through meaningful content.

Brinton et al.(1989) present five rationales for integrating the teaching of language and content. First, this approach provides the language forms students need. If a student is interested in economics, the best way for a student to learn economic concepts such as supply and demand, is by reading books and discussing economics. As students study economics, they learn the vocabulary and language structures associated with that subject area. Secondly, even if the content area of study involves language that is difficult, students are more apt to be motivated to learn because of their interest in the subject matter.

A third rationale for teaching language through content is that this approach ensures that teachers build on the background knowledge of the students. Most students have some knowledge of the subject areas that interest them. Fourth, this approach ensures that lessons include contextualized language use rather than fragmented studies of usage. That is, students are involved with language in the context of authentic texts instead of doing exercises or drills on language forms presented out of context.

Brinton, Snow, and Wesche (1989) argue that for teachers to take this approach they must use authentic texts, those that are not specifically designed for language teaching but, instead, are written as literature to be enjoyed, or as informational material related to some subject area. Teachers select particular language structures or functions found in the texts to focus lessons on. This approach begins with learner needs and interests. It requires teachers to find creative ways to make content areas understandable for students whose English proficiency is limited.

A final rationale for teaching language through content comes from second language acquisition theory. Krashen (1982) argues that students acquire language when they receive comprehensible input that contains items slightly beyond their present level of proficiency. The input can come from reading or from listening. As they study different content areas by reading texts in English, discussing the content, and writing about the subject area, students naturally acquire English.

Teaching language through content is not something new. As Brinton et al. (1989) point out, most early language learning came when travelers or scholars recognized the need to learn a new language to meet daily needs or to engage in studies of texts written in foreign languages. In addition, teachers recognize that for students to fully develop their first language, study in all areas needs to include a focus on both content and language. In England, for example, the Bullock (1975) report stressed the importance of language across the curriculum. "A major finding of the committee was that first language instruction in the schools should cross over all subject matter domains" (pp. 5–6). In other words, every teacher was both a content area teacher and a language teacher.

In second and foreign language teaching, there developed a number of courses referred to as English (or more generally, language) for specific purposes. For adult students, many courses were designed to teach the language of a specific subject area. For example, engineers might take a course in English for engineers. Doctors might study the English needed to talk with patients and write prescriptions. This approach appealed to groups interested in specialized fields of study because the classes were directly tied to their area of interest.

Another example of teaching language through content comes from immersion education. In Canada, for example, young students learn either French or English in immersion classes. Teachers focus on academic content and use a number of techniques to make the content accessible to students who have limited proficiency in the language of instruction. In the United States, there is a growing interest in dual immersion or two-way bilingual programs in which all students learn a second language. In these programs, as well, language is taught through academic content.

There are a number of books that can help teachers to teach language through content. Figure 2–1 describes several recent publications that offer explanations of content-based language teaching.

Many books on teaching second or foreign languages describe ways to teach language through content. Not all books take exactly the same approach, of course. There are always questions about how much a teacher should focus on content and how much on language. Should

Brinton, Donna and Peter Master, eds. 1997. *New ways in Content-Based Instruction*. Alexandria, Virginia: TESOL.

Part One includes a chapter on the theoretical background of content-based instruction. There are sections on K-12 instruction; postsecondary instruction; and teacher preparation, assessment, and research. Part Two deals with practical issues of implementing content-based instruction in different settings, and Part Three has articles connecting content-based instruction with other approaches.

Crawford, Alan. 1994. "Communicative Approaches to Second Language Acquisition: From Oral Language Development into the Core Curriculum for L2 Literacy." In *Schooling and Language Minority Students: A theoretical framework*, edited by Charles Leyba. Sacramento: Evaluation, Dissemination and Assessment Center.

Crawford's chapter helps show teachers how to move students into content-area studies and provides a good explanation of how to help students develop academic literacy in a second language.

Enright, D. Scott, and Mary Lou McCloskey. 1988. *Integrating English: Developing English Language and Literacy in the Multilingual Classroom*. Reading, MA.: Addison-Wesley Publishing Co.

Enright and McCloskey's book contains many practical ideas for elementary teachers, including ways to organize the classroom for thematic instruction.

Law, Barbara, and Mary Eckes. 1990. *The More Than Just Surviving Handbook*. Winnipeg: Peguis.

This book offers many practical ideas for both elementary and secondary teachers of English language learners, written in a teacher-friendly style.

Peregoy, Suzanne F., and Owen F. Boyle. 1993. *Reading, Writing, & Learning in ESL*. New York: Longman.

Peregoy and Boyle's book is subtitled "A Resource Book for K-8 Teachers" and that is what it is. The authors offer good suggestions for teaching reading and writing across the curriculum for both elementary second language students.

Richard-Amato, Patricia, and Marguerite Snow, eds. 1992. *The Multicultural Classroom: Readings for Content Area Teachers*. White Plains, NY: Longman.

The chapters include both theory and practical ideas. The book has four sections: theoretical foundations, cultural considerations, the classroom: instructional practices and materials, and reading in specific content areas. This last section contains several chapters, each focusing on a different content area. The last two sections of this book, in particular, contain many practical ideas for implementing content-based language teaching.

Scarcella, Robin , and Rebeccah Oxford. 1992. *The Tapestry of Language Learning: The Individual in the Communicative Classroom.* Boston: Heinle & Heinle.

Although the title suggests a communicative approach, Scarcella and Oxford include many useful charts and practical ideas that would be easy to implement in a content-based language classroom.

Snow, Marguerite, and Donna Brinton, eds. 1997. *The Content-Based Classroom: Perspectives on integrating language and content.* White Plains, NY: Longman.

This book focuses on university-level content-based instruction. It offers a very good theoretical grounding for teaching language through content.

Stryker, Stephen, and Betty Lou Leaver, eds. 1997. *Content-Based Instruction in Foreign Language Education.* Baltimore: Georgetown University Press.

Books that provide examples of content-based instruction in foreign language settings are rare. However, this book shows how teachers of many languages (Arabic, Croatian, French, Indonesian, Serbian, and Russian among others) with students at different proficiency levels are using subject matter content rather than grammar to teach language. This is a practical book with many actual classroom descriptions.

Figure 2–1   *References for Content-Based Instruction*

teachers directly teach some grammatical points, or will students acquire the language as they study different content areas that interest them? Even though there is some disagreement on these points, there is widespread agreement on the value of content-based language teaching.

In fact, TESOL, the international organization for Teachers of English to Speakers of Other Languages, recently issued a series of goals and standards for students in public schools pre K-12. The second goal of Standard 2 is "To use English to achieve academically in all content areas." This goal states that "Students will use English to obtain, process, construct, and provide subject matter information in spoken and written form"(TESOL 1997).

There are good reasons and there is strong support for teaching language through content. The principles we develop in subsequent chapters are chosen to help guide teachers as they teach language through content, and all the principles work best when teachers are teaching language through content. This approach is consistent with teaching whole to part, centering on the learner, making learning meaningful, including all modes, creating opportunities for social interaction, and including students' primary languages and cultures in the lessons. This approach only works if teachers have faith that students can learn both language and content together.

We already described Problem Posing, an approach to teaching language through content designed for adults. The content for Problem Posing comes from the social concerns of the students. In this chapter we review how content-based language instruction has been developed in public school settings with elementary and secondary students. We also consider the special challenges of content-based instruction in settings where English is a foreign language.

From ESL and Sheltered English to ELD and SDAIE

Even though content-based instruction may be the logical response in a context where students need to learn both school subjects and English, it is a relatively new approach. As content-based language teaching became more widespread, it evolved. In the past, students with limited English proficiency were often pulled out of regular classes and taught ESL until they developed an intermediate level of conversational proficiency. Usually, ESL instruction focused on developing the social functions of language (greetings, requests, and so on) and everyday vocabulary (clothes, games, household items, and so on). Teachers used programs like the Idea Kit or the Rainbow Collection, which have pictures and small group lesson ideas, at the elementary level and textbooks published especially to teach ESL at the secondary level. However, the problem was that the conversational language proficiency students developed didn't prepare them to compete academically in mainstream classes.

When the responsibility for teaching English learners shifted to the regular classroom teacher, at least in the primary grades, no major problems seemed to surface. Lower-grade elementary teachers were often successful in involving English language learners in instruction because the techniques they use are often similar to those recommended for use with English learners. With young children, there is always the challenge of making lessons understandable and getting the students involved. Primary teachers are more focused on student development than on transmitting the body of knowledge associated with a particular academic discipline.

Older students, though, particularly at the intermediate and secondary levels, face greater demands to learn academic content. At the same time, teachers of older students often use techniques, such as lecture and longer reading assignments, that prove difficult for students with limited English proficiency. These teachers generally teach a single subject, and they see their job as teaching that academic content area, not as developing their students' English proficiency.

When we have worked with intermediate and secondary teachers, we have presented a list of suggestions for making their instruction more comprehensible for their English language learners (see the following list). The focus on using techniques to make input comprehensible is an important one. It is based on the theory of second language acquisition developed by Krashen (1982). This theory emphasizes the role of input. Language develops naturally in humans when they receive messages they understand. This may reflect an innate predisposition in humans for language acquisition. The reason for teaching language through content is to provide the input students need to develop academic as well as conversational language.

1. Use visuals and realia. Always try to move from the concrete to the abstract.
2. Use gestures and body language.
3. Speak clearly and pause often, but don't slow speech down unnaturally.
4. Say the same thing in different ways (paraphrase).
5. Write key words and ideas down. (This slows down the language)
6. Use overheads and charts whenever appropriate.
7. Make frequent comprehension checks.
8. Have students explain main concepts to one another working in pairs or small groups. They can do this in their first languages.
9. Above all, keep oral presentations or reading assignments short. Collaborative activities are more effective than lectures or assigned readings.

We encourage teachers to use techniques such as those listed. However, these techniques apply best in situations where teachers are giving a lecture, and lecture is not the most effective way to help students develop academic concepts. Instead, students develop concepts and academic language most easily during collaborative social interaction. Both Kagan (1986) and Holt (1993) argue that second language students make significant gains in language, academics, and social skills and also build self-esteem in classes where they work together collaboratively.

If teachers take into account the importance of teaching language through content, making the input comprehensible, *and* getting students to work together collaboratively, a new view of curriculum emerges. Teachers can no longer simply use a set of techniques to make their lectures more understandable. They must also restructure their classrooms to ensure that students are actively involved in working together to solve problems.

Sheltered Instruction

In the early 1980s, the number of limited English proficient students in public schools increased, and both researchers and teachers recognized the need for programs that would meet the linguistic and academic needs of these students. Krashen and others developed a program model for older students that included a component called sheltered English (Freeman et al. 1987, Freeman and Freeman 1991, Krashen 1985). This model was designed for students at an intermediate level of English proficiency with adequate primary language academic preparation. In schools that use sheltered instruction, English language learners are taught some subjects in their primary language, some in sheltered classes, and some in mainstream classes. As students become more proficient in English, they are transitioned from primary language instruction to sheltered instruction, and then they are mainstreamed. For example, students might take social studies classes at first in their primary language. Later they take a sheltered social studies class, and eventually they are mainstreamed into social studies classes with native English speakers.

Over time, the term *sheltered* developed two different meanings. In some schools, the English language learners were put in one class. Teachers knew their students were not fully proficient in English, so they used special techniques to help students understand the academic content. Students were "sheltered" in that they didn't have to compete with native speakers. In other schools "sheltered" referred to the delivery of academic content, not the class composition. Teachers in classes with both native and nonnative speakers of English used special techniques to make their subject understandable. Many teachers found that this style of teaching benefited all their students, not just their English language learners. Whether second language students were grouped together for instruction or mixed with native speakers, many teachers began to reconceptualize their way of teaching.

Sheltered instruction is a step in the right direction because students' needs for content and for language are both taken into account. Sheltered classes help many intermediate and secondary students to succeed. However, teachers of sheltered classes face various problems. Some students are put into sheltered classes before they develop an intermediate level of proficiency in English. Many of these students are not at grade level in their primary language. As a result, teachers have to go more slowly or risk losing their students. Because teachers of sheltered classes are seldom able to cover as much content as mainstream teachers, they often sacrifice academic content to meet language needs.

In addition, many content area teachers who are asked to teach sheltered classes are not adequately prepared. A high school biology teacher, for example, might be given a two or three hour inservice on sheltered techniques and then be expected to work effectively with English learners. This is simply not enough time. In some schools, mainstream teachers coordinate with ESL teachers, but they are seldom given the time needed to plan together. Often, ESL teachers are not confident in their knowledge of academic content areas such as math and science, so that adds to the difficulty of team teaching.

Even students who succeed in sheltered classes often flounder when mainstreamed. They are generally behind in the content, and they have difficulty catching up because the mainstream teacher doesn't use the techniques that the English learner still needs. In fact, the real problem is that students simply need more time to develop linguistic, cognitive, and academic proficiency. Extensive studies by Thomas and Collier (1995) showed that students need at least five years to score at the fiftieth percentile on standardized tests given in English in different subject areas. Older students often don't have five years before graduation, and few are given five years before being completely mainstreamed. Primary language instruction is essential for these students, but it is seldom available. Sheltered instruction helps, but it can't make up for the time needed to acquire enough English to compete academically with native English-speaking peers.

Despite the research showing how long it takes for students to develop academic proficiency in a second language, the blame for poor student performance is laid on the sheltered instruction (and instructors). One of the main criticisms is that sheltered classes are "watered down." Often the criticisms are leveled by mainstream teachers. In essence, rather than rethinking the curriculum or attempting to adjust their own teaching techniques to accommodate students who are still learning English, these teachers blame sheltered classes. This "blame the victim" response surfaces regularly in the history of ESL and bilingual education. Such a response can't be expected to solve the problem.

A New Approach: ELD and SDAIE

The charge that sheltered classes are watered-down versions of mainstream classes has caused educators to rethink the goals of content-based instruction. Is the goal content or is it language? Should students in a sheltered biology class be learning English through studying biology, or should they be learning biology through the medium of English? It seems unreasonable to assume that students with relatively low levels of English proficiency can learn as much biology as their native English-speaking peers within the same time frame. Furthermore, it seems unreasonable to expect students without much primary language science background to succeed in a high school science class. However, it might be possible for students at intermediate to advanced levels of English proficiency who have an adequate academic base in their first languages to learn the same amount of biology as native speakers.

A good way to think about what might be reasonable for these two groups of students is to picture yourself going to Japan next week. If your level of Japanese is low or nonexistent, you wouldn't want to be in a sheltered biology class competing with native Japanese students. The teacher could use wonderful techniques to make the content comprehensible, but if she tried to cover the normal biology content, you probably wouldn't receive a high grade in the course.

On the other hand, if you have a reasonable level of proficiency in Japanese, you might succeed in the sheltered class. Of course, it's not just your knowledge of Japanese that would make a difference. Your success also would depend on how much biology you had studied in English. That knowledge would transfer over to the new setting. Success might also depend on your study skills and your test-taking skills. Collier (1995) pointed out that linguistic, cognitive, and academic proficiency are interrelated. Students whose English language abilities are not highly developed can't be expected to do well in academic classes in English.

The problem with many sheltered English programs was that students with quite different levels of English proficiency and primary language education were lumped together in the same class. No matter how well teachers used sheltered techniques, they could not succeed with all types of students, even though individual students often did very well. This common situation led educators to distinguish between two kinds of content-based ESL instruction. The first type of class, English language development (ELD), is designed for students with lower levels of English proficiency and less primary language academic development. In ELD classes, the focus is on learning English through content instruction suited to the level of the students' academic background. The second type of class, Specially Designed Academic Instruction in English (SDAIE), is for students with intermediate to advanced levels of English proficiency and grade-level academic development in their primary language. SDAIE classes are content classes taught using special techniques to make instruction comprehensible. The primary goal of ELD classes is language development, and the primary goal of SDAIE classes is academic development.

ELD and SDAIE are similar. Both include language *and* content. However, there are significant differences. Figure 2–2 compares and contrasts approaches to teaching English language learners.

Some Considerations for Developing ELD Lessons

In ELD classes, the students are at beginner or low intermediate levels of English proficiency and/or are significantly below grade level in subject area background in their first language. For that reason, teachers provide first language support whenever possible, especially to help students with key ideas and concepts. In addition to using techniques to make oral input comprehensible, most ELD teachers organize the curriculum around thematic units. This helps students to develop needed academic vocabulary for different subject areas.

Teachers also choose materials carefully. Books with photographs or pictures and somewhat limited text are generally appropriate. It is important, however, to be sure that students do not perceive the books as "baby" books. Texts should include illustrations or photographs of older students. When teachers decide to use texts originally written for younger children, they give clear reasons for using those books. For example, students may practice reading the books for a cross-age tutoring time with younger students, or students could be encouraged to read the books to younger siblings at home.

Above all, ELD teachers allot more time to studying a theme or unit than they would take with native English speakers so students can begin to develop the vocabulary and language structures needed for the content area. By providing extra lessons on a topic, ELD teachers ensure that students have more opportunities to interact using the language associated with the content area.

Student Characteristics

ELD	**SDAIE**
English proficiency beginner to intermediate	English proficiency intermediate to advanced
L1 academic proficiency not considered	L1 academic proficiency at grade level

Focus of instruction and evaluation

ELD	**SDAIE**
Teach language through content with emphasis on language development	Teach grade-appropriate content using special techniques to make the language understandable
Evaluation focuses on language	Evaluation focuses on academic content

Most Often Used at

ELD	**SDAIE**
Elementary or secondary	Secondary

Some Differences

ELD vs. ESL	**SDAIE vs. Sheltered**
ELD is language instruction based on content. It is usually taught by the regular classroom teacher.	SDAIE classes provide grade-level appropriate content instruction taught by content teachers.
ESL may be based on content or the focus may be on some aspect of language itself, either the grammar or social use. It is often taught by a pull-out specialist.	Sheltered English classes are content-based but are often at a lower academic level than the corresponding mainstream class.

Figure 2–2   ELD *and* SDAIE

ELD *Lessons Around the Theme of the* Migrant Experience

Sue teaches a fifth grade ELD class in a rural school in the central valley of California. All of her students speak Spanish as their primary language. She wanted to draw on her students' background, and after she found several books about the migrant experience, she decided that a theme around migrants would be perfect for her students. While only a few of Sue's students were part of a migrant family, many of them worked in the fields. Many had relatives who were migrant workers. Several students had been in California for only a short time and had little schooling in their native rural Mexico.

Sue began the theme with a book to inspire her students. The author, now a poet and college professor, spent some of his childhood as a migrant child in the local area. Sue first asked one of her strong Spanish readers to read the bilingual book, *Calling the Doves: El canto de las palomas* (Herrera 1995) in Spanish. Then, she asked the students to write down what the book made them think of; the students shared this writing in pairs. Students could do this initial writing and sharing in either Spanish or English. During the whole class discussion in English that followed, students eagerly described personal experiences that were similar to those in Herrera's book. Next, Sue read the book in English. She asked the students to notice the artwork in particular. After Sue read the book, students discussed the images and shared more of their experiences.

The next day Sue brought in two more books, *El camino de Amelia* (Altman 1993) and the English version, *Amelia's Road* (Altman 1993). Again, she began by asking a student to read the book to the class in Spanish. Sue asked the students to notice the illustrations in this book and to compare these illustrations by Enrique Sanchez with those by Elly Simmons in *Calling the Doves: El canto de las palomas*. After the reading, the students were asked to work in pairs listing English words to describe how the colorful illustrations in the two books were the same and how they were different. After the pairs of students brainstormed, the whole class made a list of the descriptive words in English. Using those words, the students each wrote a paragraph description in English of an experience they remembered from their childhood. Because of the reading they had done, many wrote about experiences in the fields. At the end of the day, Sue read the English version of *Amelia's Road* to her class. The earlier Spanish reading, the discussion, and the writing activities helped prepare her students to understand more of the English text.

The following day Sue brought in another book about laboring in the fields, *Working Cotton* (Williams 1992). This story tells about an African-American family working in the cotton fields of California's central valley. The students compared and contrasted the three books they studied so far. Sue organized the students' ideas in a three-circle Venn diagram that represented the similarities and differences among the books (see Figure 2–3).

A last book that Sue shared with the class on this theme was *A Migrant Family* (Brimmer 1992). This book has photographs of a migrant family and tells about the difficulties of living the life of a migrant. Because there is more text in *A Migrant Family* than in the other books, Sue read it to her students in three sections. At the end of each section, Sue

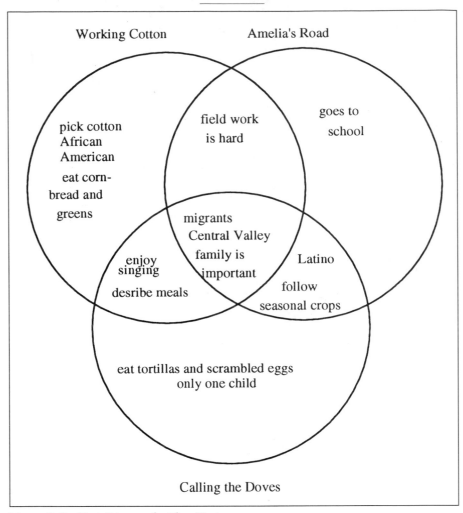

Figure 2–3   *Venn Diagram for Three Stories*

asked the students to write summaries and share them with their class-mates. After completing all their reading, the students decided they wanted to interview family members and friends who had lived or were living as migrant workers.

Sue helped her students to brainstorm a list of questions for their interviews. They decided to work in teams to conduct the interviews. The students got permission from the people they interviewed to publish something about them. Then, using the information they gathered, each team wrote a section of a class book on the topic of the migrant experi-ence. In most cases, the students conducted the interviews in Spanish, but they did their write-ups in English. The students worked hard on this project. For each section, they worked in teams to draft, revise, and edit. Also they went back and took pictures of several of the people they interviewed to use in the book.

The entire theme was extremely successful. Sue chose a topic that built on her students' background experiences. The support they received in their first language was just enough to help them bridge into using English as they wrote and discussed further. The students and their teacher were so proud of the book that they wrote based on the interviews that they shared it with the principal and parents at open house.

Sue's focus was more on language development than on content, even though this unit connected well with her social studies curriculum. She extended the unit to provide her students with many opportunities to use academic English for real purposes. The books Sue chose introduced vocabulary that students drew on to develop their questionnaire. The book project gave students additional opportunities for productive use of the language they were acquiring. Publishing the book for others to read, motivated students to learn English writing conventions.

Some Considerations for Developing SDAIE Lessons

SDAIE is the second type of instruction for English learners, especially for students at the secondary level. These classes are for students with intermediate to advanced levels of English proficiency and near grade-level academic development in their primary language. SDAIE differs from ELD in that the focus is on academic content, not on language development. Students must deal with the content and textbooks that mainstream classes use. SDAIE classes are content classes taught using special techniques to make the instruction comprehensible. In addition, teachers pay special attention to helping students deal with academic texts in English. This often means creating lessons so students can develop strategies for effective content-area reading.

SDAIE Lessons Around the Theme of the Migrant Experience

"Mi meta en la vida es ser un mayordomo en el fil" (My life's goal is to be a foreman in the fields). This is a response that Mary, a bilingual, high school English teacher in a rural community got all too often from migrant students. Mary explains a dilemma she often sees: "The biggest reason that these students have so much trouble in school is that people think they are proficient in reading and writing English just because they speak English. Once this assumption is made, the trouble begins." Mary knows that unless her students can achieve academic success and show to themselves as well as to their teachers that they can be readers and writers of academic English, they will probably drop out of school and take minimum wage jobs.

Like Sue, Mary also developed a unit on the migrant experience. The Hispanic high school students in her SDAIE English class were going to read *The Grapes of Wrath* (Steinbeck 1967). Mary wanted to help the adolescents understand the text and make connections between it and their personal experiences or the experiences of people in their community. She started by drawing on her students' experiences and, at the same time, helping them build background for the novel. She read the poem, "Border Towns" (Durán 1994). She put a copy of the poem up on the overhead projector and then asked students to write a reaction to the poem. Then the students discussed the poem in groups of three and shared their responses with the whole group. They talked about how it felt to be called a "wetback" and expressed their sympathy for the undocumented people trying to cross the border into the United States. The students also discussed a videotaped beating by policemen of undocumented immigrants. Recently, the videotape was shown on a local television station. Students also discussed the recent newspaper coverage of wage disputes among local farm workers.

Next, the students read "Salvador Late or Early," a one-page excerpt from Cisneros' (1991) *Woman Hollering Creek*. This description of a poor, gallant, rural Hispanic child who is totally ignored by the schools and Anglo society caught the students' attention. Mary asked the students to write their reactions to this excerpt and then discuss their ideas in small groups. While the reading and writing were in English, students could use Spanish in the small groups to clarify ideas. Then, the students picked out phrases and descriptive words that created powerful images. Each group wrote their choices on an overhead transparency and explained to the whole group why those images were so vivid for them.

The following day Mary began class by reading *Lights on the River* (Thomas 1994) the poignantly told and beautifully illustrated story of a migrant family. Mary chose this book because the illustrations and the text paint a vivid picture of the difficulty of migrant living. Then, she showed her students three other books about migrant life, *Voices from the Fields*, (Atkin 1993), *A Migrant Family* (Brimmer 1992) and *Earth Angels* (Buirski 1994). Each book is a photographic essay of migrant life. Mary had two copies of each book, so she divided the class into six groups. She asked each group to choose sections of the book to share with the class. The groups selected both photographs and text that conveyed important points. Again, some students used Spanish as they discussed their choices and prepared for their presentation, but they gave their reports in English.

Altman, Linda Jacobs. 1993. *Amelia's Road*. New York: Lee & Low Books Inc.

Altman, Linda Jacobs. 1993. *El camino de Amelia*. Translated by Daniel Santacruz. New York: Lee & Low Books.

Atkin, S. Beth. 1993. *Voices from the Fields: Children of Migrant Farmworkers Tell their Stories*. Boston: Little, Brown and Company.

Brimmer, L.D. 1992. *A Migrant Family*. Minneapolis: Lerner Publications Company.

Buirski, Nancy. 1994. *Earth Angels*. San Francisco: Pomegranate Artbooks.

Cisneros, Sandra. 1991. *Woman Hollering Creek*. New York: Vintage Press.

Herrera, Juan Felipe. 1995. *Calling the Doves: El canto de las palomas*. Emeryville, CA: Children's Book Press.

Steinbeck, John. 1967. *The Grapes of Wrath*. New York: Penguin Books.

Thomas, Jane Resh. 1994. *Lights on the River*. New York: Hyperion Books for Children.

Williams, Sherley. 1992. *Working Cotton*. Orlando: Harcourt Brace Jovanovich.

Figure 2–4   *Migrant Bibliography*

After their presentations and further discussion, Mary's students read Steinbeck's novel. Their reading assignments were not too long each night, and each day students shared (in groups of three) their written journal responses to the reading. Because Mary's students live in areas similar to those Steinbeck described and because Mary had worked to build background concepts and vocabulary before her students began the novel, they were able to make many important connections and to discuss and write about the novel, showing a depth of understanding. As a final project, the students chose sections of the novel to write up in play form which they dramatized.

Mary's SDAIE English class worked with the same content that mainstream English classes at their grade level were reading. The techniques she used to introduce the novel and get students involved helped them understand and appreciate a novel that they might otherwise have considered tiresome and irrelevant. Mary used a number of effective teaching strategies as she worked with her students to provide content-based language instruction. Her focus was on content instruction in the areas of literature and writing, but she also paid special attention to the language needs of her students. Figure 2–4 lists the books Mary and Sue used in their units on the migrant experience.

Elementary Teachers Teach Language
Through Content: Diversity and Nutrition

At the elementary level the line between SDAIE and ELD often blurs, especially in self-contained classes with students who represent a range of English proficiency levels and a range of levels of prior academic knowledge. In these settings, teachers find ways to teach both language and concepts by organizing curriculum around themes. By building on student interests and experiences, teachers help students move beyond their present level of proficiency in English while they are learning academic language and concepts. At this level, it is more useful to refer to SDAIE or ELD students rather than classes. Whenever possible, teachers allow students to respond to assignments in different ways, and they base their evaluation more on content knowledge for SDAIE students and more on language development for ELD students, even though both groups are learning both language and content.

Roberto is a third grade bilingual teacher who teaches much of the content and reading in his class in Spanish. However, he knows that his students need to transition to an all English classroom soon. He also knows that their ability to read, write, and speak Spanish helps them as they study in English. His unit on "Diversity and Nutrition" is an example of how he carefully chooses materials and topics that help his students develop academic concepts and linguistic proficiency in English. Like Juan Carlos, whose cultural food lesson was described at the beginning of this chapter, Roberto avoids teaching traditional lists of English words or having students memorize dialogues about foods. Instead, he involves students in analyzing the eating habits of a variety of cultural groups.

To introduce a unit on nutrition and to encourage students to begin talking about the topic of the food traditions of different cultures, Roberto read El sancocho del sábado (Torres 1995) (Saturday Sancocho) to his third grade students. Then, he asked them if they had eaten a dish like the sancocho described in the book. Some students explained that their families prepared sancocho but their sancocho had some different ingredients. Other students enthusiastically described ingredients and preparation of stews and soups their relatives served, including typical Mexican stews like posole and menudo. To stimulate further discussion of traditional foods, Roberto read Todos cocinan arroz (Dooley 1993) (Everybody Cooks Rice) to his class. This reading stimulated lively discussion as students talked about their favorite rice dishes.

As the discussion in Spanish progressed, some of the students complained that they did not like certain dishes or particular ingredients within them. Then, Roberto moved the discussion to English and read the students "In the mood for a favorite food," one of the playful poems from the collection, *What's on the Menu?* (Goldstein 1995). The students brainstormed in English a list of foods they liked and did not like. Next, students interviewed one another about those foods, asking which they liked and which they disliked. Then, they graphed the class results following a suggested math activity from the *Descubrimiento/ Finding Out*, (Santillana 1986) program, "Diagramando lo que te gusta"(Diagramming What You Like).

Because spaghetti came up often as a favorite food, the students and the teacher looked for stories and poetry about pasta. They sang, "On Top of Spaghetti" using the big book (Tillotson 1997) and enthusiastically repeated together the Jack Prelutsky poem, "Spaghetti! Spaghetti!" (Prelutsky 1996). Two students also located two more poems from *What's on the Menu?* that were about pasta, "Italian Noodles" and "Ready for Spaghetti."

Next, Roberto showed the students a large poster of the food pyramid. He asked students to look at the pyramid, talk together in pairs, and then tell him what they noticed. Students immediately pointed out that pasta was at the bottom and "You should eat lots of bread and pasta." They also pointed out that the pyramid showed "You shouldn't eat too much greasy or sweet stuff." Roberto asked the students to think about spaghetti and traditional dishes like *sancocho* and *posole* and decide if they were nutritious or not. Students noted that all the dishes included different sections of the food pyramid. Several students added that they ate bread or tortillas with their *posole* or spaghetti.

Because bread can be an ideal topic to get at the idea of the rich diversity in eating, Roberto read his students the big book version of *Bread, Bread, Bread* (Morris 1989). Students were interested to see different shapes of loaves of bread, tortillas, French bread, and even pretzels and pizza among the photographs of breads eaten around the world. The teacher also put up a poster, "Los panes del mundo" (Breads of the World) for students to look at and discuss.

Roberto's goal for this discussion of the varieties of bread people eat was to have his students begin to understand the value of their different eating customs and the eating customs of others. To further this discussion about different eating customs around the world, the class read *Good Morning, Let's Eat* (Badt 1994), a book rich in photographs that tells what people eat for breakfast all over the world. They also read "Sandwiches around the world," an excerpt taken from, *Crayola Kids*, a children's magazine.

Using the English version of *Todos cocinan arroz* (Dooley 1993), *Everybody Cooks Rice* (Dooley 1991), Roberto continued with the theme of eating around the world. In the book, the main character goes from house to house, and in each home is served rice prepared in the style unique to a particular culture. Drawing on this plot line, Roberto divided his students into groups. Each group chose one section of the book and reported on the special rice preparation described in that section.

Roberto turned to the foods that were representative of his students' Latino backgrounds. He read *Chato's Kitchen* (Soto 1995) and students listed the traditional Mexican foods the "cool cats" from the barrio prepared to try to trick the mice at their dinner. They also read *Judge for a Day* (Gonzalez-Jensen 1997) in which an Anglo boy hesitates to judge in a Latino food contest because he is afraid the dishes will be too spicy. He is amazed to learn of the variety of Latin American food that is not spicy at all. In fact, it is the spicy Texas chili that really burns! *From Father to Son* (Almada 1997) fascinated the students as they read about the art of making Mexican *pan dulce* (sweet breads). Later, their interest led to a field trip to a local *panadería* (Mexican bakery). To conclude the unit, students wrote about traditional family dishes and decided whether they were nutritional or not. The students found that most dishes were, indeed, very good for their health. As a final activity, each student brought a sampling of a favorite family recipe, and the class shared a traditional and nutritious meal together. Figure 2–5 lists the books Roberto used in his nutrition unit.

Roberto chose a content theme of interest to his students, one for which they already had background knowledge. By reading a variety of literature around the same theme, Roberto's students built up their English vocabulary of terms that refer to food, food preparation, and health matters. The students increased their content knowledge in the areas of both health and social studies. Perhaps the greatest benefit of the unit for Roberto's students is that they came to appreciate their own cultural tradition as well as the traditions of other cultural groups.

Several teachers we have worked with in our multicultural city have expanded on nutrition units. One adult education teacher had her students bring in traditional recipes for favorite foods. Together, the class talked about the recipes and translated them into English. The published booklet includes a Russian sponge cake, a Laotian papaya salad, a Cambodian fish dish, a Hmong pork recipe, and a Mexican meatball soup dish.

Other teachers have asked immigrant parents to come into the classroom to talk about and cook different ethnic foods for their classes. Some teachers end a multicultural unit with a meal that includes foods from many cultures. One high school SDAIE class collected ethnic recipes from the students in the school and put together a very professional ethnic cookbook to sell. The success of this project helped both the students and their families feel a new pride in their heritage. In addition,

Almada, Patricia. 1997. *From Father to Son*. Crystal Lake, IL: Rigby.
Badt, Karin. 1994. *Good Morning, Let's Eat*. Chicago: Children's Press.
Dooley, Norah. 1991. *Everyone Cooks Rice*. New York: Carolrhoda Books, Inc.
Dooley, Norah. 1993. *Todo el mundo cocina arroz*. New York: Scholastic.
Goldstein, Bobbye S., ed. 1995. *What's on the Menu?* New York: Puffin Books.
Gonzalez-Jensen, Margarita. 1997. *Judge for a Day*. Crystal Lake, IL: Rigby.
Klien, Ann. 1994. "Sandwiches from Around the World." *Crayola Kids*.
Morris, Ann. 1989. *Bread, Bread, Bread*. New York: Mulberry Books.
Prelutsky, Jack. 1996. "Spaghetti! Spaghetti!" In *Celebrate*, edited by J.
     David Cooper and John J. Pikulski. Boston: Houghton Mifflin.
Soto, Gary. 1995. *Chato's Kitchen*. New York: Scholastic.
Tillotson, Katherine. 1997. *On Top of Spaghetti*. Boston: Houghton Mifflin.
Torres, Leyla. 1995. *El Sancocho del Sábado*. New York: Farrar Straus Giroux.

Figure 2–5   *Nutrition Bibliography*

others in the community began to appreciate different nutritional habits. Anglos may eat large quantities of bread and potatoes instead of rice or tortillas, for example, but students see that each cultural group relies on certain staple foods. When teachers validate the customs of different cultures, they validate the students who represent those cultures at the same time

Content-Based Teaching with Languages Other than English

In previous sections, we defined and gave examples of content-based instruction for English learners. In this section, we show how this approach can apply to students learning other languages by providing an example of an ELD lesson with a twist; this is also an SLD (Spanish language development) lesson. The strategies would be the same for ELD or SLD, but in this lesson the teachers are working with limited-Spanish proficient students and attempting to teach them content in both English and Spanish.

We chose this example for two reasons. First, we want to emphasize the importance of using students' primary languages. This helps students reclaim their linguistic and cultural heritage and builds self-esteem. It also highlights the importance of bilingual students as human resources in any classroom. Second, we suggest that teaching language through content organized around themes using learner-centered and interactive methods is a valid approach that applies to students of any language.

Denette

Denette was a monolingual fifth grade teacher in a rural school with a high Hispanic population. The school did not have a bilingual program, and ELD was only provided on a pull-out basis for a half hour each day. This meant that it was up to the classroom teachers to provide comprehensible content instruction in English. Because Denette understood the benefits of primary language instruction, she looked for ways to support her students' first language, Spanish: "My dilemma has always been, how do I, a monolingual teacher, provide the best language instruction for my second language learners when I do not speak their language?"

All of Denette's fifth graders were mainstreamed, and none were pulled out for ELD. Many of them claimed that they no longer spoke or understood Spanish, much less read or wrote it. Denette wanted to find a way to restore pride in her Latino students' linguistic and cultural heritage, and to introduce her English-only students to Spanish. Her goal was to help all her students to develop both linguistic and academic competence.

Denette found a creative solution to her own lack of bilingualism by collaborating with Ann, a bilingual undergraduate college student who planned to become an elementary teacher. Denette knew that together she and Ann could provide instruction in two languages. They planned a unit of study around earthquakes, a topic of interest to Denette's fifth graders. The two big questions Denette's students posed were: "What causes earthquakes?" and "What should we do if an earthquake hits?"

As they organized the unit, Denette and Ann gathered articles and stories in English about earthquakes. Over the next few weeks, Denette involved her students in the earthquake study. Students chose an article or story to read alone or in pairs and then discuss with the class. These readings and discussions helped students build background knowledge for the earthquake study. In the sections that follow, we describe some of the lessons Denette and Ann designed together to promote Spanish language development and teach content. Both their goals and their methods also are appropriate for teachers whose goal is English language development.

Earthquakes!

To introduce academic Spanish, Ann passed out an article about earthquakes from the Spanish *Scholastic News*, "¿Qué pasó aquí?" ("What Happened Here?") (1995), and Denette led a discussion about possible reading strategies students could use to comprehend a text in a new language. One goal of this lesson was to help students develop the strategies they need to read any difficult material they encounter. Many students rely on trying to sound out words or resort to looking them up in a dictionary. Denette and Ann wanted the students to learn to rely on extralinguistic cues, such as pictures; linguistic cues, such as cognates; and human resources beyond themselves or their teacher. Denette asked her students, "What can you do to understand this article if you do not read Spanish?" The students volunteered the following ideas:

Look at the pictures.

Look for words that are similar to English words.

Buddy up with someone who knows some Spanish.

Look at the pictures, then the words, then the pictures again.

Then, the students were divided into groups of three. Denette didn't think any of her students could read in Spanish, but she put one student she thought could speak some Spanish in each group. She asked the students to work together to read the article. Denette reminded them to use the strategies they brainstormed. She also told them that after they read and discussed the article they would be called on to report back on what they learned and on the strategies they used.

The whole class discussion that followed the activity revealed that the students understood the academic content of the article written in Spanish and used the strategies the class listed. One group commented, "We saw the *Scholastic News* and looked at it, and we saw that it was in Spanish so we saw the pictures and looked at the words and found out what it meant." The students went on to explain how they found connections between English and Spanish words. By expanding the discussion to include not only academic content but also the strategies students used to understand the content, Denette and Ann helped students develop both language and academic competence.

What surprised Denette was how much Spanish some of her students could read. Different groups commented on how important the Spanish speakers had been. They shared how the Spanish readers only had to give a few key ideas. The more proficient Spanish speakers shared their pride in teaching someone else Spanish. One student commented, "I felt proud about myself when I taught Ashley and Marcos how to read in Spanish." By creating a situation where her students could demonstrate their primary language competence, Denette built their self-esteem. Her new awareness of the strengths of these students also led her to involve them fully as language experts in subsequent activities.

The next activity Denette and Ann developed dealt with plate tectonics, which Denette introduced the previous week. She reviewed plate tectonics using overhead transparencies for visual support. Then she told the students to turn to the back of their *Scholastic News* and follow along as Ann explained the instructions in Spanish for a science activity. The students worked in their groups, again relying on the Spanish speakers for clues, to follow the illustrated instructions and build a structure representing plate tectonics by placing blocks on top of two books. The books represented the plates under the earth. The students wrote a hypothesis (in English) about what they thought would happen to the structures as the books were moved in different ways. The students moved the books in different directions and recorded differences in how the structures collapsed with each type of plate movement. Each group recorded their results to test against their hypothesis. Afterwards, the whole class met, and the groups reported and discussed their results.

Again, during whole class discussion in English, Denette and Ann helped students reflect on both the academic content they learned and the process they used to understand the content, including working with others and using different strategies to comprehend instructions written in a second language. Once again, the Spanish speakers in Denette's class made an important contribution.

For the final activity, students acted out earthquake scenes. They formed groups of five, with at least one proficient Spanish speaker in each group. Then Ann passed out descriptions of different scenes where people were experiencing an earthquake. These were written in Spanish on a strip of paper. They included situations such as "You are in a bus on the way to school, and an earthquake begins." "You are in your math class, and the floor starts to shake." "You are out on the playground playing a game with your friends when you feel the earth moving."

The students read their scenes in groups and then discussed the best way to react in that situation. Then they chose a way to pantomime the scene and their response. The object was to act the scene out in a way that classmates could guess the situation. The students decided how to present their scenes and practiced them. Then each group acted out a scene, and the other groups wrote their guesses down in Spanish with the help of the group expert. After each performance, Ann collected the guesses and announced the winning group or groups.

To end the exciting day, each student responded with a quick write (spontaneous writing for a short period of time) to answer the questions: "How did your day go? What was it like if you did not speak Spanish? Did you surprise yourself in how much you could comprehend today?" Student responses were consistently positive. For example,

Ashley commented, "I loved the way I learned new Spanish words. I only know a tiny bit, but Jesse helped me." Terry wrote, "I am a second language learner, and I like learning languages because it helps us talk to other people." And Jesse concluded, "I felt proud of myself."

The theme study Denette and Ann's students participated in helped them learn science content. The students were actively engaged in answering questions they helped to raise. What made this theme study effective is that Denette considered her students' linguistic and affective needs as well as their academic and cognitive needs. By including Spanish in her lessons, Denette more fully involved all her students. Ann's use of Spanish in the classroom seemed to legitimize the language and functioned as an invitation for students with some Spanish ability to use their primary language in class. As one student commented, "Well today it went wonderful. Because I knew Spanish a little, but now I know much more." In addition, students with higher levels of Spanish proficiency were regarded as important resources by their classmates.

This theme study provides a good example of an approach to language and to curriculum that best exemplifies ELD lessons. In this case, the language being developed was Spanish, so this was ELD with a twist. What is important, though, is not which language is used, but how both language and content can be learned together when teachers engage students in meaningful curriculum organized around interesting themes.

Content-Based Instruction in EFL Settings

Teaching language through content sounds wonderful for students in the ESL setting, but for those who teach EFL (English as a Foreign Language), it's different. They cannot simply take ESL strategies and activities and use them successfully.

We heard this concern over and over as we traveled, lived, and worked in Latin America over the past five years. We spoke to groups because they were interested in hearing about innovative approaches to teaching English, and they had heard or read about content-based approaches such as whole language, the use of literature to teach language, and sheltered English instruction. As we explained how teachers in ESL settings implemented content-based language instruction, EFL teachers expressed their interest but also raised concerns. In the following section, we discuss some of the challenges these teachers face in trying to move toward teaching language through content using a sociopsycholinguistic orientation. Then, we provide some examples of ways that teachers in Venezuela have met those challenges.

Challenges for Content-Based Teaching in EFL Contexts

Taking a sociopsycholinguistic orientation and teaching language through content is particularly challenging in EFL settings for a variety of reasons. Most EFL settings have several of these challenges.

- Often, there are limited resources available that reflect literature/content-based practices.

- Many countries have depressed economies, so available materials often seem extremely expensive; money to buy available materials is extremely limited.

- Available materials are often out-of-date textbooks that reflect a traditional grammar-based approach to language teaching.

- The official government curriculum reflects a traditional approach, and teachers do not know how to reconcile that with a new orientation.

- The official government curriculum calls for more current, innovative approaches, but teachers lack training to implement it.

- There is limited time allocated for teaching English in schools.

- Teaching conditions are often poor. Problems include large class sizes, heavy teaching schedules, low salaries, and poor physical conditions in the schools.

- Because of the lack of opportunity to use English, many teachers' English proficiency may be limited.

- Because of the lack of teacher training opportunities, teachers may teach as they were taught—usually through grammar translation or audiolingual methods.

- Teachers often teach the language found in textbooks rather than the language students need to communicate or compete academically in an English-speaking environment.

- The emphasis is on learning skills, not on acquiring the language.

- National and international examinations of English proficiency are based on the content of traditional approaches to teaching English.

- Teachers often have to work several jobs to make a living. This makes collaboration, planning of themes, and sharing of materials difficult.

- Parents have definite expectations for their children's English learning. They expect traditional approaches and traditional homework assignments.

- Administrators of innovative programs find it difficult to coordinate complicated teaching schedules, overwhelmed teachers, and limited resources.

- Students may see little relevance in learning English if they have limited opportunities to use English outside school or to interact with native speakers.
- It's hard to learn language outside the cultural context of native speakers of the language.

Some of these challenges exist in the ESL setting as well: the reluctance to move away from state mandated curriculum, poor teaching conditions, the tendency to teach as we were taught, and the emphasis on skills. In the EFL setting, however, teachers are more likely to face strong pressure to follow official guidelines; they are more likely to face poor teaching conditions (especially in public schools); they are more likely to have been taught English with a traditional method, and they are more likely to be surrounded by other teachers who teach English as a set of skills.

Other challenges are unique to the EFL setting. These may include limited access to content-based materials in English and pressure to use grammar-based textbooks with the result that students don't learn the language they need. EFL teachers have limited time for teaching English. Some teachers are limited in their English proficiency. Administrators trying to implement current practices find their efforts to change schools affected by these challenges and by the pressure of parent expectations. Because many teachers in EFL settings work in private schools, the parents are essentially the customers, and their demands must be taken into account for schools to survive. Added to all these constraints is the difficulty of teaching language outside its cultural context. Because English does not have immediate use and purpose, many students are not motivated to learn the language because they don't see it as relevant.

Despite these challenges, content-based teaching from a sociopsycholinguistic orientation is possible in the EFL setting. Next, we describe ways that elementary EFL teachers as well as teachers of adult EFL in Venezuela, adapted their curriculum and their approach so that they could teach language through content.

During our year in Venezuela, we became aware that teaching language through content offered not only possibilities but huge challenges as well. We worked with teachers in a K-6 public school who wanted to help their students, but struggled against the odds. The average salary for an elementary school teacher was about $150 a month. Inflation rates were high, and the salary barely covered food and housing. The schools had very few supplies. Children brought their own paper and pencils if they could afford them. Paper for art projects and bulletin boards was very strictly rationed. No copy machines were available at the school. The only books were some bland government texts in reading, social studies, and science. The official reading program consisted of copies of four literature titles for each grade level. Often, these small paperbacks never reached the school or, if they did, they never got past the librarian.

We talked to the teachers about how people learn and what kinds of materials support reading. We showed them children's books in Spanish and English, including big books we brought from California. They responded enthusiastically, but they also knew that access was almost impossible. Teachers literally couldn't afford to buy books for their classrooms. When we explained, for instance, that a big book in Spanish or English cost around thirty dollars, they were aghast at the expense.

It was clear we needed to look for alternatives to the beautiful materials we have in many ESL settings. We talked with the teachers about alternative materials to help support a quality reading and writing program that would teach language through content. The teachers came up with the following list:

- Initiate a campaign to buy a set of big books in Spanish and English for the school. Each student could bring the equivalent of ten to twenty cents to begin a general fund.
- Investigate if grants to buy books might be available from various industrial firms or educational agencies.
- Make big books by hand, referring to commercial books for ideas.
- Have students put together class sets of big and little books around themes the whole class is studying. Preserve the books for continued use by covering them with contact paper.
- Cut out pictures from magazines to create stories that can be made into books.
- Choose an interesting theme and find newspaper articles on this theme. Mount articles onto heavy paper or cardboard.
- Invite experts in the community to share ideas and materials.
- Establish pen pals with students in other schools or other countries.

These teachers became enthusiastic about adopting a new orientation toward teaching. Despite the challenges they faced, they saw that these ideas would help their students learn both language and academic subjects.

Another group of teachers we worked with in Venezuela were adjunct faculty members of the Universidad de los Andes and were teaching English to older learners, from teenagers to adults. This was a large program of over one thousand students who registered for different levels of English about every three months. The teachers attended workshops we gave on successful practices, including a workshop on teaching language through meaningful content. Each week we met with teachers to help them implement a meaningful curriculum.

The director of this program adopted a textbook series that was based on a combined notional-functional and communicative approach. A series of characters are introduced in the first lessons and their stories unfold throughout the series in the dialogues of each lesson. Lessons center around traditional functions such as introductions, apologies, and requests. Suggested activities are interactive and include such things as discussing pictures in the text, interviewing classmates, and asking and answering questions.

For the most part, the teachers in the program were young and had no background in language teaching pedagogy. They were selected primarily for their English proficiency. They used the textbooks rather traditionally, going through the exercises with their classes mechanically. Then, they came to our weekly meeting complaining there wasn't enough in the lessons to fill up the class time. When we probed, the teachers admitted that their students did not speak that much English nor did the quick run through the lessons seem to teach them much.

As a group, we decided to take each lesson and brainstorm ways to extend it and make it more authentic. Even though the extended lessons were not content-based because there was no science, social studies, or literature within most of the original lessons, the ideas the teachers came up with got them and their students more involved and excited about English. For example, Figure 2–6, EFL Lesson Application, shows extensions and ideas the group brainstormed for a typical lesson. Note that the themes and structures taught in the lesson are fairly traditional. The extensions the teachers came up with helped personalize the learning, drew on students' backgrounds, included authentic reading activities, and involved students in concept development through comparing and contrasting.

Taking a sociopsycholinguistic orientation and teaching language using authentic materials and drawing on student interest and backgrounds is a challenge for teachers in EFL settings. This is because most language textbooks teach the language and culture of the target language generally. Not much can be done to personalize lessons and allow students to really draw on their background and strengths. When teachers adapt their lessons using successful practices, they offer students a better chance for success.

Lesson Ideas   Level 1   Unit 3   Lesson 1

Theme / topic   **Structures**

Families   possessive adjectives

Physical characteristics   noun plus possessive

Occupations   which questions with present tense of *be*

Nationalities   negative statements with *be*

Possessions   present tense of *have* descriptive adjective
                                 with *be* and *have*

Ideas to Extend Book Activities

Ex.

1   Students introduce own family members using family photographs

1   Diary entry on family members (describe your family)

4   Discuss/ chart students' marital status

5   Draw your family tree

6   Interview in pairs about families, report, survey, chart

Related Activities

Look at society page in newspaper (in Spanish) and describe in English.

Look at marriage and birth columns in paper. Discuss family relationships and customs of marriage, birth, etc.

Discuss birth order and preference and naming customs in your family,
in Venezuela. . . compare with U.S./British customs

Do a "Find Someone Who..." with family information (example: "Find
someone who has more than eight brothers and sisters. . . .) Students
must ask "Do you have more than eight brothers and sisters?" Do as
interview and chart the class results.

Materials that Could Be Used

Family photos (and teacher's family)

Book on families

Newspaper/ magazine columns (*Hola*, etc.)

Questionnaire for interview about families

Evaluation Ideas

Diary entries about family members

Family trees (oral, written)

Interview results (oral, written)

Figure 2–6   EFL *Lesson Adaptation*

Despite the challenges, we are convinced that for EFL and ESL teachers, the best approach is to follow the principles for success while teaching both language and content. In each of the following chapters, we explain, in depth, one of the principles that guides successful practice.

THREE

Learning Goes from Whole to Part

◆

Introduction

Picture a fictitious classroom filled with thirty inquisitive second graders, many of them English language learners. The teacher is conducting
a lesson centered around a food theme. First, she passes out some
pieces of oregano. She asks the children what they can tell her about it.
They look at the oregano, they smell it, they feel it. "It's green and it
smells funny," says Manuel. "I think I know what it is, it's *perejil* (parsley)!"
pipes up María. The teacher records the children's answers on a large
piece of butcher paper.

She collects the oregano and passes around some mozzarella
cheese. The children know that this is cheese, that it's white, and, after
tasting it, that it doesn't have much flavor. Francisca declares that it is
definitely not *queso Oaxaca* that her mother uses to make enchiladas.
Again, the teacher records the children's responses. Garlic and tube-
shaped Italian sausage follow the mozzarella, and then comes tomato
sauce. The children are interested, but they aren't sure where all this is
going. The teacher passes out uncooked, wide noodles with scalloped
edges. The noodles are brittle and dry. They look nothing like the
noodles the Laotian students in the class eat daily.

"Now," the teacher announces, "we are going to cook a special
meal. Using all these things you have looked at, we will make lasagna.
How do you think it will taste?"

"Yucky!" shout several students. "I'm not going to eat it," claims
Mo. "Nothing you passed out smelled good or looked good either."

"It might be good," countered Alicia. "Noodles and tomato usually
means Italian food, and I like spaghetti."

"You always cook things we like," added Mai. "I'll try it."

The students in this class are intrigued by the food the teacher
passed around. They try to use their past experiences with food to pre-

dict what lasagna will be like. However, despite the fact that they have smelled and even tasted each of the ingredients, they can't mentally put the odors and tastes together into a final product. The individual ingredients of oregano, garlic, sausage, mozzarella, and tomato sauce simply don't add up to the taste of lasagna.

This lesson might be part of a unit in which children study foods from different cultures, like the units described in the last chapter. In many ways, the lesson is consistent with our list of principles for success. The children are engaged. There is lots of talk. The children read what the teacher writes on the butcher paper. Later, they will cook and eat the lasagna. They will write about the experience.

Although this is a good lesson in a literal sense, on a metaphorical level it suggests why some educational practices make learning hard for students. The teacher presented all the ingredients that make up lasagna. Even though the students experienced all the parts of the recipe in isolation, they couldn't predict what the whole, the lasagna, would be like. The taste of lasagna is different from the tastes of its constituent parts. Knowing about the parts doesn't ensure knowledge of the whole.

In this chapter, we look more closely at the commonsense view that, when we break a subject down into parts, we make learning easier. We argue that the whole is more than the sum of the parts and that students, especially English language learners, need first a sense of the whole to understand the parts. The whole provides an important context in which the parts are naturally embedded. When curriculum is developed through themes based on significant questions, students naturally begin with the whole, the big question, and move to the parts as they search for answers. Teachers who follow principles for success help students by teaching whole to part.

To explain whole to part teaching we do three things: First, we consider what first and second language researchers say about how learning both oral and written language takes place. Then, we look specifically at the importance of context, which provides the whole, in second language learning. Finally, we give examples to show how teachers with many English language learners adopt principles for success by organizing curriculum around big questions as they teach whole to part.

Language Learning Takes Place Whole to Part

The process of acquiring a first or a second language involves moving from whole to part, although it sometimes doesn't look that way on the surface (Freeman and Freeman 1994). In learning oral language, for example, babies first utter single words like *Mama* or *milk*, then they produce two-word sentences *want milk*, and only later develop complete sentences. This suggests that language develops from the parts, the single words, to the whole, complete utterances.

Although it is true that children first utter single words, those words often represent complete ideas. *Milk*, for example, could mean I *want some milk*, I *spilled the milk*, or *That's milk over there*. Vygotsky (1962) believed that word meanings develop in a functional way from whole to part:

> In regard to meaning . . . the first word of the child is a whole sentence. Semantically, the child starts from the whole, from a meaningful complex, and only later begins to master the separate semantic units, the meanings of words, and to divide his formerly undifferentiated thoughts into those units (p. 126).

Children start with ideas that they express in a single word, and later they learn to use more words to express that idea. They add more details with time and move toward the conventional adult way of speaking. When children first start to use written language, they often write a single letter to represent a whole word. This is true also for children learning to write English as their second language. In early stages of writing English, Sonia, a native Greek speaker, wrote "lwtmh" to represent "I *went to my house*." (Cambourne 1988, p. 46). As students write more, they begin to represent words by first and last sounds. Manuel, a second grader recently from Mexico, wrote the following as the teacher dictated the weekly spelling list:

1. an
2. bs
3. bn
4. fs
5. fs
6. gn
7. kl
8. ls
9. on
10. ps

Unfortunately, Manuel's teacher did not know about writing development and did not recognize that Manuel was representing the whole with first and last letters. The words the teacher dictated were *animal, birds, bison, feathers, furs, gone, kill, laws, ocean,* and *plant.* Manuel did not receive credit for any of the words he wrote. Fortunately, his student teacher at the time, Denette, was studying early literacy and recognized Manuel's strengths. Denette pointed out to the teacher that Manuel was developing important hypotheses about English spelling.

Students who are encouraged to write using their own hypotheses about spelling often move next toward representing each syllable with a letter as Rinette, a first grader from Mexico, did with LDBG for *ladybug*. Finally, students come to realize the alphabetic principle, that letters represent individual sounds, not syllables or words. Although students do not move neatly through these stages, these examples are typical of learners who experiment with representing their ideas through writing. Throughout the process of their written language development, students always first represent the whole, not the parts. We describe writing development in both English and Spanish more fully in our book *Teaching Reading and Writing in Spanish in the Bilingual Classroom* (Freeman and Freeman 1997).

In the development of both speech and writing, children begin with a whole and only later develop an understanding of the constituent parts. Goodman (1986) explains this phenomenon. He says that when we learn language we are "first able to use whole utterances" and that "only later can we see the parts in the whole and begin to experiment with their relationship to each other and to the meaning of the whole" (p. 19). Parts are harder to learn than wholes because they are more abstract. We need the whole to provide a context for the parts. Of course, what is difficult is deciding what is a whole and what is a part. For example, second language teachers may feel they are providing the whole by having students memorize dialogues rather than focusing on individual words. Again, a dialogue is not what we mean by a whole.

Traditional approaches to reading begin with small parts and build up to the whole despite research evidence, from first and second language development, that shows children start with the whole and gradually add the parts (Ferreiro and Teberosky 1982, Goodman 1996). For example, phonics approaches start by students matchings sounds with letters to decode words. Students are expected to combine word meanings to reach the meaning of the whole text. Whole word approaches start with the words. Students often memorize sight words using flash cards. Again, they are expected to combine word meanings to get at the meanings of texts. Actually, many programs combine phonics with sight words. Phonics works with words that have a regular sound-to-spelling match and sight words are useful for words such as *of* or *one* that occur frequently but do not follow regular phonics patterns.

This part-to-whole approach is not consistent with natural learning patterns. Adults who are proficient readers can break reading down into parts to present to students one part at a time. They do this in an attempt to make reading easier, but because students naturally learn whole to part, the approach actually makes learning harder. This is true for both young second language learners learning to read in a new language and for older students who can already read in their first language. These students in particular too often focus on individual words, looking words up in their bilingual dictionaries, and writing in the definitions. Instead, they benefit from reading more rapidly with a focus on getting the meaning of the whole piece. As they become more proficient, they can attend more to the parts.

Too much attention given to the parts does not lead to increased reading comprehension. The following example shows that even when we know all the words and can understand individual sentences, we may not be able to make much sense out of text. We often give teachers the following paragraph to try to make this point.

> With hocked gems financing him our hero defied all scornful laughter that tried to prevent his scheme. "Your eyes deceive you," he had said. "An egg, not a table correctly typifies this unexplored planet." Now three sturdy sisters sought proof, forging along, sometimes through calm vastness, yet more often over turbulent peaks and valleys. Days became weeks as many doubters spread fearful rumors about the edge. At last, from nowhere, welcome winged creatures appeared, signifying momentous success.

When readers first encounter this text, they usually complain that it is poorly written, that it doesn't make any sense, and that the parts don't go together. They understand all the words, but they can't tell us what "hocked gems" refers to or what the phrase "an egg, not a table" means. When we ask them to tell us what would help them understand this text, they often ask for a title. These readers have all the parts, but they need the whole, the main idea. They know intuitively that titles often supply that information. If we supply a title such as "Columbus' Voyage to America," the parts come together for most readers. Instead of perceiving the story as a series of unconnected sentences, the readers see that the text is cohesive and coherent.

One last consideration should be mentioned here. When we work with English language learners, the above passage about Columbus could present an additional problem. For immigrant students who have no knowledge of Columbus, the title is not a useful clue. The reference to Columbus provides the whole only if we have the requisite background knowledge and experience. For our second language students, "Columbus" may simply be one more unconnected part. They need more than a title as background for understanding this passage.

To summarize, part-to-whole instruction makes learning hard for several reasons. First, it is hard to understand the individual parts outside the context of the whole. Second, the whole is more than the sum of the parts, so even if we know all the parts, as we did with the passage about Columbus, we may still not understand the whole. Third, and most important, if we give students only the parts, they may decide they are not interested in them because they don't know what the whole might be like. That's what probably would happen to us if we first experienced lasagna one part at a time the way the children did in the lesson we described. As a result, teachers who follow principles for success attempt to teach reading and other subjects whole to part.

Skills and Acquisition Approaches

Another way to think about the difference between a part-to-whole approach to teaching reading—or language more generally—and a whole-to-part approach is to consider the underlying assumptions about how learning takes place. Those who advocate a part-to-whole approach see reading as a set of skills to be learned and applied in a sequential manner. In contrast, those who take a whole-to-part approach view learning to read as a process of acquisition. They assume that, like oral language, written language is acquired rather than learned. These two views are summarized in Figure 3–1.

As Figure 3–1 shows, the two approaches show contrasts in their theoretical perspective and in their view of the teacher's role.

The skills model is based on behavioral psychology. Learning is thought to result from the formation of stimulus-response bonds. The teacher's job is to drill students and to make sure that the exercises hold students' attention, that they are frequent, and that they last as long as possible. Teachers who follow a skills model break tasks into manageable parts and present the parts in strict sequence. They test each section, and, if some students fail, they reteach and retest. If (or when) students have trouble, teachers plan extra exercises, usually at a lower level of difficulty. Grammar plays an important role in this model because knowledge of grammar is thought to help students develop the needed skills.

The skills model applies equally well to learning oral or written language. We already saw how a skills approach formed the basis for empiricist methods like ALM. The same set of beliefs also applies to teaching reading. The written language is divided into parts to be mastered. The problem with the skills approach is that for both oral and written language, students may master individual skills and, in the end, not develop

Skills and Acquisition Approaches to Teaching

Skills–Theory	Acquisition–Theory
Learning results from forming Stimulus → Response bonds	Acquisition results from activating the UG in natural language use.
Bonds are built when the stimulus is vivid, frequent, and long-lasting.	Language develops as speakers engage in meaningful communication.
Tasks should be broken into small parts and sequenced.	Language is most easily acquired when it is kept whole.
Knowledge of grammar increases mastery of language skills.	Linguistics is an appropriate subject for inquiry, but explicit knowledge of grammar has little effect on oral or written language development.
Testing success varies with recency; knowledge is not retained.	Testing should be authentic; acquired language is retained.
Role of the Teacher	*Role of the Teacher*
Provide stimuli that are vivid, frequent, and increase time on task.	Provide demonstrations (comprehensible input) in a functional social or academic context.
Break tasks into parts and sequence the parts.	Keep learners cognitively engaged, and keep language whole and meaningful.
Teach/test/reteach retest.	Observe and document students' development.
Intervene if students have trouble.	Mediate by providing scaffolding in the Zone of Proximal Development to promote growth.

Figure 3–1   *Skills and Acquisition Approaches*

against grammar?

functional use of the oral or written language that they need for communication or for learning in school.

In contrast, the acquisition model is based on current research in linguistics and psychology that suggests that humans have an innate ability to develop language proficiency. They do this when the language centers of the brain (what Chomsky called the "universal grammar" [UG]) are activated. As students use written language for real purposes, their abilities develop and are refined. The study of language, from this perspective, is as valuable as any academic content area study would be, but traditional grammar instruction is not thought to improve performance in reading or writing (for a detailed discussion of the kinds of grammar teaching that may improve writing, see Weaver 1996). Teachers who follow an acquisition approach use authentic assessment measures, such as portfolios.

Teachers play an important role in the acquisition model. They provide the demonstrations students need. They read to students and with students. They plan many different activities where they write, and students write. They carefully observe student development and provide the help students need at the time they need it. They do this by asking questions or directing students' attention to certain details of written language. This type of teaching constitutes a kind of mental scaffolding. Teachers work in what Vygotsky called the "Zone of Proximal Development," the area between what students can do alone and what they can do in collaboration with an adult or a more proficient peer. In the next section, we describe how one teacher puts this first principle for success, teaching whole to part, into practice as she teaches reading following an acquisition model.

Teaching Reading Whole to Part

In René's first grade classroom, language is kept whole. Her thirty-five students represent five different ethnic groups, including African Americans, Hispanics, Hmong, Anglos, and Laotians. Although many of the children enter René's classroom at the beginning of the first grade unable to read, they all leave as readers.

Print is visible everywhere. There are books of different sizes in the book racks, charts with poetry and songs, lists of the students' favorite children's authors with the books they have written, stories written by the children, and a message board for leaving messages to other classmates. The teacher and children read, write, and talk together daily. René reads favorite stories that the children memorize and read with her, with peers, or by themselves in the book corner. (This early memorization is a stage of reading and is not the same as the conscious memorization that goes on when, for example, one memorizes a poem.) The students read several books by one children's author and discuss how that author's books are the same or different. They read songs and poetry from charts.

The children write their own stories, representing whole words by single letters, by letters representing the first and last sounds, and by letters representing syllables as they move toward conventional spelling. Although various children may be at different stages of the writing process at any given time, they read their stories to their teacher and to each other.

They read and write messages for the message center. The children are constantly writing, reading, and discussing whole texts of interest to them.

When asked how she teaches reading, René explains that she doesn't teach reading directly. Her students learn to read by reading, not by being taught sounds or words in isolation. Not all children in her classroom become independent readers at the same time, but the constant exposure to the reading of whole, meaningful texts eventually leads all her students, including her second language students, into reading. Her students become skilled language users.

whole language

Principles for Success: Teaching Skills in Context?

In René's classroom, students develop literacy using a whole-to-part approach. However, the question she is most commonly asked is, "How do you teach reading skills with your approach?" People who ask this question may assume that René's approach is just another way to teach skills such as phonics or vocabulary. The assumption is that teachers such as René simply teach these skills in context. However, as Edelsky, Altwerger, and Flores (1991) point out, getting to the parts and teaching the skills is not the goal:

> What one child learns is not necessarily what other children are learning, and most importantly, what is taught or learned is triggered by what the children need for the language they are actually using at the time. That is, to become skilled language users, the focus of both teachers' and children's activity is whatever purposes the children themselves are trying to accomplish. By contrast, to learn language skills, children work on exercises according to a curricular sequence, and above all, the focus of teacher's and children's activity is the skill (p. 38).

Did this with Michelle

The goal for teachers such as René is to enable students to become skilled language users. Her goal is not to teach separate language skills. The focus on skills has been largely the result of confusing causes and effects. For example, good readers develop a knowledge of phonics. But children don't need to practice phonics to read and write. Children in René's classroom pick out sounds from their reading and write by sounding out words. Good readers develop large vocabularies. But children do not need to develop large vocabularies to learn how to read, write, and speak. René's students carry on class discussions using sophisticated vocabulary, and they write using a wide range of words. The focus is always on the whole, on communicating through reading and writing as well as speaking and listening, and in that process the students develop the parts, the sounds, and the words.

As students read and write whole texts, they become more aware of the parts. Teachers may help learners focus on these parts. When René works with her students as they are writing, she often asks them the beginning sound of a word they are trying to write. When the children are reading, she asks what sounds letters make. However, she only asks these questions about words that occur in the stories children are reading or writing and only when those questions help students understand or express an idea. The focus on parts is not designed to refine or practice specific skills. For a detailed account of how a teacher provides phonics instruction as René does, in the context of authentic reading and writing, see *Looking Closely: The Role of Phonics in One Whole Language Classroom* (Mills et al. 1992)

As they work with their teacher, René's students learn more about literacy. Goodman and others (1987) describe learning as "coming to know through the symbolic transformation and representation of experience" (p. 98). The knowing cycle involves three stages: perceiving, ideating, and presenting. René's students perceive written language as they read. Beginning readers don't really "see" all the words or letters, but when they write as well as read, they begin to "read like a writer" (Smith 1982). That is, they begin to perceive the smaller parts of words. In this process, they also ideate, or build concepts about words. They do this as they talk about reading and writing with their classmates and their teacher. In their writing, the children present their ideations to others. By examining students' written presentations, teachers can assess children's conceptualizations of print.

Involving students in reading and writing complete texts allows them to come to know as they move through the three stages of the learning cycle. Teachers who follow principles for success understand that language is learned best when it is kept whole. When we break that whole down, we make learning more difficult. We are attempting to do for students what they must do for themselves. Instead, we must allow learners to construct their own understandings of literacy processes. The goal of literacy instruction is to produce skilled readers and writers, not to teach reading and writing skills.

Two Scenarios of Second Language Classrooms

Experienced teachers realize that attempts to transmit knowledge directly by teaching skills or attempts to divide knowledge up for the learner only subvert natural learning processes. These approaches do not make learning easier. Then what should the teacher's role be if learning develops whole to part? To help illustrate the differences between whole-to-part and part-to-whole approaches, we will contrast two classrooms of second language learners.

Scenario One

Betty teaches English language development (ELD) in a large, inner-city high school in California. Her students are mostly Hispanics and Southeast Asians who have varied educational backgrounds. Betty's class is a fairly traditional one in which students work to improve their linguistic competence, their ability to manipulate linguistic units, rather than their communicative competence (Hymes 1970). To do this, Betty uses several part-to-whole activities to build vocabulary and improve grammatical accuracy. For example, students memorize and repeat dialogues, complete worksheets, study word lists, and take spelling and grammar tests.

In a typical period, Betty turns on the tape recorder as soon as the bell rings, and the students listen to the ten-line dialogue from the week's lesson. After listening to the dialogue, the students repeat each line after the speaker on the tape while looking at the dialogue in their books. Then, Betty turns off the tape and asks the students to practice the dialogue in pairs for five minutes. Next, Betty leads oral substitution drills from the dialogue. She reads a sentence and asks the students to give the contracted form:

Teacher	Students
I am hungry.	I'm hungry.
She is laughing.	She's laughing.
They are in class.	They're in class.

After the students practice the drills orally, they do a written exercise on contractions in their workbooks. During the last fifteen minutes of the class, Betty dictates a list of vocabulary words from the dialogue and asks the students to write sentences using the words.

Scenario Two

Lonna's classroom is also a high school classroom for English language learners. Her students come from many countries, although the majority are Southeast Asians whose first languages are Hmong, Laotian, Khmer, and Thai. Lonna's class is a content reading class, and her goal is to prepare her students to be mainstreamed into regular content classes. Lonna believes that her students must be involved in authentic, meaningful reading and writing to become competent readers and writers of English. In this class, students read whole texts on topics that are important to them and then write about their reading. There are no isolated vocabulary lists, no oral repetition drills, no grammar lessons. A description of a unit on newspapers gives an idea of how Lonna approaches teaching (Freeman and Freeman 1989).

A general discussion of the purpose and value of the newspaper began the unit. A speaker from the local paper came and explained to the class the various parts of a paper, such as the headlines, the masthead, the index, and the different sections. During this talk, students examined the various sections of the newspaper, because the school purchased enough newspapers so that each student could have one. In addition, Lonna arranged a field trip so the students could tour the local newspaper office.

Later, Lonna posted on a bulletin board an article, which recently appeared in the local paper, about the Ban Vinay refugee camp. Her students, many of whom had lived at the camp, read the article with interest. When Lonna invited students to write about the article, the response was enthusiastic. Mai began her response by reflecting on her experiences at the camp:

> My memories of Ban Vinay in Thailand is very sad. When we live in Ban Vinay my brother is very sick. He almost died there. We were very poor. We have to get in a line to get our food. I was very small at that time. When we get in line, all the older people always step over me, because I was so small they couldn't see me.

Lonna posted Mai's writing and that of her classmates on the board around the news article. This activity generated a great deal of interest. English language learners from other classes across the campus came to the room to read the news article and the student responses and then added their own writing.

Lonna created an activity in which learning moved from whole to part. In the Ban Vinay lesson, students responded to a whole article, not part of an article or an adapted, simplified version of an article. Full, unadapted texts provide more comprehensible input than adapted or simplified texts (Goodman and Freeman 1993). The students' written responses were full pieces of writing, not constrained or limited by the teacher. Both Graves (1994) and Calkins (Calkins 1994, 1991) argue that only when writers produce whole texts from the start do they develop an adequate understanding of the writing process. Lonna used a whole-to-part approach to reading and writing instruction.

The two scenarios provide examples of part-to-whole and whole-to-part teaching of second language students. In the first scenario, Betty used a modified audiolingual method as she had students repeat dialogues and practice drills. She also worked on isolated grammar points and lists of words. Lonna, by contrast, kept language in authentic con-

Don't adapt?

text. To understand this approach more fully, it is important to consider the role of context in learning. All learning occurs in a context, and the richer that context, the easier the learning.

Cummins' View of Language Acquisition

Research on second language acquisition by Cummins (1996, 1981) helps highlight the important role context plays in developing language proficiency. The reason we advocate a whole-to-part approach to teaching is that this approach enriches the context. Cummins explains that learners may develop two types of proficiency. Conversational proficiency is the ability to use language in face-to-face communication, whereas academic proficiency is the ability to carry out school-related literacy tasks. The following list outlines differences between these two kinds of language proficiency.

Conversational and Academic Language
(*Based on Cummins* 1989)

Conversational Language: The ability to speak English (or another language) when there is a lot of context.

- in conversation
- in games
- when there are visuals
- when they already know about it in their first language

Students need approximately two years in order to be able to understand and talk in context-rich situations.

Academic Language: The ability to use English (or another language) when there is very little context.

- reading textbooks, novels without photos or pictures
- writing long compositions
- understanding a long presentation without visuals
- understanding new concepts

Students need four to nine years to use the new language in order to learn, read, and write academic materials such as science and history.

As this list shows, conversational proficiency develops during casual talk when situational context cues are present to aid comprehension and when the topic is familiar. Academic language, on the other hand, may take longer to develop because there is less contextual support and students may have less background knowledge of the content. To explain the difference between academic and conversational proficiency, Cummins developed a framework that places any instance of language use into one of the four quadrants on the chart presented here (Figure 3–2).

Cummins found that it took immigrant students about two years to develop conversational proficiency (quadrant A) but five to seven years to reach grade level norms in academic tasks (quadrant D). A closer examination of the two scales Cummins uses to define language proficiency provides additional evidence for the need to teach whole to part.

In Figure 3–2 the horizontal scale places instances of language use along a continuum from context-embedded to context-reduced. Cummings (1996) explains what he means by context-embedded on his continuum.

> in context-embedded communication the participants can actively negotiate meaning (e.g. by providing feedback that the message has not been understood) and the language is supported by a wide range of meaningful interpersonal and situational cues (p. 58).

An example of context-embedded language is a discussion between a salesperson and a customer deciding which of several sweaters to buy. The two can negotiate meaning by referring to the sweaters as well as by using gestures, changes in intonation, and so on.

Cummins contrasts context-embedded language with context-reduced.

> Context-reduced communication, on the other hand, relies primarily (or at the extreme of the continuum, exclusively) on linguistic

	cognitively undemanding language	
A *2 years Conversation*		C
context embedded language	————————————	context reduced language *5–7 years*
B	cognitively demanding language	D

Figure 3–2   *Cummins Quadrant*   *Takes 5 years to get to D*

cues to meaning, and thus successful interpretation of the message depends heavily on knowledge of the language itself (p. 58).

A telephone conversation is an example of context-reduced language. Although callers can infer meaning from intonation, they can not rely on facial expressions, gestures, or references to things both people can see. In schools long readings, standardized tests, and lectures are examples of context-reduced academic language.

Cummins emphasizes that to facilitate the development of academic proficiency, teachers must provide context-embedded instruction and recognize that "human relationships are central to effective instruction" (p. 73). He believes good instruction includes building on students' background knowledge and interests, using strategies to make the input comprehensible, encouraging active language use, facilitating cooperative learning and peer tutoring, and organizing around themes. This is what Mary and Sue did with the migrant units described in Chapter Two. Rather than teaching isolated language parts, then, the role of the teacher is to keep language in meaningful contexts and to ensure that students are working with the whole of language, not simplified parts.

Providing Context to Support Language Development

One way to embed language in context is to provide the kind of extralinguistic support found in authentic language use. For example, if two children on the playground are talking about who is going to use the swing first, their conversation is embedded in the situational context. The extralinguistic cues include objects (such as the swing), actions, (such as pointing) gestures, and intonation cues.

Teachers of English language learners know that the greater the contextual support provided by objects and actions, the lower the necessity for students to rely solely on their new language. In traditional language classes, teachers frequently provide extralinguistic cues by developing lessons around things and people found in the classroom, including the teacher and the students. Furthermore, teachers may bring objects from home into the classroom or ask students to bring things in to talk about. For good reason, "show and tell" is popular in both mainstream and second language classrooms.

When conversations are about things or people that are not present, teachers can provide context by bringing in pictures that show people and places outside the classroom. If teachers are reading to students, teachers may use big books that contain illustrations all the students can see.

Acting out situations that do not occur naturally in the classroom is another way teachers can provide context. Such role-play allows students to communicate without relying solely on the spoken words. Furthermore, teachers may use gestures such as holding a hand to their ear to mimic talking on the telephone, and, in this way, enrich the context.

In some cases, the only context available is linguistic. Cummins uses the term *context-reduced* rather than *decontextualized* to describe cases in which the primary context is the language itself. He recognizes that language offers a range of possible contextual support. An expository text or a lecture is easier to understand if there is an introduction that outlines the main points. Stories are easier to understand if they follow a familiar pattern. Children who have heard many stories learn these patterns. Often stories begin with "Once upon a time . . .," then a problem arises, and usually there is a resolution with a happy ending. As students come to understand this pattern, subsequent stories become more predictable.

Language is also more context-embedded when the number of participants in a conversation is reduced. Anyone who studied a second language and then tried to use that language outside the classroom knows that one-to-one conversations are much easier to engage in than group discussions. Within the classroom, as well, when teachers can work with individuals or small groups of English language learners, they provide greater contextual support than when they work with the whole class.

Teachers of second language students also may use the students' first language to provide contextual support for the second language. Bilingual teachers often use a method called preview, view, review. In the first phase, they preview the lesson in the students' first language. This helps ensure that the students understand the big picture. It helps them follow the "view," the actual lesson, conducted in their second language. Finally, the teacher may provide additional context for the lesson by reviewing the main concepts again in the first language. ELD teachers who do not speak all the languages of their students find the preview/view/review method helpful, and they ask students, paraprofessionals, or parents to provide the primary language support. Following, we outline the preview/ view/ review method.

Preview/View/Review
Preview
First Language

The teacher gives an overview of the lesson or activity in the students' first language. (This could be giving an oral summary, reading a book, showing a film, asking a key question, etc.)

View
Second or target language [English]

The teacher teaches the lesson or directs the activity in the students' second language.

Review
First Language

The teacher or the students summarize key ideas and raise questions about the lesson in their first language.

Teachers facilitate language learning when they keep authentic language in context by providing either extralinguistic or linguistic cues. This approach contrasts with many methods of language teaching that rely on simplified materials. Attempts at simplifying language forms or functions often result in inauthentic language. Practice with simplified language forms may cause students to form false ideas about natural language. Above all, simplification limits the range of cues available and reduces the context. The importance of the role of context in developing language proficiency becomes more apparent when we examine the way in which context is related to cognitive demand.

Cognitively Demanding Language

The second dimension Cummins uses in Figure 3–2 to define language proficiency is a scale from cognitively undemanding to cognitively demanding language. Cummins explains that this continuum "is intended to address the developmental aspects of communicative competence in terms of the degree of active cognitive involvement in the task or activity" (1989, p. 12). At an early stage, an activity may require a high level of cognitive involvement. Over time, as the task is mastered, the activity becomes more automatic, and the cognitive demand lessens. The scale is intended to be developmental in that a task that is demanding at one stage becomes less demanding at a later stage.

For example, certain aspects of phonology or syntax are very demanding for a three-year-old but relatively undemanding for a six-year-old. A three-year-old may have trouble pronouncing a word with r and say *wabbit* rather than *rabbit*, but rs generally present six-year-olds with no problems. When a person acquires a second language, tasks that are at first cognitively demanding are later less demanding. For example, second language learners might struggle with using the auxilaries *do* and *does* to form questions. After using English for a while, learners acquire these forms and use them easily without having to stop and think about the structure of the question they are forming.

78

It is the amount of conscious attention or cognitive energy that determines how cognitively demanding a task is, and this helps explain why certain subjects are not, in themselves, more demanding than others. It is true that some subjects are more complex than others. Calculus is more difficult than algebra. Furthermore, to study some topics it is helpful to study other topics first. However, while different topics have different potentials for the demands they might place on a person, the demand a particular topic makes depends on a person's previous experiences with that topic. To a mathematician, both algebra and calculus may seem quite easy.

Teachers who work effectively with English language learners are aware of the time it takes students to develop academic language. They understand the importance of presenting cognitively demanding concepts in context-embedded language. For example, a teacher might involve students in reading a number of interesting stories by a single author. Krashen (1993) refers to this as narrow reading. Narrow reading focuses on one topic or one author. By the time teenagers reach the second or third *Sweet Valley High* book, they are familiar with the vocabulary, and they can easily predict many elements of character and plot. They have built up a context from reading the earlier books in the series. The language of the new book is context-embedded, so it is less cognitively demanding.

Teachers who follow principles for success always embed language in a meaningful context. They know that their English language learners are capable students who need a challenging curriculum if they are to fully develop their academic potential. At the same time, they recognize that their students' limited English proficiency can make learning more difficult. For that reason, these teachers teach whole to part. This helps ensure that even demanding concepts will be presented in a context that helps students understand the lessons and develop the academic English they need to succeed in school.

A Shift Toward Whole-to-Part Language Teaching

The recognition that all learning, including language learning, involves a gradual process of differentiating the parts out of the whole has led to a change in second language teaching. Instead of beginning with discrete bits of language, teachers attempt to expose students to a wide range of the target language. They use specific techniques to make the new language understandable. These teachers embed the linguistic elements of communication in a rich nonlinguistic context. They recognize that language is easier to learn when it is kept whole. Plunging a student into a new language, the old sink-or-swim method, is not the best way to teach. Instead, these teachers create situations in which students dealing with the full range of the target language get clues from the context that help them make sense of what they are experiencing. In Krashen's (1982) terms, such teachers make the input comprehensible.

In addition, teachers who follow principles for success, even when they are teaching a class called English language development (ELD), keep language in the context of academic content. They recognize that language is best learned in the functional context of use. There are three good reasons for teaching language through content. First, students get both language *and* content. They develop academic proficiency at the same time that they develop English language proficiency. Second, language is kept in its natural context. As we study any subject, we learn the concepts and the vocabulary related to that subject. And third, when teachers teach language through content, they provide students with real reasons to learn the language. Rather than focusing on the language, they create situations where students can use language for authentic purposes.

Secondary Teachers Teaching Whole to Part

In a summer program for high school students that we observed, the teachers were encouraged to apply whole-to-part teaching in their content classrooms for second language students (Freeman et al. 1987). Rather than having their students focus on language or memorize bits and pieces of information about biology or history, these teachers taught language through content by concentrating on key concepts.

In a U.S. history class, Rob began the unit on the American Revolution by asking students to talk about what revolution meant, why countries had revolutions, where there were revolutions right now, and finally what they knew about the American Revolution. Both Rob and the students brought in current periodicals with articles about present-day revolutions. Rob read the students a short story about the American Revolution to help make the characters and setting of the period come alive. He also showed a film about the American Revolution. Then, students read the social studies text and compared what they read with the information about revolutions they already had gathered. Next, they worked in groups to decide what the major causes of the American Revolution were, what events and people were important to the outcome, and how the American Revolution could be compared to other revolutions discussed in class.

Rob was working with students who had not been successful in previous classes. They were language minority students and had scored low on standardized tests. However, they did well in Rob's class. Part of their success can be attributed to the rich context Rob provided. Rather than teaching isolated vocabulary, he introduced the vocabulary in context as he built a strong background for concepts such as "revolution" long before the students encountered that term in their social studies text. By itself, the textbook offered context-reduced language, but the class activities provided the context that made the textbook understandable.

In another class, the biology teacher organized a number of activities in which his students worked in cooperative groups and examined real plants and animals. For example, one day the teacher brought in a variety of fruits and vegetables. The students, working in small groups, studied the samples. They began with very general observations. Bananas had only one outer layer of skin while onions had many layers. Oranges could be divided into equal sections, but turnips were not so conveniently organized.

As the students examined various fruits and vegetables, they categorized them according to different criteria. They became more adept at making accurate observations, either directly or under a microscope. They began to see the world as a biologist sees it and to ask the kinds of questions a biologist might ask. As their investigations continued, they worked in teams to explore particular aspects of the topic that interested them.

These activities provided the whole, the context, the students needed to develop the concepts and the language necessary for their study of biology. The language was embedded in experiences with real fruits and vegetables, and students received added support from one another as they interacted in small groups. The teacher did not rely exclusively on the textbook but, instead, opened the whole world of biology to his students and yet did it in a way that helped them understand it.

Teaching Whole to Part
by Organizing Around Big Questions

Teachers who follow principles for success teach whole to part. They recognize the importance of providing context-embedded, cognitively-demanding instruction for all their students, and especially for their English language learners. Several writers provide detailed descriptions of how teachers organize curriculum around themes (Manning et al. 1994; Gamberg 1988). Whitmore and Crowel (1994) and Kucer, Silva, and Delgado-Larocco (1995) provide specific and concrete ideas about using themes with linguistically diverse students. Freeman and Mason (1991) suggest organizing themes around big ideas and powerful contrasts. The following list includes a number of reasons for organizing around themes based on big questions.

Reasons to Organize Curriculum around Themes Based on Big Questions

Students see the big picture, so they can make sense of English language instruction.

Content areas (math, science, social studies, literature) are interrelated.

Vocabulary is repeated naturally as it appears in different content area studies.

Through themes based on big questions, teachers can connect curriculum to students' lives. This makes curriculum more interesting.

Because the curriculum makes sense, English language learners are more fully engaged and experience more success.

Because themes deal with universal human topics, all students can be involved, and lessons and activities can be adjusted to different levels of English language proficiency.

When teachers organize curriculum around significant questions, they involve students in solving meaningful problems. For example, students might investigate questions such as "How will today's garbage affect future generations?" "Who belongs in this country and who should be allowed to stay?" or "Why do some people spend time, money, and energy to tan themselves but hate people who are born tan?" As students explore these relevant questions, they develop higher levels of cognitive, academic, and language proficiency.

How Are We Alike? How Are We Different?

Two big questions that are especially suitable for students in multilingual and multiethnic classes are: "How are we alike?" and "How are we different?" In the following sections, we describe several activities, resources, and strategies teachers can use to develop a thematic unit around these big questions with students of different ages and different levels of English proficiency. In the next chapter, we return to this theme and provide additional examples from a secondary ELD class. A bibliography of books for this theme is listed in Figure 3–3.

Primary Language Preview

If possible, provide a preview to the questions by reading an appropriate piece of literature in the students' first language. For younger Spanish speakers *Canción de todos los niños del mundo* (Ada 1993)(*Song of All the Chil-*

Ada, Alma Flor. 1993. *Canción de todos los niños del mundo*. Boston: Houghton Mifflin Company.

Cheltenham, Elementary School. 1994. *Todos somos iguales...todos somos diferentes*. New York: Scholastic.

Cheltenham, Elementary School. 1991. *We are all alike...We Are All Different*. New York: Scholastic.

Grande Tabor, Nancy María. 1995. *Somos un arco iris: We Are a Rainbow*. Watertown, MA: Charlesbridge Publishing.

Knight, Margie. *Talking Walls*. 1992. Gardner, ME: Tilbury House.

Morris, Ann. 1996. *On the Go*. Boston: Houghton Mifflin.

———. 1992. *Houses and Homes*. New York: Lothrop, Lee and Shepard Books.

———. 1990. *Con cariño*. Carmel, CA: Hampton Brown.

———. 1990. *Loving*. New York: William Morrow.

———. 1989. *Bread, Bread, Bread*. New York: Mulberry Books.

———. 1989. *Hats, Hats, Hats*. New York: Lothrop, Lee & Shepard Books.

Rotner, Shelley, and Ken Kreisler. 1997. *Faces, Invitations to Literacy*. Boston: Houghton Mifflin.

Rotner, Shelley and Ken Kreisler. 1997. *Rostros*. Boston: Houghton Mifflin.

Shea, Pegi. 1995. *The Whispering Cloth: A Refugee's Story*. Honesdale, PA: Boyds Mills Press.

Wood, Audrey. 1997. *Quick as a Cricket, Invitaciones*. Boston: Houghton Mifflin.

Figure 3–3 *Bibliography for Alike/Different Theme*

dren of the World) provides an excellent introduction to the big questions by comparing children around the world involved in their everyday activities. Another excellent bilingual Spanish/English book for elementary age students is *Somos un arco iris: We Are a Rainbow* (Grande Tabor 1995). In this book, the voices of immigrant students tell how in their country things are one way and in this country they are done another way.

If appropriate books are not available in the first languages of students in the classroom, have students brainstorm ways that people are alike and different. Students can work in different language groups with or without a primary language tutor. It might be good to begin with how people from their countries are the same and different from people in a particular English-speaking country. Students could illustrate some differences and even make picture books so that they could share in English ideas developed in their first languages with others who do not speak their language.

Resource Books in English

In English, draw from the students what they brainstormed or read about in their first languages. To expand on the ideas they developed, bring in books in English that expand on this theme. An excellent book for younger learners is *We Are All Alike: We Are All Different*, a book that is translated into Spanish and could be used as a preview (Cheltenham 1994, 1991). Another book to get lower and upper elementary age students discussing the questions is *Faces* (Rotner and Kreisler 1997). This book, also available in Spanish as *Rostros* (Rotner and Kreisler 1997), shows children of many races, countries, and ages doing things that all children love doing.

For older students, including adults who are learning English, the Ann Morris books are excellent because the photographs of people from around the world include many adults. In addition, the themes are significant, and the text is limited. Several of these books that would support the alike and different theme include: *Hats, Hats, Hats* (Morris 1989), *Loving* (Morris 1990), *Bread, Bread, Bread* (Morris 1989), *On the Go* (Morris 1996), and *Houses and Homes* (Morris 1992).

Some upper elementary teachers with students who have greater English proficiency use the book *Talking Walls* (Knight 1992), which contains information about walls erected by different cultural groups, from the Great Wall of China to the walls built by the Incas in Cuzco. Study of this book leads to questions of how cultural groups are all similar and yet all different.

After reading and discussing these books, write "People" at the top of an overhead transparency or large piece of butcher paper and "Alike" and "Different" underneath to form two columns. Have the students list words or phrases they know in English or learned from their reading that would go into each column. Be sure to keep this list up as a resource as students engage in other activities based on these questions.

Find Someone Who. . .

In order to personalize the characteristics and activities that make people alike and different, have the students brainstorm questions in English that they can use to find out about members of their class in a "Find someone who . . ." activity. In this activity, students ask each other questions that are not obvious from looking at one another to find out more about their classmates. For example, students might use their brainstormed list to " Find someone who likes to eat eels." or "Find someone who lives in an apartment." or "Find someone who plays tennis." or "Find someone who has fish as pets." In the process of doing this activity students practice English as well as practicing forms for asking and answering questions.

Legacies

Once students find out and share about their classmates, they begin to think about their own unique qualities. They can do this through an activity that begins with bringing in objects and drawing them. "Legacies" is an activity that helps students share and value their diversity (Hakuta and Diaz 1985). Younger children work in pairs to talk about keepsakes they have that they might pass on to grandchildren when they grow up. They draw pictures of their keepsakes. The pictures can be assembled into a class book. Older learners talk about objects or values passed down to them by relatives, and they can bring in keepsakes from their homeland that they talk or write about. Their writing can be gift wrapped to symbolize the cultural gift their ancestors left them.

One teacher introduced the idea of legacies with the book *Whispering Cloth* (Shea 1995). This story tells of a Hmong child in a refugee camp learning the art of *pa'ndau*, an elaborate embroidery story cloth. The girl in the book has difficulty deciding what story to weave into the cloth. Finally, she tells her own story, adding details her grandmother reminds her of. This book led naturally into the study of family and cultural arts and crafts. Children brought in sewing, knitting, painting, carving, and beading projects that their relatives had done; the children shared these in their first language and in English with their class.

Shiloh, a teacher education candidate studying second language acquisition at our university, experienced the power of legacy sharing personally. Shiloh was a parent volunteer in a kindergarten class of thirty-five students. About half the kindergarteners were native English speakers and half were Spanish speakers. In the class, there was also one Hmong girl, Choua. In the first three months Shiloh worked in the classroom, Choua did not utter one sound despite efforts of the teachers, aides, and the other children. Eventually, the other children refused to play with Choua, and they stopped trying to talk to her. Shiloh's own son in the class proclaimed that Choua couldn't talk and was "weird." With the permission of the teacher, Shiloh planned to help Choua share her legacies by centering the curriculum for one day around Hmong culture.

> First, I explained the Hmong culture using pictures and *pa'ndau*, embroidered story cloths. In explaining the stories of the war and migration into America, the children expressed interest and began

asking questions. My explanation helped them understand why the Hmong people came to America, and I believe seeds of tolerance were planted. Secondly, I brought in Hmong art, pictures of the cultural dress, and dolls dressed traditionally. The children played with the dolls and then created their own Hmong costume by coloring clothes for a paper doll form I provided. Finally, we proceeded to discuss the similarities between Hmong food and American food. The children made and ate sticky rice with sugar.

Shiloh provided activities that helped the other children to value Choua. Although Choua remained silent through the activities and was not ready yet to share her own legacy, the power of Shiloh's sharing of Choua's cultural legacies became clear afterwards. In a moving interview with Yvonne, Shiloh told Yvonne she can never tell the story without crying:

> At the end of the day, I went over to Choua. Though Choua's voice could not be heard, she mouthed clearly, "Thank you, Miss Shiloh." Every time I come into the classroom now, Choua's eyes follow me, she comes up to me, takes my hand, and smiles at me. I know how important that day was to her.

Creating Metaphors

Another way to get at the concepts of *same* and *different* is to work with metaphors. An excellent class book that introduces metaphors is *Quick as a Cricket* (Wood 1997). In this text, the narrator describes how he is "big as a whale" or "shy as a snail." After reading the book and brainstorming other ways animals can be like people, students can choose an animal, draw it, and describe how they are like the animal. Then the students can put the individual pages together to make a book. During this process, if students have a high enough level of English proficiency, they can arrange the pages to create a rhyming pattern like *Quick as a Cricket*.

It is important to allow students to preview in their first language at the beginning of any investigation of big questions and then review, summarize, and ask questions in their first languages when they are finished. This not only helps them consolidate and clarify their learning but also helps them see how much they have learned. "How are we alike?" and "How are we different?" are universal questions. As students engage in a variety of activities based on these questions, they gain greater cognitive, academic, and linguistic competence in two languages.

Conclusion

In this chapter we examined the commonsense assumption that learning goes from part to whole. The part-to-whole approach to instruction predominates in many schools. Teachers and textbooks attempt to make learning easier by dividing it up into bite-sized chunks for student consumption.

We argue that part-to-whole approaches to teaching and learning, are logical, but they are not based on psycholinguistic research. The parts are more difficult to learn outside the context of the whole. In many cases, students lose interest in the whole after they struggle with the parts. Tasting oregano, tomato sauce, and mozzarella doesn't whet their appetite for lasagna.

Teachers who follow principles for success keep language whole. They know that complete texts are richer in context than adapted or simplified language. These teachers also recognize that an important part of learning is the process of constructing meaning by determining which parts count. They believe that students will only develop a love of reading or writing or social studies if they have the opportunity to read and write complete texts and discuss big questions.

These teachers realize that whole-to-part teaching is good for all students, but that it is especially important for second language students. These students need context-embedded language so that they can understand instruction. They need to see the whole so that they know what to do with the parts. They need to be immersed in meaningful activities, not submerged in the grammatical details of a new language.

Whole-to-part teaching is not easy because school days are fragmented. Standardized tests encourage teaching bits and pieces of subjects. In some places, part-to-whole instruction is even mandated. Furthermore, teachers may have never personally experienced learning in a whole-to-part classroom and, in many schools, few other teachers may be trying to teach from whole to part. Yet, despite the obstacles to this approach, teachers who follow principles for success reject the commonsense view that learning progresses from part to whole and attempt to teach whole to part, because they know this makes learning easier for their students.

FOUR

Lessons Should Be Learner-Centered

◆

Where's The Food

I am very sick of third cluster. Do you know why, because when Room 28 comes for lunch we always have bread or cheese, and that is not fair. You guys have good food, but not us. I am very mad! The menu says we are having pizza, but I come in and we have bread and cheese. Would you like that? I don't! If you were in third cluster you would be sick like me, because I am waiting in line and I am very hungry. So you have to make more food so third cluster can get some too. If you gave people extra, you have to give us too. I am not trying to be mean, just give people fair food.

Tou Vang

Figure 4–1   *Where's the Food?*

This item in 28 *Times* (October 1997), a newsletter published in Mike's sixth grade classroom, Room 28 at Roeding Elementary School, is an example of students writing about what is important to them and what is part of their world. The publication of this newsletter is just one of the many ways that Mike helps make the instruction for his students learner-centered.

Because most of Mike's students are English language learners coming from a variety of first language backgrounds, it is critical that the curriculum draw on their backgrounds, their interests, and their strengths. Mike knows that reading is one key for their success (Krashen 1993). Students read and discuss poetry that catches their interest and inspires them. They enjoy books by Jane Yolen, Jean Little, Shel Silverstein, Jack Prelutsky, Gordon Korman, and Paul Fleischmann. Mike also invites his students to read fantasy and realistic fiction by imaginative authors including Louis Sachar, Jerry Spinelli, Roald Dahl, Scott O'Dell, and Gary Paulsen. To draw them into realistic accounts of United States history, they read Jean Fritz's historical biographies. To reflect on world history, they read several picture books: *Hiroshima No Pika, Sadako, The Thousand Paper Cranes* (Coerr 1979), and *Faithful Elephants* (Tsuchiya 1988). Mike taps into his students' backgrounds and interests by choosing a variety of fiction and nonfiction books that deal with universal themes and that represent different levels of reading difficulty.

He also organizes his class so that all students, including his English language learners, can show what they have learned. He does this by involving them in various projects. Students use a variety of ways to demonstrate what they learned: art, drama, models, video, and writing. In addition to the publication of the newspaper, 28 *Times*, Mike's students are immersed in varied and exciting learning experiences.

The projects change from year to year. Recent projects included:

- "Eureka—A History of California" was the title of a student-created museum, which included a range of exhibits, full-sized dioramas with students acting in scenes, and student-docent led tours for parents and other students in the school.
- "T.I.M.—The Incredible Machine" was an exploratorium of simple machines that students created for first and second graders in the school to come and experience.
- "Under the Sea" was a student-created, oversized, moveable diorama with animated sea creatures. The exhibit began with a California coastal tide pool and moved out under the waves into a kelp forest and finally into the murky depths of the Pacific Ocean.
- "28 Roeding Mall" was a Christmas venture. Student entrepreneurs raised money by making and selling a variety of items including

Christmas cookies and candies, ornaments, Christmas cards, and stickers. The students created business names, logos, and newspaper advertisements for 28 *Times*. They included a shopping guide with full page advertisements. Besides distributing their guide throughout the school, students scripted and produced a radio commercial aired over the school intercom and a video commercial shown to the student body during the lunch hour a day before the mall opened. Two days before the Christmas break, students opened their mall and sold their products.

Each of these activities helped Mike's students learn important academic content. The projects provided students with authentic purposes for learning, multiple means to present their knowledge, and real audiences who appreciated the results. In deciding how to develop each project, Mike followed Dewey's (1929) advice that "the child is the starting point, the center, and the end" (p. 14) of all curriculum decisions. Mike's classroom exemplifies a second important principle for success—*classes* should be learner-centered rather than teacher-centered.

Y. Goodman, a leader in the field of children's language and literacy development, said that the cartoonist, Bil Keane, can summarize years of her research in one cartoon. This principle is illustrated in Keane's "Family Circus" cartoon in which Billy leads his younger sister, Dolly, into the house after school explaining to their mother, "Dolly's school would be better if they didn't have that lady up front talkin' all the time."

Mike is not "up front talkin' all the time." In fact, Mike is behind the scenes nudging, encouraging, directing, and cheerleading. He follows Wells' (1992) advice to "lead from behind." He knows that his students learn best when they take ownership of their learning. The idea of the teacher as the source of all knowledge standing "up front talkin' all the time" follows from commonsense assumptions of how schooling should be. With English language learners, the temptation to have a teacher-centered classroom arises because the perception is that the teacher has the English proficiency the students need. Therefore, all knowledge must come from the teacher. However, it is important to remember that English language learners are not deficient just because they do not speak English. They bring a rich and varied background of experiences and talent to the classroom. Teachers who follow principles for success find ways to use their students' knowledge, including their first language and culture, even when the students do not speak English.

To explore this idea of a learner-centered curriculum for English language learners, we first look at additional examples of student publishing, one specific activity used in many learner-centered classes. Then we suggest a method for organizing lessons by using a questioning lesson plan format. We also include a checklist teachers can use to see if lessons follow the principles. We describe a sample unit that is strongly learner-centered. This unit is organized around the questioning lesson plan and involves students in writing and publishing materials based on their lives and interests; it also involves students in reading and writing about others whom they admire. We conclude by discussing a unit developed by a secondary teacher around a learner-centered theme.

Publishing: A Learner-Centered Classroom Routine

Students like to write about themselves. Teachers with immigrant students, especially, have discovered that students want to tell about their own experiences, and that they can do this through writing (Fu 1995). The article from the newsletter published in Mike's classroom is just one example of the type of publishing possible and the kinds of topics that students find important to write about. Student publications can include newsletters, individual books for the classroom library, whole class books, books for school distribution, books with hardback covers, and even professionally published books. All of these help English language learners share their experiences with others.

Publishing can be as simple as a very small, hand-printed, and hand-illustrated book and as complex as a professionally published collection of student writings. Topics can vary from concerns and interests students have about their daily lives to the philosophical retellings of life-changing experiences. Sometimes publishing is done in a language other than English. In learner-centered classes, students choose to write in their first language or in English about their own experiences and about the things they have learned. When teachers publish their students' own stories, other students can read them, and in this way, the reading and writing curriculum becomes learner-centered.

Simple Classroom Publishing: From Handmade Books to Newletters

In many classrooms students publish books frequently. Often a "publishing corner" occupies a place in the classroom where students can find pieces of paper of various sizes, shapes, and colors; also they can find many types of writing implements, including multicolored pens, pencils, and markers. During a daily writer's workshop time, students write, share, and edit various kinds of writing, including books. These pieces of writing are often read to the rest of the class by the author during an "author's chair" time. For young emergent writers, a book may be a series of a few pictures or it may be the result of a language experience activity in which the student dictates the story, the teacher acts as scribe, and then the student illustrates the finished book. For older learners who have a great deal of experience writing and publishing their own work, a book might consist of many pages and be divided into chapters. What is important is that the students choose their own topics, develop their ideas, revise and edit their work, and celebrate one another's writing as respected authors.

Mike explains how a writer's workshop functions in his class:

> The core of my philosophy for writer's workshop is the belief that children should be treated like real writers. Students are asked to keep a list of writing ideas that they have generated. They are asked to consider a writing genre from many we have discussed and demonstrated. With their idea in mind, they share with a small group what they plan to write. At this point, they actually write an initial rough draft. Students are encouraged to keep a collection of several "open" drafts so if they should get stuck with one, they have another to fall back on. After working on the rough draft, they meet with two different peer partners of their own choosing and one adult at home to get some feedback. After, doing some revision, the student meets with four peers and the teacher in a Content Conference where the author reads his/her piece for content ideas. The student then revises using suggestions from the Content Conference, self edits, and asks for peer editing by one or more peers. Students then make a final copy of the piece which is the "copy for assessment." The piece then is assessed by a student author initially and then with the teacher. This piece is then published. Publishing is student choice which could be an individual book with white tag cover and folded, stapled white bond paper inside. Occasionally students make pop-up books or do desktop publishing with digital photography and scanned images.

A workshop approach to writing is especially successful with students whose first language is not English. Students can choose what is important to them, and the students' messages are accepted and valued even when the form is not completely conventional. To include even non-English-speaking students, some teachers encourage their students to write stories in their first language. Another way to support student writing is to organize so students can co-author books. Carolina, a student teacher in a fourth grade classroom, suggested that three of her reluctant Spanish speaking writers collaborate on a book. The result is the handwritten and illustrated book *Viva Tijuana* (*Long Live Tijuana*). Some of the pages are shown in Figure 4–2. This book shows the value the writers place on their own country and how they are learning to compare life in Mexico with life in the United States.

Figure 4–2   Viva Tijuana

What impressed Carolina about the writers of this book was the ownership and pride they took in the project. Not only did they dedicate the book proudly to "all the families that know spanish," but they also ended their book with self-portraits and a personal greeting from each of the authors, "¡Ola! Nuestros nombres son Jorge, José y Hector. José tene 9 ayos Hector y Jorge tenen 10 anos. ("Hello! Our names are Jorge, José, and Hector. José is 9 years old Hector and Jorge are 10 years old.") Although the book is filled with nonconventional forms in both Spanish and English, the story is readable and the finished product gave each of the boys confidence in himself as a learner.

In Julie's high school ESL class, students also publish books on topics of interest and concern to them. After a discussion on pollution, Carmela wrote and published a creative story that included her solution to the problem (Figure 4–3).Included here are two of the pages from her book.

Carmela relies on her knowledge of Spanish to "invent" several syntactic and semantic forms in English. For example, she uses *contamination* for *pollution* because *contaminación* is the Spanish word for pollution. She says, "In one country about the here exist a very big Ghost the name Smog," which draws on the Spanish structure "En un país por aquí existía una fantasma que se llamaba 'Contaminación'" (In a country around here there was a ghost who was called Smog). Although Carmela frequently relies on her knowledge of her first language as she writes in English, her story and illustrations show that she is becoming confident in English. By allowing Carmela to publish and share her book, Julie is giving her second language student the opportunity to begin to express thoughts and concerns in her new language.

Both *Viva Tijuana* and *The Ghost of Contamination* are very simply constructed books. On plain white paper, students drew their own illustrations with marking pens and hand wrote their texts. Covers for their books were designed on construction paper and stapled around the pages. In some classrooms, the student books that are published look more like professional books. Students write the text of their stories, plan where they want illustrations and then type the text. After the text is typed on separate pages, students illustrate their books. The covers for these books are cardboard, covered with decorative pieces of wallpaper or contact paper. The pages are either stapled or sewn so that the final product looks more like a commercially produced book. As computers are almost always now standard equipment for schools and classrooms, teachers find it easier to do more sophisticated desktop publishing of books and even to do class newsletters.

Newsletters are one way of allowing students to share their experiences in writing. Books published by the class may have a somewhat

Figure 4–3   *Ghost of Contamination*

limited audience, whereas newsletters usually are duplicated and distributed more widely. They are often sent home to parents, to neighborhood organizations that the students are involved in, or to other classes in the school. Sometimes newsletters are even mailed across the country to other classes.

Topics that appear in newsletters might vary widely. In the issue of Mike's class newsletter 28 *Times*, in which the editorial "Where's the food?" appeared, articles included world news about the death of Mother Teresa and Princess Diana, interviews with the new principal and new librarian, the upcoming celebration of the school's 100th birthday, the need to get good grades to play football, the advantages of school uniforms, recommended children's literature, favorite recipes, school sports events, word plays, and even computer-generated cartoons. One other example from 28 *Times*, that clearly shows how English language learners respond with passion and enthusiasm when their writing is centered on topics of interest to them is shown in Figure 4–4.

In EFL settings, particularly in private, bilingual schools, newsletters are an important means of informing parents and showing them student progress in two languages. A good example comes from *Woodlands News*, the newsletter for a new school in Montevideo, Uruguay where teachers follow principles for success and teach language through meaningful academic content. The newsletter is a showcase for student work.

A recent issue includes riddles, nonfiction writing, poetry, and a short story. For example, younger students wrote simple riddles following a form, such as this one by Nano Argenti:

> It is an animal
> It jumps and it is green
> It lives in a hole.

Older students wrote paragraphs about dinosaurs, showing what they had learned during a theme study. As part of an environmental unit, one class wrote a poem about the earth. The Woodlands newsletter includes writing in both Spanish and English. It even features poems written by one of the teachers and by the director of the school.

Formally Published Books

Teachers who publish student work use formal as well as informal formats. Sometimes individual books have clothbound covers and pages with typed text. Often these books are made part of the class library and are checked out like books written by professional authors (Calkins 1994, 1991; Graves 1994, 1983). What is important about classroom publications by English language learners is that they draw on the students' experiences and give teachers a picture of their lives. Themes for the books are chosen by the students and often center around their experiences coming to a new country or adjusting to the country after arrival. A description of four different formal publications will give an idea of the potential of this kind of activity.

We Came to America (McConnell 1984) is a collection of the writings of fourth and fifth grade refugee students assembled by the Migrant

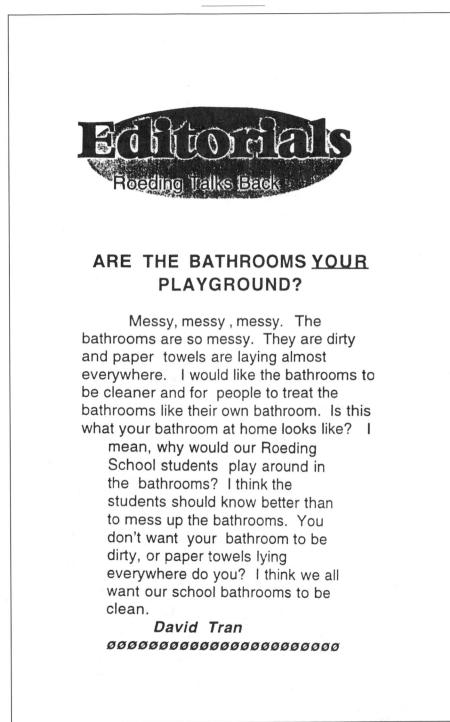

Editorials
Roeding Talks Back

ARE THE BATHROOMS <u>YOUR</u> PLAYGROUND?

Messy, messy , messy. The bathrooms are so messy. They are dirty and paper towels are laying almost everywhere. I would like the bathrooms to be cleaner and for people to treat the bathrooms like their own bathroom. Is this what your bathroom at home looks like? I mean, why would our Roeding School students play around in the bathrooms? I think the students should know better than to mess up the bathrooms. You don't want your bathroom to be dirty, or paper towels lying everywhere do you? I think we all want our school bathrooms to be clean.

David Tran
ØØØØØØØØØØØØØØØØØØØØØØØØØØ

Figure 4–4   *Bathrooms*

Education Program in Fresno County, California. Frances McConnel, the teacher who coordinated the project, explains its purpose and effectiveness in her preface:

> As a small child, one of my favorite stories was the true story of how my grandparents came to America. . . . My students are all Laotian or Hmong. They began telling me some of their stories of how they came to America, and I could hardly believe my ears. When I suggested they write these stories for me, it was like striking oil. Some of the children couldn't write fast enough. It was as if they had bottled it up inside, and now it could finally all come out.

Thirty children published their illustrated stories in the book that was typed and spiralbound with a construction paper child-illustrated cover. Phouvieng's writing (Figure 4–5) will give an idea of what the stories were like. This book was very popular among teachers who wanted to encourage their students to write. As a result, it was reprinted. Although the idea is a simple one, the book became a powerful teaching tool.

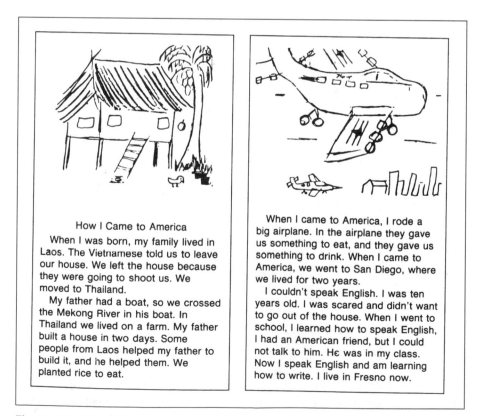

How I Came to America

When I was born, my family lived in Laos. The Vietnamese told us to leave our house. We left the house because they were going to shoot us. We moved to Thailand.

My father had a boat, so we crossed the Mekong River in his boat. In Thailand we lived on a farm. My father built a house in two days. Some people from Laos helped my father to build it, and he helped them. We planted rice to eat.

When I came to America, I rode a big airplane. In the airplane they gave us something to eat, and they gave us something to drink. When I came to America, we went to San Diego, where we lived for two years.

I couldn't speak English. I was ten years old. I was scared and didn't want to go out of the house. When I went to school, I learned how to speak English, I had an American friend, but I could not talk to him. He was in my class. Now I speak English and am learning how to write. I live in Fresno now.

Figure 4–5   *How I Came to America*

THE BIG EXPERIENCE

By Gabriel Martinez

Stories from the ESL Students of

Roosevelt High School, 1990

Figure 4–6   *The Big Experience*

Drawing on the experience of teachers like Frances, who had published books with younger children, Bunny Rogers decided that her high school ESL class could also publish a book. The students chose the title The Big Experience and participated in all aspects of the publication, including the cover design (see Figure 4–6).

In *The Big Experience* students wrote about a time they were afraid, needed help, or were happy. In the introduction, Bunny expresses what she hopes the publication will accomplish:

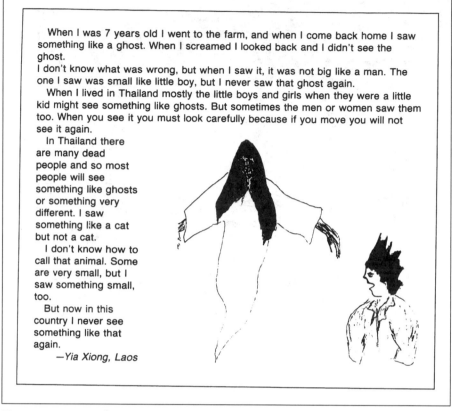

When I was 7 years old I went to the farm, and when I come back home I saw something like a ghost. When I screamed I looked back and I didn't see the ghost.

I don't know what was wrong, but when I saw it, it was not big like a man. The one I saw was small like little boy, but I never saw that ghost again.

When I lived in Thailand mostly the little boys and girls when they were a little kid might see something like ghosts. But sometimes the men or women saw them too. When you see it you must look carefully because if you move you will not see it again.

In Thailand there are many dead people and so most people will see something like ghosts or something very different. I saw something like a cat but not a cat.

I don't know how to call that animal. Some are very small, but I saw something small, too.

But now in this country I never see something like that again.

—*Yia Xiong, Laos*

Figure 4–7   *Yia's Ghost Story*

It is hoped that all who read these pages will be touched, as we have been, by the eloquence and indomitability of the human spirit as expressed by these young people.

Through pieces in this publication, students shared topics of interest and concern to them, such as Yia's ghost story (see Figure 4–7).

New Americans is a publication by Wayland Jackson's middle school ESL class. This is the third year that his seventh and eighth grade students produced a hardcover book that contains photographs of students and the school, as well as drawings done by the students to illustrate the typed stories and articles. All of the students worked on putting the book together, including typing the text and organizing the artwork and pictures. Several students worked after school and during their vacations to help meet deadlines. When the text was done, the local library bindery bound the book with a hardback cover. Then, the students used the books in their class as one of their textbooks. The low cost of publication was covered by sales to students, parents, and community members.

A short piece written by José Valencia and illustrated by Vang Lor (Figure 4–8) shows how second language learners write and draw about what is important to them. Students who enroll in Wayland's class each year realize they probably will be involved in a book project. They enter the class ready with ideas. The books always have a particular theme centered around the lives of new immigrants and their past experiences. One year, Wayland and his students decided to write a book on folk medicine. The students began their research enthusiastically, but the project was abandoned after a freeze killed the plants their family members grew for the home remedies. The next year Wayland and his students began another book. This time the students and the teachers together decided that the book would have no theme. They agreed that writing has to come from the experiences and interests of each writer. Although some students chose to pursue the previous year's theme of folk medicine, others chose topics that were directly relevant to them, including jobs, family activities, concerns about gangs, and the problems of poverty.

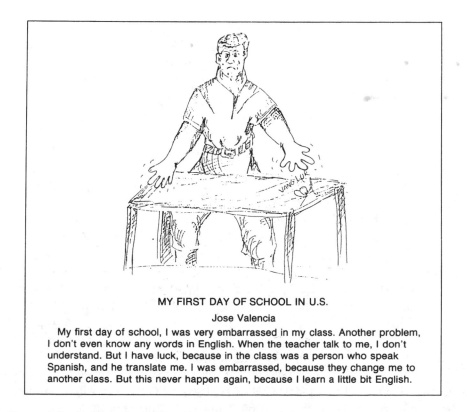

MY FIRST DAY OF SCHOOL IN U.S.

Jose Valencia

My first day of school, I was very embarrassed in my class. Another problem, I don't even know any words in English. When the teacher talk to me, I don't understand. But I have luck, because in the class was a person who speak Spanish, and he translate me. I was embarrassed, because they change me to another class. But this never happen again, because I learn a little bit English.

Figure 4–8   *José Valencia and Vang Lor*

Katsuyo Howard (1990, p. xi) begins her preface to *Passages: An Anthology of the Southeast Asian Refugee Experience* with this poignant quotation. "Another Hmong student leaves my office with tears in his eyes, saying, 'This is the first time that someone has listened to my story. I thought nobody was interested in listening to me.'" This book contains accounts of the trials and sufferings of many Southeast Asian students now attending college. The book was written to inform others and to help the authors come to terms with their own, often traumatic, experiences. Howard dedicates the volume to "all of you who are finding your own ways to bring peace and understanding to the earth." *Passages* demonstrates that there are benefits of student publishing for students at any grade level.

Classes that are learner-centered often include book projects that feature student writing. The writing may be a collection of individual stories around a common theme or a collection of writing centered on the students' own interests and experiences. In other cases, the writing may focus on what students are studying. One class we observed published a book on various sea creatures as the culmination of their unit on oceanography.

With electronic mail availablity, books can be shared with schools around the world and become interactive! Mike's class published on the Internet. He subscribes to the Scholastic Network. One especially interesting project Mike found posted on the Teacher Connection page was a "Chain Book." The class joined with fifteen schools around the country via the Internet. Together, they created a chain book. The first class, from Shreveport, Louisiana wrote the introductory chapter. Then, each of the other classes developed the story line of the chapter written by the first class. They kept the same characters and extended the plot. In addition, each chapter reflected the school and the city where it was written; so readers learned about different parts of the country.

For example, Mike's class wrote the second chapter. First, they read and discussed Chapter One. Then they decided on the incidents to be included in their chapter. They were sure to bring in their city and their school to add a unique local flavor. The Fresno chapter helped dispel myths about California. Fresno does not have a beach, and all the characters are not blonde surfers. When they finished, they mailed the first two chapters on to the next school, in Williamsburg, Virginia. In fact, one challenge was to find a way to get the characters to the next site. The chain continued until the book was completed.

Whether the books are fiction, stories of students' lives, or summaries of students' research, all of these publications are learner-centered because they draw on student interests and strengths. For many

English language learners, these publications are a first step toward future school success. Book projects fit well with the sociopsycholinguistic orientation we advocate. This approach views learning as transactional, a process in which the activity of both the teacher and the learners is important. The teacher does not simply facilitate learning for students. Instead, the teacher learns with the students as they explore knowledge together. Topics for exploration may come from either the students or the teacher, and together all members of the class, including the teacher, determine how to find answers to the questions they pose. Students learn language in the process of exploring content area questions.

In classes where teachers and students work together to negotiate curriculum rather than following a traditional curriculum format, structure is still needed. Many teachers would be uncomfortable simply playing each day "by ear" and exploring whatever comes up. This is one reason that teachers of English language learners teach language through content. They know that a long-range plan is needed for learning to take place. Both the teacher and the students can help create the plan. In the next section, we discuss one way to organize curriculum that is consistent with a transactional approach and that is learner centered, yet still carefully structured.

Questioning Strategies Begin with the Student

One way to engage students' interest as they learn language through content is through the use of students' questions. Clark (1988) pointed out that curriculum should involve students "in some of the significant issues in life" and therefore encourages teachers to design their curriculum around "questions worth arguing about" (p. 29). These are what we refer to as big questions. Clark suggests questions for different grade levels such as, "How am I a member of many families?" (K–1); "What are the patterns that make communities work?" (2–3); "How do humans and culture evolve and change?" (4–5); and "How does one live responsibly as a member of the global village?" (6,7,8).

Sizer (1990) draws on this idea by suggesting that organizing around "Essential Questions" leads to "engaging and effective curricula." In social studies, U.S. history teachers might begin with broad questions such as "Who is American? Who should stay? Who should stay out? Whose country is it anyway?" (p. 49). Sizer suggests larger questions for long-term planning and smaller, engaging questions to fit within the broader ones. For example, an essential question in botany might be "What is life, growth, 'natural' development, and what factors most influence healthy development?" A smaller, engaging question might be

"Do stems of germinating seedlings always grow upwards and the roots downwards?" (p. 50).

In each of the preceding examples, the goal is to make the curriculum learner-centered rather than teacher-centered by involving students in answering relevant, real world questions that they help to raise. This inquiry approach to teaching and learning involves students in their own learning in a way that mandated curriculum does not (Short et al. 1996). In the following section we suggest a way of using questions for day-to-day lesson planning and then give a sample unit based on this kind of questioning approach to planning. We should add that in a learner-centered class, the questions come primarily from the students; however, as a member of the learning community, the teacher also can raise questions.

Mike's curriculum centers on big questions. Last year Mike's students were fifth graders. They began the year by brainstorming possible topics to study. Several of the suggestions dealt with the topic of discovery, including the discovery of America and the country's beginning. There also was interest in the various cultures that make up America. The class pulled these together into a theme around the question, "What IS American?"

Mike introduced the unit with Jean Fritz' (1987) book, The Double Life of Pocahontas. Students compared the book with the Disney movie, "Pocahontas." Mike encouraged students to look at both the book and movie and discuss the author's point of view and how history is presented differently by authors and movie makers.

Mike expanded the theme by having students read different picture books that dealt with Native American cultures including readings on the Aztecs. He also read the class a book about Sir Francis Drake. Then, the students role-played scenes of the exploration of the New World from different points of view. Mike explained what the class did:

> We role played student interpretations of the English position for coming to the New World versus that of the Native American reaction. The social studies text was used as a resource for its maps and many pictures, helping to bring more visual information to the students. In addition, we used some slides of Jamestown and Plymouth colonies shared by a teacher who had lived in the area before coming to Fresno, and some video footage I recorded from Discovery channel about the early colonies. We made a five foot map of the eastern coast, and began to identify the English colonies as we read about them in other Jean Fritz books, and also the approximate locations of the different Native tribes mentioned. I was able to get some historical information from the Internet on Pocahontas and her tribe and shared it, too.
>
> We moved from there into the differences in the colonies, economically, politically, and in their beliefs about the church. Students divided themselves into the three different colonial areas,

and then returned to the textbook using a "jigsaw" activity, allowing each group to discover information about their colonial area and share it in some creative way with the class. This activity allowed me to demonstrate how to "read" a nonficion text for the purpose of gathering information. Students shared the information in a variety of ways, including a group which acted out parts of different person-alities they felt demonstrated the key aspects of their colonies and a group that put on a kind of colonial news broadcast informing its colonial listeners as to important topics of the day.

Mike's class continued the study of "What IS American?" through an examination of issues of slavery in the colonies, and the Revolutionary War era. After four months, the students wanted to find a way of sharing their findings about America's beginnings by creating some kind of ex-hibit. They finally decided on using a variety of ways to share. Some made static art displays, others made small dioramas, still others wrote and acted out scenes. One group wrote and narrated a video they put together with a series of slides. The students dubbed it, "A Multimedia Museum of Early American History." Tours of the exhibit were extended to about five classes, ranging from first to fifth grades.

After the presentations, Mike asked students to reflect on what they learned in this unit during a final discussion of the original question, "What IS American?"

> Students felt that they had not really found a single answer to their question, but instead had actually found many new questions along the way. They also felt that their question was something that was still being defined as new immigrant groups joined their cultures, languages, and traditions with those of other groups who were al-ready here. They saw that no group came without conflict, prejudice, and racism. It seemed to bring the history home for them as they looked around the room and saw the incredible diversity within their own classroom. One student responded, "I think America is us. We are all different, yet all the same. That is what makes us special, that is what makes us American."

Questioning Lesson Plan and Principles for Success Checklist

Teachers at all levels, including creative teachers like Mike, are required to do long-term and day-to-day planning. Too often the day-to-day plan-ning becomes routine, a kind of exercise completed because it is re-quired by administrators. In our work with teacher education candidates, for example, we have found that student teachers are tempted to fulfill the requirement of preparing lesson plans by making lists—lists of page numbers students will read; lists of exercises students will complete; lists of activities students will do; or lists of materials that will be needed.

Although we try to get away from this mechanical type of lesson planning, we also realize that it is critical that all teachers have some plan for the general direction in which the curriculum is headed. Teachers must be able to show administrators, parents, and other teachers that their curriculum does fulfill district and state guidelines. At the same time, teachers who follow principles for success are aware of the importance of keeping the learner at the center of all curriculum decisions. A method for planning that we suggested for student teachers and that we recommend for experienced teachers is the "Questioning Lesson Plan" that follows. This lesson plan format is designed to help teachers reconceptualize curriculum as a series of questions generated by the students and the teacher as they explore topics together. This format also encourages teachers to remain focused on the major concepts they are studying. It asks them to consider how each lesson might connect to broader themes. Planning lessons with this format is one way teachers can put principles into practice. In addition, we suggest that they use the following Principles for Success Checklist to review their lessons. The checklist is a series of questions based on the principles.

Questioning Lesson Plan

1. *What is the question worth talking about?* (Can the topic for this lesson be formulated in a question? What is the engaging smaller question that fits into your broader question for your overall theme?)

2. *How does the question fit into your overall plan?* (What is the broad question/theme that you and your students are exploring over time? How does the smaller, engaging question support the concepts you are working on with this broad question?)

3. *How will you find out what the students already know about the question?* (What are different ways your students might show what they already know about answering the question? You might brainstorm, do an experiment, interview someone, and so on.)

4. *What strategies will you use together to explore the question?* (What are ways the question might be answered? You and your students might read, do an experiment, brainstorm, ask an expert, work out a problem together, and so on. Ask the students if they have ideas about how to answer the question.)

5. *What materials will you use together to explore the question?* (List the resources, including people, that students might use to answer the question. Again, ask the students if they have ideas about this.)

6. *What steps will you and the students take to explore the question?* (In order to be sure that you are keeping in mind principles about learning, consult the Checklist. Do the activities you suggest incorporate the principles?)

7. *How will you observe the students' learning?* (What are some different ways to evaluate the process of your students' learning? Be sure to consider alternatives to traditional tests including group presentations, a group produced book or newspaper, the results of an experiment, a drawing or schemata, and so on.)

Principles for Success Checklist

1. Is curriculum organized around "big" questions? Do lessons move from whole to part?

2. Are lessons learner-centered? Is there an attempt to draw on student background knowledge and interests? Are students given choices?

3. Is the content meaningful? Does it serve a purpose for the learners?

4. Do students have opportunities to work collaboratively?

5. Do students read and write, as well as speak and listen during their learning experiences?

6. Are students' primary languages and cultures valued, supported, and developed?

7. Are students involved in activities that build their self-esteem and provide them with opportunities to succeed?

Critical to any lesson plan is the idea of learner-centeredness. When lessons begin with students' interests and experiences, students are naturally more motivated to engage in learning. If they are not interested in learning something, their learning is apt to be short-term rote memorization at best. We also hope that students' interest is not based simply on the desire to do well on a test or get some other kind of extrinsic reward, but instead we hope that students will "buy into" the curriculum because they honestly are interested in answering the questions that they helped raise. When students do this they are engaging in inquiry (Short et al. 1996). We found that teachers who plan lessons with the Questioning Lesson Plan and review them with the Checklist encourage inquiry and a learner-centered curriculum.

An example of a questioning plan that draws on student interest and involvement comes from Kelly, a fourth grade teacher in a small farming community. Kelly's class has several Hispanic students whose first language is Spanish. The students' facility with English varies greatly; yet, Kelly wants to be sure to involve all her students in her lessons regardless of their English proficiency.

Kelly and her students were working on the theme of drugs. Their broad question was, "How do drugs affect my life?" As they explored this topic, the class looked at the surgeon general's warning against smoking and the effects of tobacco on health. The question of why people still buy cigarettes and smoke despite the medical evidence arose naturally from the students during discussion. Kelly thought that if she and her students looked at different advertisements, they could see how the media uses propaganda. Following the Questioning Lesson Plan, Kelly's unit on drugs might look like this:

Questioning Lesson Plan

1. *What is the question worth talking about?* How does the media (newspapers, magazines, television in Spanish as well as English) use propaganda to encourage smoking?

2. *How does the question fit into your overall plan?* The students realize that tobacco is a drug that is harmful, and they need to be aware of the ways the media encourages this unhealthy addiction in their lives. This ties in with two broad questions: How do drugs affect our lives? How does propaganda affect our lives?

3. *How will you find out what the students already know about the question?* We will see if we can remember seeing any cigarette advertisements. What language were they in? Where did we see them? What were the advertisements about? We will look for advertisements and write down what they are about or, if possible, bring them to class.

4. *What strategies will you use together to explore the question?* We will brainstorm what we saw in the media. Students will interview people and collect advertisements. We will use cooperative groups as we discuss and look at advertisements. We will compare and contrast different advertisements. Students might make up their own advertisements about smoking.

5. *What materials will you use together to explore the question?* Magazines/ newspaper advertisements in both English and Spanish; video.

6. *What steps will you and the students take to explore the question?* (Consult the Checklist to be sure each step is consistent with the principles).

   a. Do a quickwrite (write for one minute anything that comes to your mind on the topic or question) on advertisements they can remember for cigarettes. (Be sure to allow for advertisements in both Spanish and English.)

   b. Brainstorm familiar advertisements.

   c. Interview others and collect advertisements.

   d. Cut out cigarette advertisements from English and Spanish newspapers and magazines; categorize them according to how they appeal to the public (i.e., smokers are beautiful, smokers are athletic, smokers are rich, and so on.).

   e. Make a bulletin board of the advertisements in their categories.

   f. Write and act out advertisements against smoking.

   g. Videotape advertisements to show to other classes.

7. *How will you observe the students' learning?*

   a. Keep anecdotal records of students' contributions to the small group and large group discussion and the bulletin board display.

   b. Group presentations (including videotapes) and written advertisements will show that the students answered the question for this lesson.

Kelly did more than facilitate this unit of study. She was an active co-learner. She was as excited and interested as the students in finding advertisements in magazines and noting down billboard advertisements as she drove around town. During class discussions and activities, Kelly added her examples. Reviewing Kelly's unit with the Checklist clarifies how a series of lessons drawing on students' questions is consistent with principled practice.

Reviewing Kelly's Unit with the Principles for Success Checklist

1. Is *curriculum organized around "big" questions? Do lessons go from whole to part?* Kelly based the unit on big questions on the effect of drugs and propaganda on our lives. She taught whole to part by starting with what the students knew about advertisements in general and then moved on to an analysis of specific advertisements.

2. *Are lessons learner centered? Is there an attempt to draw on student background knowledge and interests? Are students given choices?* Kelly chose a topic she knew her students were interested in. The students wrote and brainstormed about what they already knew. Then they chose specific advertisementss to bring in and discuss. They also chose the advertisement to make up for the video.

3. *Is the content meaningful? Does it serve a purpose for the learners?* This topic was one students were very interested in because there is a great deal of pressure on them to use various kinds of drugs, including tobacco.

4. *Do students have opportunities to work together collaboratively?* The students interacted in several of the activities, particularly in creating the advertisement.

5. *Do students have an opportunity to read and write as well as speak and listen during the lesson?* Yes, all four modes were included. In addition, the students used drama and the visual arts as they made the video.

6. *Are students' primary languages and cultures valued, supported, and developed?* The discussion of advertisements in Spanish focused on their culture. Spanish speakers translated the Spanish advertisements. Groups could choose to do their anti-tobacco advertisement in English, Spanish, or in both languages.

7. *Does the teacher demonstrate a belief that students will succeed?* Yes, especially with the video for the other classes. The students realized that Kelly had confidence in what they could do.

With units such as this, which are learner-centered and encourage participation, students often contribute in ways teachers cannot plan for. One of Kelly's students interviewed his grandparents about smoking. When they realized what their grandchild was doing, they offered to loan the class a video that included cigarette advertisements from a television show produced in the 1950s. With this resource, students were able to compare advertisements for cigarettes before and after the surgeon general's warnings was required; they also looked at the difference in the claims that advertisements made in the past and make today. Several students were surprised that there was a time when cigarettes were advertised on television. They began to raise questions about who regulates media—questions that could form the basis for future units.

Another interesting and unexpected outcome of looking at advertisements came from the Spanish-speaking media. The students noticed that there were more advertisements for smoking in Spanish language magazines than in English magazines. This led to a discussion about whether more Hispanics smoked than Anglos and what the reasons for this might be.

Lessons such as those that Kelly involved her students in are learner-centered because they draw on student interests, provide choices, include experiences from the students' own lives, promote the active involvement of all the students, and encourage students to creatively share with peers what they are learning. These kinds of activities could lead to others; for example, teachers and other adults who smoked could be interviewed to get their opinions on the effect advertisements have on them. Recent court cases finding tobacco companies guilty of false advertising and the revelation of the attempts by tobacco companies to get government subsidies could lead to other interesting directions for this unit, especially for students studying U.S. court and legislative systems. Guest speakers from the American Cancer Society and other health organizations could be invited to come to the class to help answer questions, such as what the research says about the relationship between secondhand smoke and cancer.

The Questioning Lesson Plan and the Principles for Success Checklist encourage teachers to take a critical look at the rationale for the activities they plan with their students as they explore different content areas. As students and teachers answer real questions that interest them, they learn together.

Me and Other Great People: A Study of Heroes

Teachers who follow principles for success and use a transactional approach to explore questions together with their students recognize that their limited English proficient students can learn language through content, especially when they see a connection between the content and their own lives. We suggested that one way to make classes learner-centered is by students publishing stories that reflect their experiences, interests, and research. We also described a learner-centered lesson plan format organized around questions worth talking about. In this section, we combine these two ideas by using the Questioning Lesson Plan format to outline a unit that involves students in reading and writing autobiography and biography. As we describe the unit, we suggest possible activities that can be adapted for different grade levels. This unit has clear ties to the unit on "How are we alike?" and "How are we different?" that we outlined in the previous chapter.

1. *What is the question worth talking about*? How am I similar to and different from others?

2. *How does the question fit into your overall plan*? This self-analysis is one step toward answering the larger question "What are my values and who are my heroes?"

3. *How will you find out what the students already know about the question*? Students can learn about themselves by reflecting on their own characteristics. They can interview or read about others to establish a basis for comparison.

4. *What strategies will you use together to explore the question*? Strategies will include responding to a book, brainstorming, interviewing classmates, reading about sports and sports heroes, and writing autobiography and biography.

5. *What materials will you use together to explore the question*? Materials include the book *People* (Spier 1980), questionnaires made by the stu-

dents, newspapers, books, and magazines about sports, a camera for taking class or school pictures, and butcher paper for charts or other displays.

6. *What steps will you and the students take to explore the question?*

    1. Begin the lesson by reading the book *People* by Peter Spier. Because the book discusses physical characteristics, interests, customs, and languages of people around the world, have the students brainstorm in groups about all the ways people in the book are the same and all the ways they are different.

    2. Move from the discussion of people around the world to those in the classroom. How are the people in the book the same as or different from each of the students in our class? How are students in our class the same as or different from one another? Have students brainstorm questions they could ask their peers for an interview to find out the interests, customs, language backgrounds, and so on, of their classmates. Then, students can interview each other and write about each other.

7. *How will you observe the students' learning?* There will be frequent opportunities to observe students as they interview, read, and write.

    A number of possible extensions for this lesson could help to answer the bigger question, "What are my values, and who are my heroes?" These would be part of the extended unit on this topic.

    1. Several activities are possible using the data collected from the interviews: (a) Find Someone Who, (b) Who Is It?, and (c) Introductions. In "Find Someone Who," students make up "Find Someone Who. . . ." forms from the interview information. These forms contain sentences with characteristics of people in the class. For example, "Find someone whose first language is Laotian" or "Find someone who likes to roller skate." Then, all students question classmates to find people who fit the descriptions and fill in their names on the forms. The descriptions also might be used as a "Who Is It?" guessing game. Students read descriptions from their interviews and the other students guess who they wrote about. In addition, the write-ups from the interviews can be used as introductions. Students tell important things and interesting stories as a way of introducing each other.

    2. For the next step, have students look at themselves and their own lives. Students ask themselves, "What things, symbols, or objects represent me?" They make posters with their names in large script and a symbol that represents them. In some classes, as a variation, students design a personal coat of arms. A next

step after the visual representation is to create a book of basic information called *All About Me*. Students brainstorm as a group the information they want to include in their individual books.

3. Following the making of individual *All About Me Books*, students might compile the information into a class book. Consider including a picture of each student with basic information printed underneath. The class pictures also could be one section of a longer book about the school that includes other people such as the principal, the vice principal, the attendance secretary, the nurse, the cafeteria staff, the custodians, and the couselors. Students could take pictures and interview these people and include them in the book.

4. Students enjoy reading about the lives of personalities who interest them; teachers or students could bring in newspapers with sections from the sports pages, entertainment pages, or teen pages. Ask the students to read articles and share what they learn with their classmates. Each student or pair of students could report on one newspaper personality.

5. Teachers might ask students to brainstorm, "What do you know about sports?" Then allow students to look through and discuss issues of *Sports Illustrated for Kids*. Working individually or in pairs, students can pick a sports hero to become an expert on and to share with the rest of the class. They might prepare a "vital statistics" chart on their hero; have each group compare heroes.

6. Other activities that encourage language development are possible using resources such as newspapers, magazines like *Sports Illustrated for Kids*, and biographies or fictional accounts of sports heroes. Students can make charts listing vocabulary specific to different sports. They can read the sports pages daily, following certain teams and then chart results of their games. Students who are experts in one sport can teach others how to read box or line scores. In *Sports Illustrated for Kids*, there are many letters written by students to sports heroes. Students can write to their sports hero and ask questions they cannot find answers to in their reading. To learn more about particular sports heroes, students like to read factual accounts of athletes' lives or read novels such as *In the Year of the Boar and Jackie Robinson* (Lord 1984), which include information about sports heroes.

7. As students become experts on sports heroes, they could produce books following the same format they used in *All About Me*. Because many sports heroes are from foreign countries or

are recently naturalized citizens, students can explore the different backgrounds of sports heroes. The question, "What does it take to make a sports hero?" can lead to interesting discussions. Students also can explore reasons that certain countries produce great athletes in specific sports.

8. As a culminating activity, ask students to write about a sports hero, and publish these accounts in a class book or newspaper. Or, have students create a collage of pictures about a particular athlete or sport. Students also can present, in dramatic form, scenes from important points in the life of the sports hero they studied.

This unit begins by asking students to reflect on who they are and then involves them in reading, writing, and talking about other people they admire. This helps second language students, and all students, consider what they can become. The activities use authentic materials such as magazines and newspapers, and this also makes it adaptable for the EFL setting. In our example, we used sports heroes. It is easy to expand or refocus this unit to include heroes from a number of other fields. The choice depends on the age and interest of the students.

Mary's "Sense of Self" Unit

We conclude this chapter with the description of a learner-centered unit from a secondary teacher. This is Mary's second year of teaching at a high school in a rural community. She uses this unit, "Sense of Self" to begin the year with her ninth grade classes of ELD, regular, and honors English. This unit is based on the same general questions as the previous units— "How are we alike/ different?" and "Me and other Great People." It shows how a creative teacher can take these ideas and adapt them to fit her teaching context while still following the principles for success.

The high school where Mary teaches has a large Hispanic population as well as a sizable group of students whose first language is Punjabi. The school schedule is organized into four block classes per day. Students take eight classes, so they see their teachers every other day. Teachers teach seven classes and have one preparation period every other day. The block schedule provides extended time for students to read, write, and talk about significant themes. However, because Mary has seven different classes, she needs to plan so that she can challenge her students academically and provide them with ample reading and writing activities without becoming completely overwhelmed in her preparation. Therefore, she organizes her classes around the same basic theme offering all her students the same kinds of challenging activities while still adjusting instruction to meet the varying language needs of her classes.

Daily Routine

Students in Mary's English classes follow a typical routine each day. Mary found that this is especially important for her ninth graders who are often intimidated by high school and its schedules and demands. Of course, this kind of routine also is helpful to English language learners because they are able to predict what is expected of them during class. The routine allows those students to spend their energies in making sense of the content of the curriculum instead of worrying about what they are supposed to be doing.

Each period begins with fifteen minutes of SSR (sustained silent reading). If students do not bring their own books or books from the school library, Mary has a classroom library of about 250 books, including short stories, poetry, and novels at different levels of complexity. In addition to traditional works, Mary's library also has short, fairly easy reading, predictable texts including "choose your own adventure" books, books from the *Goosebumps* series (Stine), or teen romances such as the *Sweet Valley High* series (Pascal). Mary agrees with Krashen (1993) that these kinds of books encourage reluctant readers to read. Eventually, less confident readers who begin with easier books move on to read what would be considered more traditional, quality literature. For students who are intimidated by reading in English, Mary has books in Spanish. This wide variety of reading materials ensures that all students are reading daily.

Mary makes an effort to include works by Latino and Latina writers in her library. For example, she found that works of Gary Soto, such as *Baseball in April: And Other Stories, Crazy Weekend, Living Up the Street* and *Neighborhood Odes* (Soto 1990, 1994, 1992, 1996) are especially relevant to her Latino students because Soto writes about everyday experiences of Hispanics.

A helpful resource for locating relevant books is *Latino and Latina Voices in Literature* (Day 1997). This annotated bibliography is organized by geographical areas and by themes. Day provides a half-page summary of each book. This is helpful for teachers wishing to preview longer chapter books.

Mary relies on books in English for her Punjabi students, and she is aware that for this group, finding culturally appropriate books is more difficult. Two books her Punjabi students enjoy are *Shabanu, Daughter of the Wind* (Staples 1989), which tells the life of a young girl whose nomadic family raises camels in Pakistan. This book and the sequel, *Haveli,* (Staples 1993) describe how families arrange marriages, a topic students

Cisneros, Sandra. 1991. *Woman Hollering Creek*. New York: Vintage Press.
————. 1984. *The House on Mango Street*. New York: Vintage
Contemporaries.
Day, Frances Ann. 1997. *Latina and Latino Voices in Literature*. Portsmouth:
Heinemann.
Pascal, Francine. *Sweet Valley High Series*. New York: Bantam Books.
Soto, Gary. 1996. *Neighborhood Odes*. New York: Harcourt Brace.
————. 1994. *Crazy Weekend*. New York: Scholastic.
————. 1992. *Living Up the Street*. New York: Dell Publications.
————. 1990. *Baseball in April and Other Stories*. San Diego: Harcourt Brace
Jovanovich.
Staples, Suzanne. 1993. *Haveli*. New York: Knopf.
Staples, Suzanne. 1989. *Shabanu*. New York: Alfred A. Knopf.
Stine, R.L. *Goosebumps Series*. New York: Scholastic.

Figure 4–9   *Mary's Multicultural Bibliography*

find fascinating. Figure 4–9 lists some representative literature from Mary's library.

At the end of the daily SSR time, students respond to their reading in their literature journals for fifteen minutes. Next, Mary reads a short piece to the class, or they read the piece themselves. Mary chooses readings related to the theme being investigated. Students talk about the reading in pairs or small groups and then engage in a general class discussion. Next, the students work on a project related to the theme. During the last fifteen minutes of each period, students write in their personal journals. Usually, Mary gives them a question to answer that is based on the reading and that involves literary concepts such as metaphor, character, or setting that Mary wants students to understand. In the next section, we discuss one unit and related activities in which Mary and her students engaged.

Developing a Sense of Self

Mary created a unit "Developing a Sense of Self" to help her high school students answer the big question "Who am I?" She knew students needed to appreciate the diversity in their school and their world, and they first should begin with understanding themselves. In addition, beginning the school year with this theme helped Mary get to know her students and helped give her insight into their lives as well as helping students to get to know one another. Mary found her students enjoyed this theme because the activities focused on them.

In the first activity, Mary asked students to interview each other and write down the answers. Then, they introduced their partner to the rest of the class. Later in the year, Mary would have students brainstorm interview questions, but at this point, she wants to be sure certain information is included. She also wants to involve her ESL students in an authentic activity that requires them to ask and answer basic information questions. For that reason, she gave students the following questions as an interview guide:

Name:

Where were you born?

How many brothers and sisters do you have?

What do you do for fun?

What is your favorite sport? Favorite team?

What is your favorite food?

What is your favorite book?

What is your favorite movie and or television show?

When you think of English class, what do you think of?

What are your plans for the future?

What is something interesting/unique about you?

Once students learned about their classmates, they began to think about their own uniqueness. One activity that helped students think about themselves and value their individuality was creating a coat of arms. Students drew an empty coat of arms with five quadrants to fill in. For each quadrant they drew or cut out a picture that revealed something about themselves and labeled it. After students completed their personal coats of arms, they shared them in pairs. They also had other students guess what some of the pictures represented. Then, students worked in groups to make a cumulative coat of arms that they shared with the whole class.

Figure 4–10 shows the coat of arms a beginning ELD student made. These pictures represented student responses to "things I love to do," "what I want to do in the future," "where I want to live in the future," and "what I like to eat." This coat of arms activity provided students with opportunities to develop English language proficiency as they shared about how they were the same as or different from their peers. It also provided the background and built vocabulary for other activities requiring more reading and writing in English.

Mary followed the introductory interview and coat of arms project with a series of other activities to engage her high school students in read-

Figure 4–10   *Coat of Arms*

ing and writing. To help students continue to build on the idea of developing a sense of who they are and to enable them to write a longer autobiographical piece, Mary introduced the autobiopoem. In this activity students write a poem about themselves following the pattern shown here:

Autobiopoem

Follow the instructions and you will see that you are a poet.

Line 1: Write your first name

Line 2: Write four adjectives that describe you

Line 3: Son/daughter of. . . or . . brother/sister of. . .

Line 4: Who feels (three words that describe your emotions)

Line 5: Who finds happiness in (three things)

Line 6: Who needs (three things)

Line 7: Who gives (three things)

Line 8: Who is afraid of (three things)

Line 9: Who would like to (three things)

Line 10: Who likes to wear (three colors or things)

Line 11: Resident of (city, street, road)

Line 12: Write your last name

Mary's students enjoyed writing and illustrating their auto-biopoems. Although students in her ELD classes had difficulty understanding all the categories and their English was not always perfect, they did an excellent job of describing themselves, their wants, and their interests in English (see Figure 4-11 Dominga's Poem and Figure 4-12 María's poem).

Although Mary realizes that her second language students acquire language naturally in the process of reading and listening, she also capitalizes on assignments like this to develop the academic concepts students need. For example, she pointed out that the four words students use to describe themselves in line two are called adjectives, and the things they need (line 6) are probably nouns. In this way, Mary increases students' academic competence as well as their linguistic competence.

To help students write longer prose pieces, Mary asked her students to list the ten best and ten worst things that happened to them. After they did this, she demonstrated on the board how to graph their list on a five-point scale. Students decided how negative or how positive the events were. For example, Monica graphed "My third grade teacher got me into reading" as a +4.5, and "I got a poem published!" as a +5, but "I have a lost uncle." as -5 and "Three of my best friends moved away" as -4.5.

Even though Mary is an English teacher, she used this activity to reinforce important math concepts, such as graphing. In the process, she also helped her ELD students build the necessary content area vocabulary.

Figure 4–13 shows the graph one ELD student created. His high point was "coming to America," but the low point was "not understanding English." He drew pictures and labeled them. His entry "somebody killed me" shows he is still developing English proficiency. He was involved in a fight with guns, and someone shot at him.

Figure 4–11   *Doming's Poem*

After students completed a first draft on graph paper, Mary showed students final presentations of life's high and low points from previous classes. Then, students completed their final high and low points projects in various ways. Some made graphs with drawings or cut-outs, others made posters, and still others put together small books or albums. One student (Figure 4-14) made imaginative use of a deck of playing cards. She used red cards for positive events (she read *Catcher in the Rye*) and black cards for negative events. The numbers on the cards indicated how high

Figure 4–12   *María's poem*

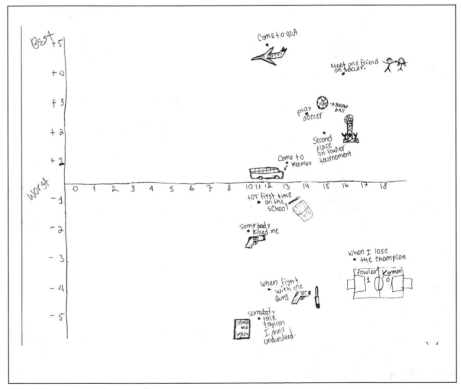

Figure 4–13   *High-Low Chart*

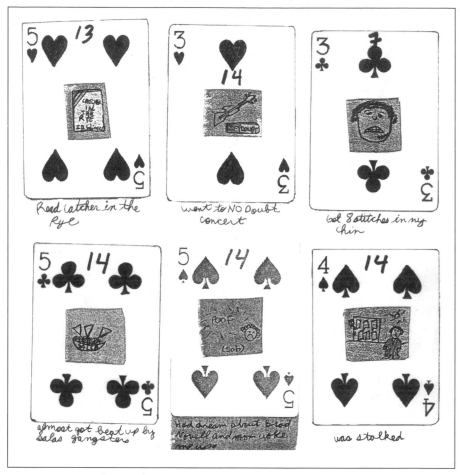

Figure 4–14   *High-Low Chart*

or low she rated the item. A Punjabi student (Figure 4–15) made creative use of computer graphics to represent his highs and lows.

During the daily reading and discussion time, Mary connected the students' life highs and lows to another activity. Students read several newspaper articles that described personal experiences. In one article, an Hispanic teenager remembered how he was teased as a fourth grader because he was fat. His descriptive writing earned him second place in the local newspaper's teen writing contest (Rios 1997). In another article, two boys described how they felt about an encounter with a homeless man. Mary and her students looked at the descriptive language in the articles and discussed how the authors helped readers feel the experience by the way they wrote.

Figure 4–15 *High-Low Chart*

Then, each student picked one of the high or low points in their lives and wrote about their personal experience, trying to be as descriptive as the authors of the article.

Because many of these incidents were highly personal, Mary let students choose who they wanted to work with for peer review, and she did not require whole group sharing of these pieces.

Readings from *The House on Mango Street* (Cisneros 1984) led to more projects around the Sense of Self theme. After reading the "My Name" selection of the Cisneros book, students researched the meaning of their own names. Then they created posters to represent what they learned about their names and presented them to the class. Mary put the posters up around the classroom.

Another chapter of Cisneros' powerful book provided Mary with an opportunity to help her students understand metaphor.

In "Four Skinny Trees" Cisneros compares herself to four trees growing outside her bedroom window. After reading and discussion, students chose a plant, animal, or object that represented them. First they drew what they chose and then wrote about it using figurative language, such as metaphors, when possible.

Mary's daily routine includes asking students to write in personal journals at the end of each period. During the "Sense of Self" unit, Mary asked students to reflect and write by answering the following questions: "How does your family contribute to who you are today?" "How do your friends contribute to who you are today?" "How does the media contribute to who you are today?" "How does literature contribute to who you are today?" These questions helped students to reflect on themselves from a variety of perspectives. Mary also used the daily reading as material for the personal journals. For example, after students read and discussed the opening section of The House on Mango Street, they wrote about their own homes, using Cisneros' writing as a model, as they expressed their feelings about where they lived.

Mary's Sense of Self unit follows the Questioning Lesson Plan and meets the criteria from the Principles for Success Checklist. Mary organized her curriculum around big questions so that she could begin with the whole and move to the parts. The unit was clearly learner-centered and meaningful. Projects drew on students' backgrounds and interests. Students were given choices about how to represent their understandings in various modalities. They often worked in collaborative pairs and groups. The very nature of the theme helped them to value themselves and each other and feel pride in their culture and language. As a result of this unit, Mary's students not only developed a sense of self but also became more capable speakers, readers, and writers of English.

Conclusion

When teachers build on the strengths of English language learners, all students benefit. Recently, a teacher education candidate at our university was placed in a learner-centered classroom. Steve wrote about what he observed when a new student arrived:

> The teacher had a new student who came from Ethiopia and spoke no English. She could not speak the student's first language . . . but rather than allowing him to languish, she chose to allow him to teach the class enough of his native language so that they could all communicate a little bit. . . . The children got excited about discovering a new language. This led to the teacher doing a unit on Africa complete with a wall-size relief mural of the entire continent. The end result was that the Ethiopian student was treated as a valued part of the class. He was able to contribute the richness of his culture while learning about his new home.

When teachers center their curriculum around their learners' experiences and interests, they build students' self-esteem. They show that they value their students by including students' lives and questions in the shaping of curriculum. In a learner-centered classroom, the potential of English language learners is expanded.

FIVE

Lessons Should Have Meaning and Purpose for Learners Now

◆

WHY DO I DESERVE MY BALL

I deserve to have my ball becous it cost alot of money. And my dad will get mad at me for loesing it. And my mom will get mad at me becous she will say that she waisted all of her money to some man for a teacher could take it away. All I want is my ball. I was playing with it when the bell rang because when I got to school evrybody had the courts and I was board so when the bell rang I started to have some fun. Becous I didn't have fun befor the bell rang. Please may I have my ball back? Thank you. Miguel

Miguel hasn't mastered all the conventions of English writing yet; however, he does know how to present an effective argument. Jane, a resource teacher, has found that the English language learners she works with produce very convincing arguments when they write to get themselves out of trouble. As a resource teacher, she is often asked to oversee children who have broken some school rule. Jane asks the students to write about the situation and then talk it through with her. In this piece, Miguel includes clear reasons why he deserves his ball back, as well as an explanation of why he was playing with the ball after the bell rang. This piece of writing is much better in many respects than the writing Miguel generally produces in class. Why is this?

We find that when students write or complete other assignments that they perceive as meeting a real and immediate need, the quality of their work is superior to what they typically produce. These are the kinds of assignments that Edelsky (1989) calls "authentic." During these assignments, students are using language naturally to fulfill real purposes, and for that reason, the assignments are meaningful to the students. Of course, not every assignment has the immediacy of Miguel's letter. But teachers can attempt to find ways to make assignments authentic.

A goal of teachers who follow principles for success is to involve students in activities that are meaningful and have a clear purpose. For an assignment or activity to be meaningful, it must be understood by the student. In the case of second language students, some assignments are not meaningful simply because the students don't understand the language of the assignment. They are not receiving "comprehensible input" (Krashen 1982). Miguel certainly understood his assignment. If he wanted his ball back, he needed to write a convincing letter.

The letter Miguel wrote to Jane also met a second condition for a meaningful assignment. Getting his ball back meant something to Miguel personally. Completing the assignment successfully served a purpose for Miguel right now. When students understand an assignment and see that it serves a function for them personally, they are more willing to take the risks involved in completing it. Older students learning a new language, for example, may not be willing to risk the embarrassment of answering the teacher's question in front of their classmates. Francisco, now a bilingual teacher, tells about his first years in a U.S. school.

> I arrived in California from El Salvador as a teenager and went to a large, inner city high school. In most of my classes, I was silent. In fact, I used to pray that the teachers wouldn't call on me. I knew I had an accent and I didn't want my peers to laugh at me.

English learners often worry about getting the pronunciation or the grammatical form wrong. Francisco also remembers the kinds of assignments he had in his classes. "I was lost most of time. We did a lot of worksheets in ESL classes, and I never really understood the purpose of the work in my assignments."

In class, Miguel, the writer of our opening essay, often produces short essays with simple words. He doesn't risk using complicated grammatical structures or words he might spell unconventionally. Yet, when he is asked to write a letter that has real meaning for him, he takes some chances. He focuses on the content, not the form. And in the process, he learns. He pushes himself beyond what he knows he can do and tries to do new things. Smith (1983) says that outside of school we learn all the time as we solve problems. By asking Miguel to write a letter, Jane helped to create a situation where Miguel used language in school to solve a real problem. As Miguel continues to use language in this way, he learns language.

Halliday (1984) pointed out that we learn language, we learn through language, and we learn about language. In this chapter we briefly discuss how second language students learn language and use language to learn when they are engaged in meaningful assignments. Then, we discuss some of the components of traditional second language teaching that are not meaningful and suggest alternatives that are more consistent with the principles for successful practice. We suggest a model for organizing curriculum that builds on the ideas we presented in the previous chapter and is consistent with a sociopsycholinguistic orientation toward learning. This model, "A Wonderfilled Way of Learning," developed by Don Howard, builds curriculum around thematic units using questions in a series of steps.

Functional Use of Language

Children learn their first language by using language to solve problems. They learn language that serves a useful purpose for them (Lindfors 1987). Often, a baby's first words identify primary caregivers—*mamá* (Spanish), or signal an immediate need—*agua* (Spanish for *water*), *mov* (Hmong for *food* or *rice*) and *mis* (Hmong for milk). As children grow older, they continue to learn the language that is necessary for them to get what they need. They also learn when to use the language they know. They gain a knowledge of the system of language and the uses and purposes for language.

By the time they reach school, children have considerable control over the forms of language. They use language for a range of purposes. They have developed different registers, different forms of language that accomplish their purposes in different contexts. In her study of children in different communities, Heath (1983) showed that although children coming to school have developed sophisticated uses of language, they may not have developed the functions of language expected in school. What they know about language doesn't help them in the new, school context; Thus, they fall behind.

Heath worked in communities where English was the first language of the children. To succeed in school, the children she studied had to learn a new variety of English, the language they already spoke. The task for a child who speaks English as a second language is even more formidable. What complicates the task is that the teacher may not recognize that the child who doesn't speak English still has language. The problem is that although the child does have language, it may be a form of language that is not useful in school.

By age five most children have learned to use the main structural features of their native language, its sound system, and a great deal of its vocabulary. In addition to this knowledge of their language, children also have knowledge of the uses of language. For example, they know how to initiate conversations, ask and respond to questions, and how to take turns in conversations. Halliday (1975) identified specific functions of language that young children use as they develop language, such as the regulatory function as they give orders, or the personal function as they describe things they can and like to do. Not only do young children give orders orally, but they also learn that print serves different functions. For example, in Katie's pre-first classroom, she asked students to draw a picture in their journals in response to a story she read to the class. After finishing his drawing, Andy made a box on his journal page, and he directed Katie exactly where to write her response to his drawing with "RTINHIR" ("Write in here.") (see Figure 5–1).

As long as they are actively engaged in school activities, children learn the language of school. They learn when it is appropriate to talk

Figure 5–1   *Andy Lopez*

and when to be quiet. They learn to talk differently with their teachers, the peer tutor, and their friends on the playground without ever being taught explicitly how to do this. This learning about the use of language continues throughout their lives. When our daughters were teenagers, for example, they spoke one register with their friends that included specialized vocabulary for describing music, cars, and their peers. However, when they were with our adult friends, they used a different vocabulary and even different grammar.

English language learners, whether small children or adults, also learn the language they need to function in a variety of different social settings, including school. Many immigrant students learn their first English words from their peers as they try to gain social acceptance. Sometimes, the words they learn are not acceptable beyond their peer group. The story of Mara's first words in her third grade bilingual classroom (as reported by her teacher) is a classic example:

> Since our classroom maintains a positive, encouraging atmosphere, it was natural for Blanca and Jessica to come running up to tattle that Mara had told them, "Shut up." . . . I exclaimed "That's great!" These were Mara's first words in English. I explained my reaction to the two girls as we went over to tell Mara some nicer ways to say "Shut up" in English. She was receptive to our offers of new ways to express herself, and she also walked away armed with new English words to meet her need for quiet or to be left alone. (Morrissey 1988)

So much more is involved in learning language than studying the vocabulary and grammar.

For adults learning English as a second language, the social, functional, everyday uses of their new language may be all they ever develop. These adult learners need to shop and find their way around. Most of their English is learned in carrying out these everyday activities. We recall Francisca, a sixty-year-old refugee from Yugoslavia, who attended Yvonne's adult ESL classes with her eighty-year-old husband. She was uncooperative with other students and usually refused to participate in English until discussions about shopping, cooking, or gardening came up. Even though she claimed she was unable to read or understand English, she found all the food bargains in the local paper and shared them each week with the entire class, including the teacher!

Those learning English as a foreign language may not learn these everyday language uses. Instead, they may only learn a formal, academic register of English. This variety does not serve them well when they come to an English-speaking country and attempt to interact in a variety of social settings. Also, in many EFL settings, English is taught traditionally, and this creates additional problems.

Students learning English as a second language acquire English as they engage in meaningful activities. They use the language they know to learn the language they need. However, our review of traditional language teaching methods, such as grammar translation or ALM, revealed that many methods do not provide the functional language students need. In Chapter One, we reviewed different orientations as well as methods that have been used in language teaching education. To understand better why many EFL students struggle with English and why most of us never learned a foreign language in school, it is helpful to review in more depth some aspects of traditional second and foreign language teaching methods.

Second and Foreign Language Teaching Methods: Grammar-Based Approaches

In natural learning situations, people seem to learn those things that are meaningful to them. They attend to whatever helps them solve their own problems. It is the learner who decides what to learn. In traditional classes of English as a second or foreign language, this process is reversed. The things to be taught in school are selected by the teacher, and those things may not be meaningful to students. The situation is further complicated if the teacher relies heavily on a textbook. Although the teacher knows the students and can respond to their needs, the textbook was written by someone who had no contact with the students.

In traditional classes, the content is the language being learned. Students focus on the language rather than on using language to solve their problems. Can you imagine telling a baby that she can't have her bottle until she identifies milk as a concrete, noncount noun? Yet, in a sense, that is what we do with English language learners when we teach them the grammar of English. We are telling them that they need to learn the grammar and the vocabulary first, and then they will get to use the language later. This reverses the natural order and makes learning a new language much more difficult.

When the content of a class is grammar, an additional problem is that most students do not understand what it is they are being taught. Smith (1983) says that people do not learn when 1) they already know it, 2) they don't understand it, or 3) they don't want to risk. When the content of a second language class is grammar, all three of these conditions for *not* learning are present. Some students already know the grammar because it was taught before. We have given classes for Japanese university-level students who knew English grammar better than we did. Unfortunately, they didn't know how to order a hamburger at McDonald's, so our class on grammar didn't help them learn the language they needed. Other students do not have any concept of grammar. They don't see how the parts—the nouns, the verbs, and the adjectives—make up the whole of grammar, so they do not understand it at all. Francisca could find the best price in town for corn, but she certainly couldn't (and wouldn't) spend time trying to find an antecedent for a pronoun. Other students are threatened by the fact that most grammar exercises have one correct answer for each question. Grammar exercises are not sufficiently meaningful for them to risk the embarrassment of giving a wrong answer in front of their classmates. In short, in language classes where the content is grammar, students are not involved in authentic tasks that encourage them to take the risks necessary for real learning.

In second or foreign language teaching, traditional grammatical approaches call for a carefully sequenced introduction of language structures and vocabulary. Grammar-based textbooks control the use of tenses and complex structures until the students have "mastered" the forms necessary to move on to more sophisticated language. This sequential system almost guarantees failure because mastery of advanced structures depends on control of simpler structures, and the class moves on whether all the students have learned a particular form or not. Attempts to control language learning create contexts in which language use is inauthentic. Students may learn forms of language that fulfill classroom functions. For example, they may learn to put a series of nouns in the blank slot during a substitution drill. However, students in controlled classrooms do not learn forms of language that will serve their purposes in the world outside the classroom.

The language used outside of school is not controlled in the same way workbook exercises and oral drills are. Outside of school, students learn to understand and use (although not with perfect accuracy) language that they need. K. Goodman (1993) explains that there is a tension between "invention" and "convention" as people learn language. As learners try to make meaning, they are, in a sense, inventing language. The forms of this "invented" language are monitored or controlled by the social conventions of language use. For example, a young child will try different ways of telling her parents what she wants until she is close enough to the conventional form to be understood. The next time that child expresses herself she will use the more conventional form that got her what she wanted.

The same kind of tension occurs with English language learners. Gustavo, an El Salvadoran teenager and family friend told us, "I am boring in my U.S. history class." When we explained to this outgoing young man that he was "bored" not "boring," we were taking his invention and helping him move toward a more conventional form. Gustavo took what he already knew about the word *boring* from having heard it and "invented" a use that was not quite conventional. Through our social interaction with him, he began to move from invention to convention.

An interaction at our university with Tong, a young Hmong man, also demonstrates the importance of social interaction, purpose, and function in learning conventional English. Tong told us about his desire to continue his education. He explained, "I first generation here to go to college. I study B.A. degree." He wanted to continue to study at our university and was trying to get the necessary forms and investigate possible programs. We immediately began to explain that we had programs for teacher education *after* the B.A. degree was completed and that he should go to the undergraduate office. He quickly explained he had *finished* a B.A. degree already at another local university. He was interested in pursuing additional studies at our school. In the course of the conversation, the past tense *-ed* ending on the verb *study* became important for communication. We pointed this out to Tong who used the past tense for the rest of the conversation when describing what he had already completed.

Unfortunately, in many traditional, grammar-based language classes, students are not given opportunities to invent or construct meaning. The language in these classes is controlled by the teacher or the text. The exercises are taken from someone else's experience. The drills are intended to teach correct forms of English, but students only acquire the correct forms when they find themselves in situations where they need them, as Tong did when he realized that we thought he hadn't finished his Bachelor of Arts degree.

This is not to say that teachers and classrooms are not important. Learners need classrooms and involvement with others. Students can learn more effectively in school than outside of school, if they are involved in authentic activities and the teacher makes the academic content comprehensible instead of presenting English as a series of grammar drills.

Alternatives to Grammar-Based Approaches

English language learners need to be offered many opportunities in school to use language in authentic ways that are interesting to them and that encourage them to interact with others. Effective teachers provide opportunities for the students to use language meaningfully: They read real books; they cook and do science experiments; they go on field trips; they have students interview guest speakers; they work together investigating topics of mutual interest; and they play games and sing songs.

Another way teachers help English language learners become more proficient at using conventional forms is by organizing pen pal letters. Because real communication is the primary goal, students are motivated to invent and use advanced forms and structures they would never use in a controlled grammar-based classroom. At the same time, because students have a real audience with whom they wish to communicate, they are willing to revise their inventions and use the conventional spelling and grammar so that their pen pal can read and understand their letters.

Sometimes the letters are between classes of students who are the same age and sometimes they are between students of different ages. One model that Yvonne used asks teacher education candidates to write to children in schools so that the teacher candidates could use the student letters in their own classes as a way to analyze the students' written language development. Erminda was a first grade Hispanic girl who wrote her first answer to her pen pal, Carolina, a bilingual teacher education student (Figure 5–2).

Erminda had a real message to convey to Carolina, and she was not hesitant to use complex conditional structures, although what she wrote would not ordinarily be expected of a first grade child writing in Spanish. She certainly had not been formally taught the conditional tense in her first language.

Translation: Caro, you are [a] good [person]. I would like to meet you. I would like to read you a story. Bye.

Figure 5–2   *Caro Pen Pal*

Another example of students using invention freely when they have a purpose for writing and when they have a real audience comes from Mai, a fourth grade Hmong girl. Mai wrote a series of letters to her teacher from the year before. Mai has an important story to tell, and she invents forms and structures to tell her story in one of her letters to her former teacher:

> On last Thursday I go swimming the teacher that tell us to learn how to swimming he was take us to 6 feet tall. When I was swimming I fall under the water about 3 or 4 min. Than is nobody can help I was cry the in my class she was cry too. Because I scraed that I dei. I thing that I go in to die and nobody wound care about me.

Despite the unconventional grammar and spelling, Mai's story is dramatic and her message is clear. She is communicating an important event, one that she could not have conveyed if her vocabulary and sentence structure was carefully controlled by grammar-based teaching.

Vocabulary Approaches

Several of the language teaching methods we reviewed in Chapter One center around vocabulary learning. Unlike grammar-based methods, these communicative methods attempt to prepare students to interact socially and to cope with academic work in schools. The beginning lessons emphasize a "survival" vocabulary of scenes and objects found in the classroom, in the home, at the park, or in the store. Publishers have developed kits that include picture cards to help students practice vocabulary and to stimulate discussions. Although vocabulary is important, these lessons are often out of the context of the students' real lives or immediate needs. New immigrants and students in EFL settings sometimes spend hours with vocabulary pictures and cards identifying household objects they may not need or use, products they never can buy, or places they cannot afford to go. The vocabulary in the lessons is chosen by someone outside the students' world who is not aware of what any particular student needs to succeed in school. Even when the vocabulary contains objects from the students' school or work world, (such as *pen, chalk, notebook, briefcase,* or *binder*) the vocabulary is not the issue. Students have no trouble learning the vocabulary, but they need more than vocabulary to compete academically with their peers or do business in a world market. English language learners do not need to be practicing isolated vocabulary that they might eventually use. Instead, they need to be offered authentic opportunities to use vocabulary in meaningful ways.

Frances, an adult education ESL teacher, shared a sample of student work with us that shows how students can stretch their vocabulary resources in writing. Second language learners can write powerfully and movingly when they are not constrained by a set of vocabulary words or asked to write on a topic they did not choose. Frances explained that one of her students, a Laotian mother, produced a two-page essay because she wanted her children to remember that life had not always been as good as it was now. Although the letter contains unconventional grammar and spelling, the vocabulary is vivid and the message is clear. The mother's voice comes through strongly as she tells of life before the arrival of the Vietnamese Communists and the contrast afterwards:

> I was born in Laos . . . before our country is beautiful country. Many American or French came visit Laos. I have a good family . . . before I was 13 years old my mother she work so hard to get money, for family to bought something. After that in 1975 Vietnamese Communists belong to the Laos They killed other people . . . they kill king and queen of Laos who did not belong with their side, they did not want people in Laos who did not belong to their side, they did not want people in Laos have own business . . . No T.V. or Video or stereo and nice cloth . . . They did not have an affordable . . . no Lord Judge or government . . . the people who belong to American side, they must kill . . . if they want to killer someone they came to the house at night time . . . they took the people to the Jungle and kill, it make me scare in my life, then I came to Thailand. When I swim the Mekong river I was afraid of many thing snakes, crocodiles leech the communists and water . . . when I were in the camp I did not have clothes or blanket a sweater and food . . . I was hungry, I have gold necklace my grandmother give it to me. before I was in Laos, I sold it and I got a few money to bought a bamboo tree to built a cabin, one day in the summer. it was very hot I walk out from the camp, 5 mile away to find wood to build a fire for cook, I sat down under the shady tree . . . it was little bit cool, for me. I look up in the sky . . . I pray to the god, please help me I want to came to America to find a freedom land, I met my husband and I marry him in the camp of Thailand, after that I came to America with my husband I got three children they was born in America, in my new life I have a new land to stay and freedom

In this piece, the author included vocabulary from a variety of topics: family, government, war, household items, animals, clothing, and weather. If this student was given a writing assignment centered around the word list for the week, she would not have the chance to use such a wide range of vocabulary. This mother had an important message to communicate through her new language, and in that situation she found the words she needed. When there is a function and an immediate purpose for the writing, the range of the vocabulary expands.

Future-Oriented Curriculum

One thing that both grammar-based and vocabulary-based approaches to language teaching share is a future orientation. Students practice forms and do exercises with language that the teacher believes the students will need at some future time. Whether it is the correct past verb form or the best synonym for *said*, the language students are using is not meeting their present needs. In this respect, the curriculum in traditional ESL and EFL classes mirrors traditional curriculum for students who speak English as their first language.

Too often, the curriculum in schools is centered on the future rather than the present needs of the students. Students are told to learn because, "Someday you are going to need to know what is being taught today." Kindergarten content is taught so children will be "ready" for first grade, first grade prepares children for second, and this future orientation continues all the way through high school or even college, where students are prepared to function in society in the future or in graduate school. At times, teachers have such difficulty in providing a rationale for an assignment that they resort to telling students they are to learn something simply because "It's on the test." And there's always a test in the future.

For English language learners, a future-oriented curriculum is particularly problematic. It is essential to get these students involved in content instruction as soon as possible. Students new to English simply cannot wait. If content area instruction is delayed until these students are fluent in English, until they speak, read, and write English perfectly, they will never catch up.

Cummins (1981), Collier (1995), and others show that immigrants need about two years to develop conversational proficiency in a second language, but it takes four or more years for students to develop academic language proficiency. These results are not surprising. New arrivals learn the language they need first. They need to communicate messages orally. It takes longer for them to develop school language, particularly the language found on standardized tests. In part, this is because they have less immediate need for such language; in part, it is because test content often has little connection to the world outside school. Collier's (1989) research showed that even students from families with strong academic backgrounds in their first language took four to eight years to acquire the language necessary to score well on standardized tests in schools.

Even if students are not required to take standardized tests, the academic language of content-area classes takes time to develop, so it is important for teachers to have reasonable expectations. If students are engaged in academic content study and if they see a purpose in studying this content, they will develop the language they need to serve their purposes. But this language development will take time.

Teachers who follow the principles we outlined offer English language learners opportunities to learn all the kinds of language they need from the start. They know that language that has strong contextual support and that is relevant, interesting, and meaningful is likely to be learned naturally. At the same time, these teachers realize that they must equip their students with much more than vocabulary and grammatical structures. They need to help their students find strategies to read chapter books with no pictures and work with content areas, such as social studies and science, that require students to understand extended discourse. These teachers realize they have to break down the walls between school and the "real" world and engage students in lessons that serve the students' present purposes as well as involving them in the content they need for academic purposes. Many teachers find that a thematic inquiry approach allows them to contextualize language and teach both language and content by focusing on topics that students choose. In the next section, we describe one way to organize curriculum by using thematic units and student inquiry. This method is consistent with the "Questioning Lesson Plan" we presented in the last chapter because it begins with student questions.

An Organizational Plan for Thematic Inquiry— The Wonderfilled Way of Learning

One way teachers working with English language learners try to make the content meaningful and functional is by organizing around a theme. "The Wonderfilled Way of Learning," an idea from Don Howard, a classroom teacher, helps teachers develop themes that focus on student interests. Howard suggests that teachers involve students in the process of organizing student inquiry by following six basic steps:

Wonderfilled Way of Learning
    Don Howard

Step 1: Ask the students: What do we know about_____?

Step 2: Ask the students: What do we wonder about _____?

Step 3: Ask the students: How can we find out about _____ ?

Step 4: With the students, work out a plan of action, and at the same time, work school and/or district curriculum requirements into the unit.

Step 5: Plan an event to celebrate what you learned together.

Step 6: Learning is continuous. From any unit, more topics and questions come up. . . . Begin the cycle again.

The first step in this process is to choose a topic. The topic may arise naturally from student questions. For example, students concerned with a water shortage might ask where their drinking water comes from. Once the topic is chosen, the teacher and students work together to combine their resources and discover what they already know about the topic. This can be done in a brainstorming session with the teacher writing on the board. Or, the teacher can put up butcher paper and over the course of several days, ask students to list things they know. As students list what they know, second language students naturally learn key vocabulary. During this time, teachers also can begin to assess students' background knowledge.

Once the students review what they know about a topic, they can begin to list their wonders. "Where does water come from?" "How much water is produced by melting snow?" "What would happen if there were no rain next year?" At this stage, teachers can help students focus on big questions. Again, these questions can be collected over several days. Also, students can talk with siblings and parents to find out what their questions are.

The third step is extremely important. The teacher does not need to provide all the answers to students' questions. Instead, the teacher works with the students to discover how they can find out the things they want to know. For example, they can read a book, watch a movie, browse the Internet, or invite in a guest speaker. During this step, students start to take responsibility for finding ways to answer their own questions.

When resources have been identified, the students and teacher work together to develop an action plan. What will they do and what will the time line be? If the teacher has certain district objectives to meet, these can be worked into the action plan. Most teachers find that as they explore a topic, students go well beyond minimum district standards. At the same time, teachers can be sure to include in the action plan any items the district requires. Because teachers are teaching both content and language, they also plan specific mini-lessons they might present on certain language structures. (For examples of these mini-lessons, see Weaver (1996 ,1997).)

Once students and teachers complete their plan, it is important to have a clear closure, a celebration of learning. This might take the form of a book or a play presented to other classes. One class we observed celebrated their unit on oceanography with a presentation for other classes and for parents. Students constructed models of sea animals to hang around the room. They wrote a book about the animals. And they shared their new knowledge with their parents and with the rest of the school.

As students finish answering one set of questions, they come up with new "wonders" and these are the basis for beginning the cycle of Wonderfilled inquiry lessons all over again. This method of organizing curriculum is different from traditional methods because it starts and ends with questions that have meaning for the students right now.

Using the steps of the Wonderfilled lessons as a guide, teachers can apply all the principles for successful practice. They draw upon students' background knowledge and interests; get the students actively involved in the decision making; get them reading and writing about what they are doing; and give them more choice and responsibility. When these conditions are met, the content automatically takes on personal meaning and purpose for each individual.

How Can I Become a Smart Shopper?

The following is a sample inquiry lesson used to introduce a unit of study organized around "The Wonderful Way of Learning." The inquiry can be adapted for students of different age levels and different levels of English proficiency and for different content areas. Although we refer to this as a lesson, it spans several class periods.

Activity One

Begin by asking the students to think about a topic. "Today we're going to talk about something we all have some experience with: money. What do you (does your family) spend money on?" Give the students a minute to jot down a list of ideas, and then allow them to share their lists in pairs. Then ask pairs what they wrote and list all the responses on the board. With the students' help, categorize the list using different symbols. A sample of a typical list dictated by adult students demonstrates this step.

+ Rice	• Movies	0 Dentist
• Swap meet	0 Medicine	• Videos
+ Groceries	+ Tortillas	0 Doctor
• Eating out	Δ Gas	√ Clothes
√ Shoes	Δ Car	0 Hospital
Δ Bus fare	Δ Mechanic	+ Fish sauce

The categories might include food (rice, groceries, tortillas, and fish sauce), transportation (bus fare, gas, car, mechanic), *health* (medicine, dentist, doctor, hospital), entertainment (swap meet, movies, eating out, videos), and clothes (dresses, shoes). Categorizing is an important academic skill and also helps students learn vocabulary by grouping similar items. This activity can be extended by having students discuss how an item might fit more than one category. For example, if families also buy food from vendors at the swap meet, that item could be marked with a symbol for food as well. Using these symbols makes the categories easy to understand, even for students whose English proficiency is limited.

The vocabulary here is generated by the students and will reflect their ability level. This kind of group language experience approach helps the teacher assess student knowledge. If the class includes students with different ability levels, the more advanced students will come up with vocabulary the beginners may not know, and this is a good chance for students to learn from each other. If the entire class is at a beginning level in their English proficiency, they can select pictures that represent things they spend money for, and the teacher can label the pictures with the English words. Then students can arrange the pictures into categories.

Activity Two

In this step of the inquiry, draw on the students' responses to the first question by asking other questions. "Where do you buy ____? Why do you buy _____ at _____ ?" Choose a category, such as food or clothes, from the first list. Students volunteer names of stores and explain why they shop where they do. List on the board or overhead projector the store names and the reasons given by students.

Activity Three

After this listing, ask "What are some things that smart shoppers do?" Students discuss this question in small groups and make a list to share with the rest of the class. Put a composite list on the board. Generally, especially in the case of major purchases, students include the idea of comparison shopping and research. This leads naturally into the next activity.

Activity Four

Give each group a copy of the magazine *Zillions*, a version of *Consumer Reports* that is high-interest and rich in context with lots of pictures appropriate for intermediate through high school classes. One feature of

Zillions is that the articles are based on research by kids. Ask the students to scan the magazine, pick out one article in which a product was researched, and prepare a brief report for classmates that includes the answers to the following questions: What product did they research? What method did they use to conduct the research? What were the results? (For other topics, other types of high-interest reading material can be used depending on age level and interest, including *World* or *National Geographic* magazine for science and social studies in English and *Geomundo* in Spanish, *Cobblestone* for social studies and history, *Zoobooks* and *Ranger Rick* for science, and *Sports Illustrated* or *Sports Illustrated for Kids* for topics related to sports. For older Hispanic students, *Hispanic* offers readings on politics, entertainment, economics, education, and health and *Latina* addresses similar topics specifically addressing issues related to Hispanic women.)

Encourage groups to begin their reports by posing a question to the whole class about their product. For example, a group reading an article rating fast-food hamburgers might ask: "What kind of hamburger do you think was rated highest—McDonald's, Burger King's, or Wendy's?"

Activity Five

Small groups of students now choose a product or service they wish to investigate. They decide on the method of research, carry out their research, and make an oral and written report to classmates. Often, students will use methods similar to those they saw in *Zillions*.

This inquiry can extend over several days or weeks. Each of these activities can be expanded. Because much of the language is generated by the students, the level of the language will adjust naturally to students' proficiency level. During the investigations, students not only interview people outside the class in the "real" world and sample and study real products, but they also read commercial print including advertisements, pamphlets, and labels. Often the results are useful to the whole class. By beginning with what students already know about spending money and asking them to explore what they might want to know about products of their own choice, the real world is brought into the classroom.

This inquiry follows the steps of the Wonderfilled lessons previously outlined. The teacher begins by finding out what students already know. This leads to "wonders" about some product. Students consider how they can find the needed information, they carry out their research, and they produce a final report for their classmates.

This same format has been used by teachers at different grade levels for other content areas. The following units from a bilingual first grade and a secondary content reading class for English language learners provide additional examples of how teachers have used the Wonderfilled lessons model.

Country/City Theme

Sam, a first grade bilingual teacher, lives in a city in the central valley of California. He decided that because many of his students came to the city from rural homes, a broad theme, "La Ciudad y El Campo"/"The City and the Country" would be meaningful for all of his students (Freeman and Nofziger 1991). The theme incorporated comparison and contrast to help students develop concepts and make connections. Sam began with brainstorming about what his students knew about the city and the country, so that he could see what kinds of comparisons the children could make and capitalize on their strengths and interests. Sam trusted that the students would guide him through the unit and provide the direction the unit would take.

Following the first step of "The Wonderfilled Way of Learning," he began with a brainstorming session. He asked the children to tell him everything they could think of that had to do with the city. He wrote their responses on a large sheet of paper as they dictated:

The City

It's big

Many persons

More things than in the country

Big buildings

Lots of cars

Raggers fight

Noise

Houses

Sometimes they don't allow pets

Lights

Zoo

Grass

The list shows what the students knew about the city. Sam's first graders drew upon their personal experiences and shared their perceptions. The addition of items such as "sometimes they don't allow pets" reflected common experiences of the children at his school, where the transiency rate is high and living in rented homes or apartments is the norm. Sam was saddened that his first graders were so aware of the rival ethnic gangs, "the blue raggers" and "the red raggers."

Sam invited the students to add to the list as they thought of things, and he left it hanging on the classroom wall where students could reach it easily. That same day, several students drew a police car and five big buildings on the butcher paper. Next to the buildings one child wrote "GOT BIG BIDES" ("Got Big Buildings"). Over the next few days, more words were added to the list as things related to the city came up in songs, literature, and conversation.

After a week of exploring what the children knew about the city, the class brainstormed what they knew about the country. The children naturally came up with contrasts with the city, suggesting ideas like "little bit of people" and "little bit of houses." They also listed things grown in the country near their city, including grapes, vegetables, and animals commonly found on a farm such as pigs, goats, and chickens. As with the list for the city, their personal experiences were reflected in suggestions such as "little food," "good people," and "old trucks."

During these first few weeks, several students chose to write stories about the city or the country. It seemed that many things that happened in the classroom or that the class read about or discussed had connections to the theme even when Sam hadn't planned them. In fact, the children were constantly telling Sam, "That's in the city" or "That's like in the country."

As Sam and his students explored their theme of the city and the country, he tried to draw upon what the children wondered and to include the children in helping to decide how they could find out about the things they wondered about. The children began to compare and contrast naturally, and one project led to another. They made maps of their school, their neighborhood, and their city. They went on field trips. They did art and science projects. All of the activities were related in some way to the theme.

AIDS: A Topic of Interest to Secondary Students

A secondary teacher working with large numbers of Southeast Asian students used the Wonderfilled lessons format with her class to study an important topic: AIDS. This topic came up when a local Hmong man committed suicide because he feared he had contracted AIDS. The students began asking questions about the disease, and the teacher saw an opportunity to help her students learn language through meaningful content.

She and the students explored this topic together. She began with what they knew and what they wanted to find out. Then, they read newspaper articles as well as more technical reports on the disease. They listened to a guest speaker and watched an educational video on AIDS. They had small group and whole class discussions. They wrote journal entries that they shared with each other or had the teacher respond to privately. Through this process the students gained a great deal of vocabulary and at the same time learned about an important and timely topic.

The Wonderfilled format can be used in many content areas. In social studies, students might explore school rules or local laws. They could begin with what they already know, list what questions they have, read and interview, share the results, and make some suggestions for change. When studying history, World War II might seem far from students' lives and interests. If the topic is taught in the traditional manner and students read social studies texts, take lecture notes, answer questions, and memorize dates of battles for a test, the topic might not be comprehensible or meaningful, especially if the students are recent immigrants who have trouble reading the texts or understanding teacher lectures. However, if the topic is introduced by asking students what they know about war in general and what they would like to find out about war, immigrant students immediately not only relate but also can be experts on a topic English-speaking peers usually know little about. Through this format, students can choose to answer their individual or small group inquiry questions and discuss and learn about important issues, such as the causes of war, the results of war, the economics of war, and how to avoid war. Using the Wonderfilled Way of Learning model helps teachers relate inquiry lessons to their students, which automatically makes lessons meaningful and purposeful

Other Examples of Teaching with Meaning and Purpose

Of course, not all curriculum for English language learners needs to be organized around the Wonderfilled lessons format. In a junior high school class, a world studies teacher began the year by reading Peter Spier's book *People* (1980). This time the book served not only as a stimulus for study on similarities and differences, but also for study of world population, individual physical characteristics, religion, recreation, housing, means of making a living, and different world languages. Then, students chose areas of special interest to them for further inquiry. They became experts in those areas and shared their expertise with their

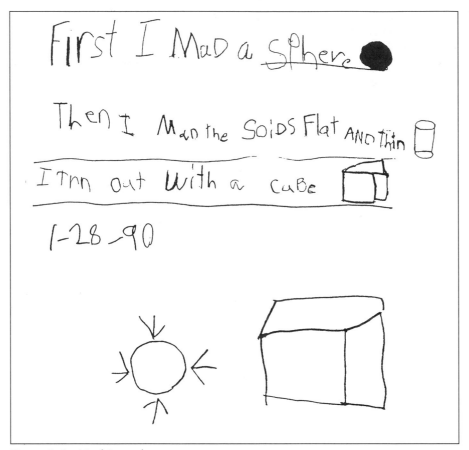

Figure 5–3   Math Journal

classmates. Here again, because students had a choice in the areas they studied, they found the study more meaningful.

One final example of how language is learned through meaningful and functional content comes from Nancy, a first grade teacher who has many Hispanic and Southeast Asian students in her classroom. Nancy was anxious to make her math time both rich in concepts and rich in language. She decided to incorporate a math journal. As students worked in cooperative groups on different concepts, they also developed language. For example, after discussing different shapes, the students were given play dough to make the different shapes they had talked about. Then, they wrote about their experience. In Figure 5–3, Xe writes about her hands-on learning, "First I made a sphere Then I made the sides flat and thin It turn out with a cube."

Conclusion

In this chapter we looked at a third principle for successful practice: Lessons should have meaning and purpose for students now. As with the other principles, immediate meaning and purpose are important for all students, but especially important for students who speak English as another language, because these students need to be engaged in activities through which they can learn both English and the academic content.

For a lesson to be meaningful, the student must understand it. Students are most likely to understand lessons that build directly on their personal experiences and interests. Teachers who follow the principles for success, though, attempt to go beyond making the lesson meaningful. Students may understand a lesson and still see no purpose in doing it. When lessons relate to their lives, students are more apt to find a purpose. In addition, when students can make choices, they can set their own purposes. They can take ownership of the learning process, and under these conditions they are more willing to take the risks that are always involved in learning new things.

Students learn as they engage in activities in which they find meaning, set purpose, claim ownership, and take risks. However, as we have shown in the examples in this chapter and in the model for Wonderfilled lessons, these processes are not generally accomplished by students working alone. Instead, students are involved in interactions with their peers. They learn from each other as well as from the teacher. In the next chapter, we look in more detail at the importance of social interaction for learning.

SIX

Learning Takes Place in Social Interaction

David is a student in an adult ESL class. His teacher, George, arranged for David and his classmates to write pen pal letters to students in a teacher education program at a local college. David's first letter to a college student (see Figure 6–1) is a powerful and poignant example of an English language learner developing language through social interaction.

David's hopes were fulfilled. He got so involved with this pen pal project that he corresponded with several college students. He wrote more letters than any of George's other students. Through these authentic, written social interactions David improved his reading and writing abilities dramatically. There was also another, perhaps even more important, benefit for him. Because of this letter writing, David began to see the possibility of becoming a college student himself. Smith (1983) wrote about the need for students to see themselves as readers, and thus become part of the "Literacy Club." These letters were one way David was able to consider entering "the club" of college-educated people.

Too often language classrooms do not offer students opportunities to interact in authentic ways. Instead, students work alone to practice language skills for future use. George's class is different. He motivates his students by providing them with real opportunities to use language to communicate.

Pen pal letters are one way that teachers create situations in which their students can develop language in social interactions. In this chapter, we review some of the research base that supports the importance of social interaction in learning; we look at how second and foreign language teaching has moved toward the promotion of social interaction; we consider ways teachers can involve students in social interaction; and we present a sample unit that engages students in social interaction as they learn both content and language.

Figure 6–1   *David's Pen Pal Letter*

Individual Versus Social Learning

The way a teacher organizes the classroom can either promote or inhibit social interaction. The list that follows on page 150 contrasts practices that encourage interaction with those that discourage students from talking and working together. English language learners need opportunities for functional use of the language they are developing, and classroom organization plays an important role in determining the possible interactions students can have.

Unfortunately, the emphasis in American education has been on individual learning, not on social interaction. We can see this individual

Restricts Social Interaction	Facilitates Social Interaction
Seats are arranged in straight rows.	Desks are arranged together in groups, or students sit at tables and chairs.
Students do not move from seats.	Students move freely around the room.
Materials are controlled only by the teacher.	Students have ownership of the room; they use and care for materials.
Teacher works with reading groups while others work individually on worksheets.	Students do shared reading, literature studies, and writer's workshop.
Work is completed by individuals for individual grades.	Students work together on group projects for group grades.
Silence is the golden rule.	Students are encouraged to talk together to share ideas.

emphasis in the way classrooms are set up with straight rows facing the teacher. Under the influence of behavioral psychology, materials were developed that further isolated students: programmed texts, mastery learning kits, and dittoed worksheets. Traditional reading instruction, in which one group reads with the teacher while the other two-thirds do seatwork, further reinforces individual learning. Even those students in the reading group are actually giving individual performances. In math classes, students begin with five problems for the day. After the teacher introduces a new type of problem, students often spend the rest of math time working individually to practice the skill that was presented. In social studies classes, students often spend the majority of their time silently reading chapters from the text and answering the end-of-chapter questions by themselves. English language learners in ELD and SDAIE classes that follow this traditional pattern have little opportunity for social interaction.

In many instances, advances in technology have increased this tendency toward individual learning. As Smith (1986) pointed out, computers often have been turned into electronic worksheets. In the mid 80's,

Smith found more than ten thousand educational software programs on the market that support this computerized, programmatic approach to instruction. Millions of computerized lessons "claim to teach facts and skills of language, arithmetic, science, social studies, art and every other subject under the academic sun" (p. 3). Students sit in front of computers that are programmed to give them endless problems in addition and countless variations on the words from their weekly spelling lists. These programs are attractive to educators. The "programs present clearly defined tasks that can be dealt with one at a time. The programs 'remember' how each child has 'progressed' from day to day and can cope with wrong answers" (Smith 1986, p. 8).

The traditional, individual approach to education does not serve students well because learning is a social activity. This is true for any area of study, and it is particularly important for language study. However, even within the area of second and foreign language teaching, there is no clear consensus on the value of social interaction.

Views of Social Interaction for English Language Learners

Second and foreign language educators have debated the role social interaction plays in language development. Krashen (1982) presented a model that describes how individuals acquire language. He argues that language is acquired when students receive comprehensible input (messages they understand) that contains language structures that are slightly in advance of their present ability level. Although Krashen acknowledges the role of social interaction in the development of thinking, he contends that language acquisition results from input, and the best source of comprehensible input is the teacher, or an interesting and appropriate book. According to Krashen, social interactions help students manage conversations better and help students refine their ideas. In addition, these interactions provide the raw material (comprehensible input) needed for language development.

Swain (1985) argued for the need for comprehensible output as well as input. She observed French immersion classes made up entirely of English speakers learning French. She noted that the native English speakers developed high levels of French, but they did not achieve native-like pronunciation. She concluded that students need the opportunities for output that interactions with native speakers provide. Furthermore, she suggested that input helps students gain control of semantic aspects of language, but output helps them with syntax, the structure of sentences. This concept of comprehensible output has been debated. Interaction with native speakers also provides a kind of input that the immersion classes lacked and might account for the lack of native-like French. Nevertheless, Swain's work underscores the importance of social interaction for language development.

Other second language educators also believe that social interaction is critical for effective language learning. In two of their four principles of language development, Rigg and Hudelson (1986) refer to the importance of the social aspects of learning:

1. People develop their second language when they feel good about themselves and about their relationships with those around them in the second language setting.
2. Language develops when the language learner focuses on accomplishing something together with others rather than focusing on the language itself. So group activities . . . are ideal (p. 117).

In a similar way, Rigg and Allen (1989) comment, "Learning a language means learning to do the things you want to do with people who speak that language" (p. viii). They strongly emphasize the importance of working with others to learn language. These educators believe that other people form a crucial element of the context necessary for language development.

Additional support for the importance of social interaction in language learning comes from a study by Long and Porter (1985). They conducted research on group work for adult second language learners and found the following five benefits:

1. Group work increases language practice opportunities.
2. Group work improves the quality of student talk.
3. Group work helps individualize instruction.
4. Group work promotes a positive affective climate.
5. Group work motivates learners.

First, they discovered that in classes where teachers used collaborative group work, individual students had more chances to try out the language they were learning. In an hour-long class with one teacher and thirty students, each student only gets one or two minutes to talk, but when students discuss topics in groups, the talk opportunities are multiplied.

Not only does the quantity of student talk increase, so does the quality. This may seem strange at first because teachers might assume that students would make more mistakes when talking with each other because the teacher would not be there to correct errors. However, the researchers found that in small groups, students took risks and tried out more advanced structures and vocabulary than when they had to speak before the whole class. In the process of using more advanced language forms, the students increased their language proficiency.

Group work helps individualize instruction in two ways. Different groups can do different activities. This allows teachers to group students according to their interests. Not every student has to do the same assignment. In this way, grouping provides students with choice and makes assignments more meaningful. In addition, when students work in groups, teachers can move around the class and answer individual or small group questions.

The researchers also found that students enjoyed working in groups. The class atmosphere improved as students moved into groups. Students relaxed. At the same time, when students became involved in activities they were interested in, they were more motivated. Furthermore, students also were motivated to help other group members. They realized that their own work was important to the success of the group.

Effective group work depends on careful organization, thoughtful selection of groups, and the active involvement of the teacher. The teacher has to think carefully through the task and give clear directions to avoid wasting time. Often groups are organized around student interests. Research shows that students learn more in heterogeneous groups than in groups where the students are very similar in ability. Once students begin to work in groups, teachers should circulate to check on progress and answer individual questions. It is also important to give groups an idea of how long they have to complete a task, and it is important to have some sort of report back period so that groups know that they are accountable for completing their work. As Long and Porter's research shows, when group work is well organized, many benefits result from the increased social interaction.

Because the ways people use language to do things varies from culture to culture, it is crucial that students in schools have a chance for social interactions with people from a variety of cultural groups. Teachers who follow principles for success value the unique way their students use words, but they also strive to make their students aware of the importance of developing forms of oral and written language that will allow them to communicate with other social groups besides their own. These teachers take an additive stance. They celebrate diversity and validate students' languages and cultures. They realize the importance of allowing students to interact with people from a variety of backgrounds to increase their language repertoire.

It is for this reason that teachers like George encourage adult ESL students, such as David, to write letters to college students. In that social interaction, all participants learned. David learned language conventions as he read the letters from the college students and then composed responses, and he learned that he might consider college education for himself some day. The college students who wrote to David began to examine some of their previously held stereotypes about immigrants. They learned that adult ESL students have aspirations and a great deal of potential.

Language Classrooms and Social Interaction

When students study a new language, they expect to be able to communicate in that language. In Chapter One, we reviewed several teaching methods that were developed to help students reach that goal. Although the methods seem on the surface to be quite different, most of them are based on the assumption that students must learn language forms or functions before they can use language to communicate. Thus, authentic social interaction is delayed.

Brumfit (1979) noted that in traditional second or foreign language classes, the goal of instruction is to develop grammatical competence. In a typical lesson, the teacher presents some grammatical structure, the students then drill on that structure, and finally, they practice it in context. For example students might replace nouns with pronouns, shift verb tenses, or change sentences with singular nouns to the plural forms. Teachers in these classes assume that students must master the grammar before they can really communicate.

Willis (1983) classifies classroom language activities into three types: citation, simulation, and replication. Citation activities involve repeating and transforming sentences. For example, a student might change a statement into a question. Simulations are closer to true communication and include such things as discussion and role-play. In replication activities, the teacher creates situations that require communication to solve a problem or play a game. However, Wilkins (1976) pointed out that even when teachers use activities such as role-play that are closer to real communication, the purpose for the role-play is often to practice some grammatical structure in context.

Teachers who ask students to engage in simulations and replications shift from a focus on developing grammatical competence to the goal of building communicative competence. These teachers often organize their courses around different language functions, such as greeting people or asking for information, rather than around grammatical forms such as verb tenses. However, although the focus shifts from grammar to communication, real social interaction is seldom evident in these classes.

Widdowson (1978) captured the difference between grammatical and communicative teaching methodologies with his terms "usage" and "use." He observed that a student might develop the grammatical competence needed to produce a sentence such as "I like to eat hamburgers." This sentence shows the student's mastery of usage. We would judge such a sentence in isolation as being formed correctly. On the other hand, if a speaker produced a sentence such as "I like eat hamburger," we would judge this usage to be incorrect.

A mastery of "usage," as Widdowson argues, is not the same as a mastery of "use." If I ask you "What is your name?" it doesn't really matter whether you answer with "I like to eat hamburgers." or" I like eat hamburger." Although the first response contains grammatically correct usage, neither answer shows correct use of the language. Widdowson and others argue that in classes for second and foreign language students, too much time is spent on "usage" and not enough time is devoted to helping students "use" the language to accomplish social purposes. Yet, that should be the goal of any language class.

Larsen-Freeman (1986) points to the need for students to engage in real communication :

> Since communication is a process, it is insufficient for students to simply have knowledge of target language forms, meanings, and functions. Students must be able to apply this knowledge in negotiating meaning. It is through the interaction between speaker and listener (or reader and writer) that meaning becomes clear. The listener gives the speaker feedback as to whether or not he understands what the speaker has said. In this way, the speaker can revise what he has said and try to communicate his intended meaning again, if necessary (p. 123).

However, even classes that involve students in communicative activities may lack real social interaction. Whether students are practicing verb forms or ways to introduce one another, the activities are not instances of authentic language. As Willis (1983) explains, in a role-play a store clerk can be downright rude with no risk of losing a customer. In authentic interaction, there are penalties for certain kinds of interactions, but no such penalties hold in a role-play.

Another difference between the kinds of interactions outside and inside typical classrooms is that in most classrooms the language forms or functions that students practice are determined by the teacher or the text, not by the people interacting. Students use the language to get better at using language. They practice certain functions so that they will be able to use them later. Students do not use language to accomplish social or academic purposes such as establishing and maintaining relationships with other people or developing their knowledge of some content area.

Therefore, Widdowson and others argued that students learning a second or foreign language should have a real purpose for the language they are learning. One way to accomplish this, as we have suggested, is to teach language through some content area such as science or social studies. A simulation activity in a social studies class is different from the kind of simulation Willis (1983) describes. In a social studies class where students are involved in simulations and role-play, students learn language as they learn about historical periods and events. An excellent source for world history and social studies simulations is *Interact* (1997). This company produces teacher and student guides and other materials that work very well in language classes as well as in ELD or SDAIE social studies classes.

Classes in which language is taught through content involve students in real communication because the focus is no longer on language forms or functions. Instead, students use language to accomplish academic purposes. If students collaborate on research projects, discuss class readings together, edit one another's written reports, and critique each other's oral presentations, the classes reflect an approach that is consistent with the principles for successful practice because the students are using language in authentic social interaction.

An excellent description of a classroom in which students engage in meaningful social interaction is provided by Wells and Chang-Wells (1992). The authors offer a detailed account of how one teacher in a class with students from many different linguistic and ethnic backgrounds helped her students develop academic English as they explored different content areas. This book contains detailed analyses of transcripts that show how teacher talk and student talk can provide the scaffolding second language students need to gain greater proficiency in English as they learn important academic content.

Activities That Promote Social Interaction

Teachers have found certain activities to be especially helpful in promoting social interaction: pen pal letters, book exchanges, cross-age tutoring, literature studies, and collaborative learning projects. Each of these activities provides students with opportunities to use oral and written language for real purposes as they interact with others.

Pen Pal Letters

The letters that George's adult ESL students exchanged with college students served a number of purposes. George taught in one community and the college class was in a different community, so letters were an appropriate way of using written language to communicate to people in other locations. When students use writing in situations such as this, they develop a better sense of the functions of writing. The pen pal letters gave George's students an audience they didn't have in their own classroom, an audience of fluent English speakers and writers. These ESL students were motivated to use conventional English because they knew this is what their audience expected. David expressed this when he wrote, "I will hope are you understand this few lines. If something (word) is incorrect Please don't take care. I try to learn something new for me." David realized that his English was not completely conventional, but he also saw this as an opportunity to "learn something new."

The college students also benefited from the exchange of letters. They were in a teacher education class and were studying about ways to work with diverse populations. They were able to see that despite making errors in syntax and spelling, George's students were intelligent adults who wanted to learn. Students such as David wanted to "go to college like you," not just work at a fast-food restaurant. The college students also had to think carefully about their own writing. They needed to find effective ways to communicate with students whose English proficiency was limited. They spent time finding topics to write about that they had in common with another group of students who were different from them in many ways but also, as they began to realize, in many ways, quite similar.

Pen pal letters serve the primary function of helping students develop proficiency in writing, but they also provide many chances for students to talk and read. In George's class, for example, the students first talked about the whole idea of writing the letters. They discussed who would be receiving them and what they might write about. They talked with their teacher and with each other about ideas for their letters. As they wrote, they read drafts to each other and talked about more effective ways of expressing their ideas. Then, when the college students wrote back, George's students first read the letters addressed to them and then shared these letters with their classmates. In these ways, the pen pal letters involved students in a great deal of writing, reading, talking, and listening.

Another group of teacher education students in Yvonne's reading and writing course wrote letters to two classes of elementary students. Although one of the purposes of the assignment was to help the college students analyze writing and spelling development over time, there were other goals for both groups. Yvonne hoped her teacher education students would come to know at least two elementary students at different grade levels and come to appreciate those students' interests and strengths. Sam and Jaime, the first and sixth grade teachers involved in the project, hoped to give their students authentic purposes for writing. In addition, Sam and Jaime wanted their students, most of whom were labeled as "limited" because they were second language learners, to begin at an early age to see themselves as having potential and to think about college education for themselves.

Yvonne's handout to her teacher education students gives an idea of how she structured the interactions between the college students and their young pen pals (Fig. 6–2).

The project was quite successful. Not only did the college students discover a number of things about their young pen pals' writing development, but they also learned important lessons about how children learn in school. Diane shared a special book her pen pal made just for her and analyzed the spelling following Wilde's (1989, 1992) questions about spelling development. Figure 6–3 on page 160 shows the pages of the book and Diane's analysis of her pen pal's spelling strengths.

At the end of her pen pal analysis, a second college student, Denette, summarized what she learned from working with Ramiro, a first grader, and Tirza, a sixth grader, "Thank you for this experience. Not only did I enjoy it but my pen pals gained from it. As a teacher, I have learned the value of practice in writing, giving choices, and bringing real purpose to writing. Kids want to learn."

Steve discovered how important the pen pal letters were to the children when he met his Spanish-speaking first grade pen pal, Paula, face to face. Steve did not realize that the many letters she sent him, which consisted of drawings, bears, and his and her names, were considered by her to each merit individual replies:

> Today the lesson of how far apart I perceive our worlds to be became painfully clear. Paula asked me why I hadn't written her as much as she had written me. I had no answer. Up until now I had felt I was doing my part by keeping up with a reply when she wrote. . . . What I didn't realize was that Paula considered EACH ONE of the papers she sent me, even if two or three were in the same envelope, to be worthy of an answer. What must she be thinking about me? Here she works so hard to put all these letters together and I only reply with one!

Yvonne, the college instructor, and Sam, the teacher in the first grade bilingual classroom, realized the value of this activity during the first meeting of the college students with their first grade pen pals at the

Each of you will have at least two pen pals. Some of you will have three. There are several things you should be doing and plan to do for this activity.

1. Always be sure to have the pen pal letters ready on the day they are collected in our class. Send yours in if you must be absent. There is nothing sadder than a disappointed child.

2. Keep all the letters you receive and make copies to hand in for your study. Also keep copies of the letters you write to see if the students use your letter in their responses. When you do your final analysis, I will want you to turn in photocopies of the letters you get and you sent.

3. On Thursday, January 25, you will be meeting your pen pals at both Lane and at Aynesworth. For that day you should be prepared to do the following:

   a. Read and discuss a short story with the first or second grader at Lane.

   b. Read and discuss a poem or story with a sixth grader at Aynesworth. For the sixth graders, we may decide as a class to do something different like reader's theater as a group or groups.

   c. Interview the first or second grader using the "Child's Concept of Written Language and Pictorial Representation" interview form. Keep the data for your final analysis. For this interview, you will need supplies: different kinds of paper, different writing utensils, etc.

   d. Interview the sixth grader using the "Writing Strategies Interview."

   e. As we study written language development, use your samples to relate your reading and our class discussions to what you are seeing.

   f. When you write up the final reports, be prepared with two sets—one for me and one for the classroom teacher.

Whatever you do, try to take into consideration what you learn from pen pal letters about your pen pals. Draw on your learners' interests and background.

Figure 6–2   *Pen Pal Guidelines*

In her spelling she consistently began and ended with the correct consonant sounds. She wrote "HS" for "house".

Other times she included consonant sounds within the word, as she did in ladybug (LDBg) and Christmas (CMtS). This is a progression in hearing and distinguishing more sounds in words.

When she wrote butterfly (BRLFI) she also heard and recognized the vowel sound "I" on the end. This is another example of "letter name spelling."

Rinette came very close to conventional spelling with "STOR" for "star."

Figure 6–3   Diane's Pen Pal

elementary school. Their description of this meeting highlights the learning that was going on:

> The sounds of both English and Spanish in the classroom create a productive buzz. . . . The adult students and young children are totally engaged in learning from each other. . . . They are seeing children, mostly second language learners from low income backgrounds, reading and writing for real purposes and sharing what they have learned with someone they care about and trust. The interest and enthusiastic support of the college student empowers the young bilingual learners (Freeman and Nofziger 1991).

Later in the semester, the first graders from Sam's class visited the college campus. They were met on the green and treated to a hamburger lunch by the college students. Then the pen pals went off together for a campus tour. The afternoon culminated in the college classroom where pen pals read books to each other, sang together, and recited poems to each other. There was little doubt that everyone learned a great deal, not only about reading and writing but also about the importance of social interaction for learning.

In some cases, pen pals who exchange letters are about the same age. One year Lonna, who teaches high school ELD classes, worked in two schools. In her classes, she often talked about things the students in the other school were doing, their games and assemblies, their clubs and dances, and their problems with English. After a short time, the students in each school developed an interest in the students in the other school. As Lonna talked, both classes felt they knew the other students. It was a natural extension, then, for the students to begin to write to one another. They wanted to ask each other questions and to know these other English language learners more personally.

Lonna helped her students write their letters. This activity included lots of talk about possible topics as well as how to express their ideas in standard English. The students were interested and put more energy into these letters than they had into any other writing assignment. They were writing to other second language learners, not just to the teacher. When Lonna delivered the letters, the students were very excited. They worked together to help each other read the letters. They wanted to know what another student said, and they were eager to write back. In fact, on days when there were no letters, Lonna reported that the students were very disappointed. The pen pal letters between her two classes helped all of her students develop their English proficiency.

When Yvonne taught beginning Spanish at the university level, she initiated pen pal letters between two of her classes. She was a bit hesitant to do this. Would her students think they were too sophisticated for this sort of activity? It turned out that university students also saw a real purpose in communicating with other students. At a large university, they were eager to meet others, and they were willing to work very hard to complete that interaction in a second language. Like Lonna, Yvonne found that students spent a great deal more time and effort in composing letters to their peers than they spent in writing formal compositions for her, the teacher. The pen pal letters served an authentic purpose. Many of the pen pals arranged to meet each other, and several became friends.

Linda teaches high school Spanish. She wanted to find an authentic audience for her students' writing, but rather than have them write to another group of high school Spanish students, she started an exchange with Susan's class of bilingual first graders. The high school students wrote to children who already spoke the language the high schoolers were studying. In the process both groups developed their Spanish writing ability. Each group had different kinds of challenges in writing and reading the letters. The pen pal activity led to many chances for both Linda and Susan to help their students develop Spanish proficiency.

Long-Distance Book Exchanges

Dan Doorn, a college professor, worked with teachers at a local elementary school to start a new kind of writing program in which students share student-authored books, rather than pen pal letters. This program, called "The Seed Pod Travelers," began with twenty bilingual students from a local elementary school. Doorn took their books to the international TESOL (Teachers of English to Speakers of Other Languages) convention in San Francisco. Copies of the student writing were picked up by teachers from around the country and taken back to their classrooms, where their own students read the books and then wrote back to the authors.

This program provided real audiences for a variety of types of writing. Students wrote stories, reports, personal experiences, poems, reader's theater scripts, and songs. Doorn reported that the authors learned a great deal from the responses they received: "One story will spark such different types of reader-response feelings. A story can prompt authentic questions not anticipated by the writer. A story may have surprising connections to similar ones re-told by readers" (Doorn 1991, p. 2).

The teachers involved reported that their students gained important insights from the "Author's mail" that they received when their seed pod books were sent to new audiences. "One girl added specific details to help her readers understand the difficult time she had at a wake for her grandfather. One boy wrote a new account of his farming chores for a California reader who also worked on a farm with his father" (Doorn 1991, p. 2). Doorn's project fostered written social interaction among English language learners around the country and in Canada.

Recently, with greater access to computer E-mail, teachers have set up long-distance exchanges over the Internet. This medium offers exciting possibilities. One teacher, for example, organized an exchange among several different schools from different parts of the country. The students at these schools all read the same book. Then they wrote a review of the book and E-mailed it to the teacher who began the program. He worked with his students to combine all the reviews into one document and then send it back out to the schools. In this way, students and teachers at different sites were able to share ideas about the literature they read. For an extended discussion of the cross cultural benefits of computer interactions, see Cummins and Sayers' *Brave New Schools: Challenging Cultural Illiteracy through Global Learning Networks* (Cummins and Sayers 1997).

Cross-Age Tutoring

Another activity that promotes social interaction is cross-age tutoring. Although there are different kinds of tutoring programs, each of these programs creates a situation in which students can develop greater language and academic proficiency as they interact with others.

Many cross-age tutoring programs link older students with younger students. For example, Charlene, a fourth grade teacher with many English language learners, arranged for her students to read to first graders weekly. The fourth graders chose books they thought were appropriate for the first graders. They practiced reading them to each other in preparation for their visit to the first grade "buddies." Many of Charlene's fourth graders were English language learners. Because the books written for the younger children often followed predictable patterns and had pictures that provided contextual support, Charlene's students were successful at reading them. Charlene was able to use these books to help her second language students develop reading proficiency in English. In choosing books, practicing reading, and discussing the best ways to work with their "reading buddies," the fourth graders had many chances to interact with each other and develop their oral skills as well as their reading ability. Other teachers and teacher researchers have developed this idea in working with English learners. Katherine Samway and her colleagues describe in detail the buddy reading system they set up in a multicultural school (Samway et al. 1995).

Charlotte, a high school teacher, extended this idea of older learners sharing books. Charlotte's secondary students were in her special reading class because they were considered to be low readers. She had them read picture books so that they could find ideas to help them create their own books. They spent a great deal of time discussing book ideas, writing the texts, and illustrating them. Then students took home the books they made and read them to their younger siblings. The results were exciting for the students and their teacher. The students became much more confident readers, and the books they created were so beautifully written and illustrated that Charlotte was asked to share the project with other teachers in her school district. For more ideas on ways to use picture books with older students, see Benedict's book, *Beyond Words: Picture Books for Older Readers and Writers* (Benedict and Carlisle 1992).

Organizing Cross-Age Tutoring

Cross-age tutoring sessions can be conducted in different ways. Sometimes students read to two or three younger children together. More often the reading is one-to-one with the older student reading first and then the younger one reading something he or she has written or has learned to read. The older students may work with the same student each time, or they may meet with different students in subsequent sessions and read the same book to different children.

More than reading is involved in tutoring sessions. Students talk together as they plan and practice before reading to their little buddies, and then there is more talk when they return to their class to debrief, to discuss the experience of working with the younger students. Labbo and Teale (1990) described a successful cross-age tutoring program they were involved with. They list the four phases of that program:

1. Preparation: The teacher helps tutors, in this case fifth graders identified as low readers, select appropriate books from the library to read to kindergarten children. The fifth graders practice reading the books, alone and in pairs, to develop fluency. The teacher helps the tutors decide how to introduce the books to their kindergarten partners.

2. Prereading collaboration: Small group collaboration time was established for the fifth graders to set personal goals, try out ideas, and receive and give feedback. They shared their books with other fifth graders and received feedback on the fluency of their oral reading and their expressiveness as well as on their use of questions and comments during discussion of the book. This time helped readers to prepare for successful sharing with the kindergarten students.

3. Cross-age reading with the kindergartners: The reading took place in the kindergarten room. Tutors from fifth grade chose their own

partners and read to them. Some tutors read the same book to a different kindergarten child each day for a week, while others read a different book during each session.

4. Postreading collaboration: After their reading sessions, the tutors met with their teacher to reflect on the quality of the storybook reading interactions. During this time, the teacher also showed the fifth graders a number of strategies they could use with the kindergartners, such as asking them to predict what the story would be about, or asking them to make connections between the characters or events in the story and their own lives.

The success of this program rested on its careful organization. The older students were well prepared to work with the kindergartners. It is interesting that both groups of students learn through this kind of interaction. In fact, they not only learn reading skills, but also social skills. One sixth grade teacher whose students read every morning to younger children commented that her students were at their "most human" during that reading time.

Research and writing can also be involved in the cross-age tutoring projects. Heath and Mangiola (1991) describe a program that adds a research dimension to this kind of tutoring program. Older students were trained to take field notes and do a case study of their reading partner. These older students, who were labeled "at risk," became critical researchers as they analyzed their own work as tutors and their students' progress. In this way, the students became ethnographers. Heath and Mangiola's book contains many helpful suggestions for teachers wishing to implement a cross-age tutoring program.

Kay, a bilingual resource teacher in a small farming community, also has shown that non-English speakers can benefit from a cross-age tutoring project. Seventh and eighth grade Spanish-speaking students read in Spanish to the monolingual Spanish-speaking kindergarten children at her school. The junior high school students who did this tutoring formed a "Teachers of Tomorrow" club. Several began to see themselves as future bilingual teachers. Their interest in doing well in English increased as these older students saw a need in the future for both their native language and English. The younger children they tutored were supported in their first language and also saw the older students as positive role models. All the students benefited from the social interaction of the tutoring.

Morrice and Simmons (1991) reported on an extensive cross-age tutoring program that went beyond reading buddies. These two teachers arranged for their grade five and primary students to meet at regular intervals during the year for various purposes. They made and read big books and giant pop-up books, they celebrated various holidays, and they worked together through a number of science investigations. They found that their students made both social and cognitive gains as they worked with each other over an entire year.

Literature Studies

In Chapter Four we described how Mike's class produced a newsletter. This was just one of many activities Mike organized to promote social interaction. Literature studies provided another opportunity for his students to work together. In Mike's class students with varying degrees of English proficiency chose books, read them alone or in pairs, recorded their reactions to the reading in literature logs, and met in small groups and with the teacher to discuss what they read. In this process, the students developed both their oral and written language proficiency.

Literature studies can take different forms (Peterson and Eeds 1990, Short et al. 1996, Short and Pierce 1990). For an extended discussion of how bilingual teachers organize literature studies, see Freeman and Freeman (1997, 1998). Another book that contains a rich description of how a bilingual teacher sets up and conducts literature studies is *Crossroads* (Cox and Boyd-Batstone 1997). This book, co-authored by a university researcher and a third grade bilingual teacher, explains in detail how to engage English language learners in meaningful literature. In this process, they learn both language and academic concepts.

In most cases, students involved in literature studies choose the books they will read, are given time to read independently (in pairs or while listening to a taped version of the book), reflect on their reading, and then meet in groups to discuss what they have read. At each step of a literature study, students collaborate. Through literature studies, reading becomes a social process, not just an individual activity.

Cooperative Learning

Whereas pen pal letters and cross-age or peer tutoring provide social interaction between classes, literature studies promote cooperative learning within the classroom. Kagan (1986) outlined three benefits of cooperative learning for second language students: increased academic achievement, improved ethnic relations, and prosocial development.

Kagan reviewed studies comparing classrooms that use cooperative learning with those that use competitive and individualistic learning structures. These studies, almost without exception, show greater gains for students in cooperative learning situations. A number of studies focused on second language students. Kagan reports that "One of the most important findings to emerge from the cooperative learning research is the strong achievement gains among minority pupils in co-operative classrooms" (Kagan 1986, p. 245). In addition, studies comparing high-, medium-, and low-achieving students show that the high achievers do about as well in the cooperative classes as in individualistic classes, but the medium and low achievers make dramatic gains. These results indicate the importance of social interaction in classrooms with high numbers of English language learners.

Cooperative classrooms also foster improved ethnic relations and prosocial development. Kagan's research shows that there is ethnic segregation in traditional classrooms, and this segregation increases with student age. However, research in classrooms that use cooperative learning showed that "The very strong ethnic cleavage observed in the traditional classrooms was reduced to insignificance" (Kagan 1986, p. 250). One reason for improved ethnic relations in cooperative classes is that in these classes teachers often teach social skills directly. Students are involved in group activities that develop positive interdependence among group members.

Cooperative Versus Collaborative Learning

Classes that use cooperative learning follow the principle of promoting social interaction. However, we distinguish between cooperative and collaborative learning. Cooperative learning activities often present material part to whole. For example, students may spend time in their groups memorizing spelling words or practicing math facts. These lessons also may be highly teacher-centered, and they seldom begin with student interests. As a result, students may not find meaning and purpose in their group activities.

Teachers who promote collaborative activities, on the other hand, follow the students' lead and view curriculum as inquiry (Short et al. 1996, Watson et al. 1989). Rather than carefully structuring classroom activities to help students learn prescribed information, teachers who follow principles for success encourage students to collaborate as they investigate subjects of interest to them. They find answers to big questions by reading together and talking together, and then they write up their findings and often also present their findings orally to others.

In Charlene's fourth grade classroom, previously discussed, children often work in collaborative groups. To culminate one of their units of study the students prepared an oceanography display to present to other classes in the school. Groups of children became experts on different sea animals of their choice. They read about the animals, visited an ocean aquarium, wrote about their sea animals for a class book, made models of the animals to scale, decorated their classroom like an ocean, and then presented their knowledge to other classes and to parents who came to visit their student-created ocean aquarium on display.

Charlene's students developed a great deal of written and oral language as they worked on this project. They conducted their research, did their writing, and made their presentations in small groups. As they worked together, both their language ability and their understanding of academic content increased much more rapidly than if they had carried out more typical individual research projects.

One common element among successful activities that promote social interaction is that they are well organized. The key to successful collaborative activities is careful planning. Teachers such as Charlene spend time with their students helping them understand how to work together effectively. With their teachers' assistance students work successfully in pairs or in groups. Later, these students work collaboratively without their teacher's help.

Using Problem Posing

One second language teaching method that emphasizes the value of social interaction is Problem Posing, which we described in Chapter One. Like the Wonderfilled lessons outlined in the previous chapter and the Questioning Lesson Plan, Problem Posing involves students in raising questions and then researching a topic of interest to find solutions. In addition, this method leads students toward social action. Wink (1997) helps us as teachers understand that our actions make a difference. We must help our students not only learn language but learn how to use language to solve problems that are significant to them.

As an example of how the Problem Posing method is used to teach social studies, we present the steps for a unit centered around the question, "How does where we live influence how we live?" (Freeman and Freeman, 1991). Throughout this sample unit, a great deal of social interaction takes place as students work together. This unit works equally well in an ESL or an EFL setting.

A Sample Social Studies Unit:
Where We Live Influences How We Live

Teachers using Problem Posing are "kid watchers" who use their knowledge of students' interests and concerns to help them pose and solve problems. In this process, English language learners develop language proficiency as they study content areas. This particular social studies unit leads students to view their own living conditions objectively and then to consider ways to improve the quality of life in their community. They accomplish this through the critical observation of different kinds of communities, including their own. Six steps are involved in organizing a unit of study such as this one that uses the Problem Posing approach:

1. Begin with the learners' actual experiences. Draw on the students' background knowledge.

2. Develop background concept(s) through actions, visual aids, discussion, and so on.

3. Begin critical observation using pictures, books, personal stories and experiences, community events, and so on.

4. Through comparison and contrast, help students to view concept(s) and how those concepts relate to their lives.

5. Research the concepts through reading, writing, interviews, discussions, films, field trips, and so on.

6. Plan appropriate action(s) related to students' lives and resulting in social change.

Steps One and Two: Introduction of the Lesson

The first activities are designed to help students develop the concept of a community as a group of people who are interdependent or interactive in some way, presumably to serve some purposes. Students begin by brainstorming answers to the questions: "Who are the people with whom you live? Play? Go to school?" This begins to develop an awareness that they are part of a series of overlapping communities: the family, the neighborhood, and the school. These communities might be represented visually by a Venn diagram, which shows that any individual is part of several communities. Students could also brainstorm and categorize the different roles community members take as they work, study, worship, engage in politics, and participate in recreational activities.

Once students begin to develop the concept of community in general, they can look more closely at a particular community. One kindergarten teacher helped her students understand their school community by taking pictures of the various people around the school: the principal, the bus driver, the cafeteria workers, the nurse. She showed the students the pictures and talked about the role each of these people played in the school community. Then the class went on a walking tour to see where each person worked. Students asked the members of their school community questions about what they did each day. When the class returned to their room, they made a class book. On each page they put a picture of one of the people who worked at the school, and underneath the picture, the teacher helped them write information about that person. The book included their favorite page, the picture of their own class.

As students study particular communities, they start to focus on how the environment influences community life. To do this, students describe their communities for someone living in another place. A fourth grade teacher in a small farming community arranged for her class to exchange pen pal letters with students of the same age living in a city in another state. In their writing, students were asked to describe their community so that their pen pal would recognize it on a visit.

In the study of communities, students with limited English proficiency can begin to build their vocabulary. Certain terms come up repeatedly. When students begin by talking and writing about their own community, they already understand many of the basic concepts and start to build the vocabulary needed to express those concepts in English. Activities such as writing pen pal letters provide a further purpose for developing the vocabulary and grammatical structures needed to express students' ideas. Because bilingual students often have lived in more than one community, they have a head start on their classmates when it comes to making comparisons. This can build their self-esteem.

Steps Three and Four: Critical Observation of Communities Using Comparison/Contrast

After students spend time building the concept of community by examining the communities they have been a part of, they analyze communities with which they have not had direct, personal experience.

For this activity, students work in groups of four or five. The groups are given pictures of different areas (rural, city, village, ocean, desert) and asked to list characteristics of these areas. Anything that comes to their minds is acceptable, including descriptive words such as *quiet, noisy, isolated, hot, dry,* and *rainy* or nouns such as *sand, water,* or *buildings.* Each group lists their words on the blackboard, on an overhead transparency, or on butcher paper.

This activity serves two purposes. For students with limited English proficiency, it provides important vocabulary, which is supported by the use of the pictures. At the same time, all the students can begin to think about the physical characteristics of different geographical areas.

Next, students list some of the needs of people living in the area they described. They brainstorm what people would need to survive and to live comfortably. This list helps prepare for the next step in the activity in which students are asked to list what they believe are the advantages and disadvantages of living in each of these areas. A typical list for the picture of the city follows.

Advantages	Disadvantages
Easy to shop	Crowded
Good entertainment	Too much crime
Live near friends	Live alone
More choices of things to do	Polluted
Easy to get places	Noisy

Step Five: Research through Reading

In another activity, the groups work with short articles about different, interesting communities. Students look for articles in magazines and newspapers to share with the class. In this case, the teacher may want to ensure that articles are available that fit the activity. In their groups, the students read to discover how various environments strongly influence the way people live. For example, people living in the arctic need special kinds of clothing and housing. People living in the tropics wear clothing, eat foods, and have jobs that reflect their environment. Each group chooses an article to report on. We suggest the following steps to guide students in this activity.

1. Appoint a recorder.
2. Look over the article in your groups. Think about the needs of the people who live here. How do they meet these needs? What kinds of homes, jobs, clothes, and so on are important? How is this place different from where you live? What would be the hardest/easiest aspect of living in this place?
3. Pick out characteristics of the place described in the article that affect what people do—how people live in that place.
4. List some of the characteristics and some examples of how the characteristics affect what people do and how they live. Put your results on a chart as shown here.

Characteristics	What People Do
_____	_____
_____	_____
_____	_____

5. Be prepared to share your responses with the whole group.

This activity is designed to encourage students to read for a purpose and to help them develop the concept that where we live influences how we live. For example, people build cities to create an environment that serves certain urban and commercial functions. The environment that is created then has a strong effect on how people in the city live. For example, students who read an article about people living in cities who use roofs creatively wrote the following.

Characteristics	What People Do
Tall buildings with large, flat rooftops	Plant rooftop gardens
	Make rooftop playgrounds
Little space for recreation	Raise animals on rooftops
High up and dangerous	Put up safety fences on the edges

Step Six: *Community Research and Action Plan*

After reading about other places and how the environment of those places affects how people live, students can refocus on their own communities. They might begin by brainstorming a list of questions: "How did our community develop the way it did?" "Why do we have the kinds of homes that are built here?" "Why do we wear certain kinds of clothes and buy certain products?" "How does our community use the resources it has?" "How does the environment relate to the jobs that adults and children have?" Answers to these questions can help students determine the advantages and disadvantages of living in their own community.

Then, students can think of ways to find data to answer their questions. Depending on student age, interest, and English proficiency this could include field trips, library research, and guest speakers. In larger cities, students might wish to concentrate on their own section of town. Students could be involved over a period of time in collecting and presenting the data. During this process, they can look for examples of how the environment affects the way people live.

In Lonna's high school ELD class, students were divided into teams. A map of the city was posted on the bulletin board with sections marked off. Each student team studied a particular area of the city. This involved traveling through that area, taking pictures, interviewing residents, and visiting places of interest as well as areas that were not interesting and areas that provided unsatisfactory environments. Then, each group reported the results of their research to the class. Because many of the students in the class were very recent immigrants, this activity helped them to learn valuable information about their new home.

Once students look objectively at their surroundings, they can begin to evaluate the quality of life in their community. They might debate the advantages and disadvantages of living there. Teachers can encourage students to develop an action plan for community improvement. The following list of questions leads students to develop projects for changing their communities.

Advantages and Disadvantages of Living in Your Community

1. List some advantages and disadvantages of living in _____.

2. How can we obtain more information about some of the things we have listed as advantages and disadvantages?

3. How do we affect the quality of life in the place we live? Positively? Negatively?

4. How can we improve the quality of life in our community?

After students brainstorm the positive and negative aspects of living in their community and as they begin to formulate their action plan, they often need to do further research to find additional information about items they listed. For example, they might list as a benefit the high quality of the recreational facilities available. A group of students could check with public agencies or the chamber of commerce to compile a list of available facilities. If "too much violence" is listed as a negative aspect, students can get statistics from the police department or the newspaper to support their contention. They may need to compare their community with other communities to make reasonable judgments.

At the same time that students are discovering more about the advantages and disadvantages of living in their community, they can begin to assess their own contribution to the quality of life. What are they doing that is positive or negative for the quality of life in their community? This question could lead to writing assignments, class surveys, and discussions.

The class might decide to take a specific plan for action, such as cleaning up or repairing an area around school. Or they might plant a garden, write letters to the editor of the local newspaper to support certain city development plans, and attend city council meetings to raise important issues. There are many possibilities, but it is crucial for social studies to result in social action, in really "doing" social studies. By using a Problem Posing approach to social studies, all students, and especially English language learners, engage in authentic social interaction, and through functional use of language they develop their content area knowledge and their English language proficiency.

Conclusion

In classrooms where teachers follow principles for success, students frequently engage in social interaction. They participate in literature studies, and they read with a buddy or a cross-age tutor. They write letters for pen pals in other classes. They form teams to investigate topics and answer questions as they explore different content areas. Together, students decide on ways to take the information they gathered and apply it to their lives. They use what they learn to help solve real world problems.

These classes buzz with a kind of controlled noise. Students constantly talk with their classmates and with their teacher, using the language or languages they possess. They learn as they engage in authentic social interaction. We close this chapter with one final example of how social interaction is making a difference for immigrant students at one high school.

International High School

In New York City there is an exciting public high school made up entirely of immigrant students who, in order to qualify for admission, must have lived in the United States less than four years and must have scored below the 20th percentile on an English language proficiency exam. Yet, 95 percent of the students graduate and 90 percent are accepted to postsecondary schools. At the end of the first three years, the dropout rate at International High School was only 3.9 percent and all 54 members of the first senior class were accepted to college for the following fall (Darling-Hammond et al. 1995).

The faculty and students of International High School believe that a secret to the success of this program is the collaborative learning and sharing that takes place in every class.

> International is committed to viewing teachers and students . . . as resources for each other, using participation in decision making and collective action as the basis for growth and development (p. 115).

The English language learners in the school are not taught English as a second language as a separate course. Instead, they learn English by studying meaningful content and by working together in small, mulitlingual, multicultural groups. "Their tasks are structured so that they must communicate ideas and directions to one another as they collaboratively produce and evaluate their work" (p. 118).

Classes are organized around interdisciplinary themes on topics such as diversity, interdependence, democracy, and government participation. The traditional subject area content is included in each theme.

For example, the "Motion" theme combines a literature course with an integrated math/physics course and a physical education course called Project Adventure, which is modeled after Outward Bound. The three courses are unified through the focus on motion.

The International High School program includes authentic assessment procedures and multiple learning contexts, including career internships. Students from fifty-four countries speaking thirty-nine different languages have come together and worked with faculty to demonstrate how sharing in their learning improves academics. This program, with its interactive focus, gives us hope that a diverse society can collaborate, as these students and faculty have, to achieve common goals. The key is that they work together. Social interaction has been an essential principle for success for these students.

SEVEN

Lessons Should Include All Four Modes

◆

As the bell rings, the twenty-eight students in this junior high ELD class settle into their seats. Bill, the teacher, has just pinned a large poster on the front bulletin board. It shows a spotted fawn lying in a meadow surrounded by yellow spring flowers. Bill addresses the class, "I'd like you to do a quickwrite this morning. Look at this picture and write down any words or phrases that describe what you see. I'll write too. You have two minutes."

These students have done quickwrites before. They open their notebooks, take out their pencils, and begin to jot down ideas. The teacher also writes on his clipboard, glancing up at the poster. At the end of two minutes, Bill announces, "Your time is up. I'd like you to stop writing. Now, I want you to share your list with someone sitting near you. Circle the things you both put down and talk about the things that are different." The students move their desks together and begin talking quietly, reading through their lists and marking off the items that they have in common and discussing the ones that are different.

After a few minutes, as student talk dies down, Bill states, "Now I want to put some of the words and phrases you wrote here on the overhead projector. Let's go around, and I'd like each pair to tell me one thing both of you had. If I put up something you don't have written down, you might want to add it to your list." For the next ten minutes Bill writes the words and phrases the students give him on the overhead projector. He continues until students run out of ideas. Some of the words and phrases are shown in here.

peaceful	fawn	deer
young	grass	spring
big eyes	calm	weak
soft fur	yellow flowers	long legs
spots	pointed ears	lying down
four legs	Bambi	baby

Then, Bill asks, "Do some of the words on our list go together in any way? For example, what words go with 'big eyes'?" The students call out other words on the list, *soft fur, spots, long legs, four legs,* and *pointed ears.* Bill puts a triangle next to each of these words. Then he asks, "Is there another group of words that go together?" This time, the students start with *yellow flowers* and then add *grass* and *spring.* Bill draws squares next to these words. The teacher and students continue categorizing the items on the list using various symbols. They notice that some items could go in two categories, so the teacher marks them with symbols for both categories. The list now looks like this:

# peaceful	* fawn	* deer
Δ* young	☐ grass	☐ spring
Δ big eyes	# calm	Δ weak
Δ soft fur	☐ yellow flowers	Δ long legs
Δ spots	Δ pointed ears	Δ+ lying down
Δ four legs	* Bambi	* baby

Next, Bill puts up a second poster. This one shows a young horse running through tall grass. Again, yellow flowers are in the picture. Bill asks, "Let's think of some things about these two pictures that are the same and some that are different. What are some things that are the same?" As the students volunteer answers, the teacher writes them on the board under the heading, "Same." The students note that both animals are young, both have four legs, both have brown fur, and both are pictures of the spring season with green grass and yellow flowers.

Then Bill asks for differences and lists them on the board under the heading, "Different." Students notice that the horse is bigger. The fur is different. The fawn is lying down, but the horse is running. They even notice a difference in perspective. The picture of the fawn is more of a close-up, so although the two animals look about the same size, the horse is really bigger.

After this activity, Bill pulls out a pile of pictures of animals. The previous week, the students cut these pictures out of magazines and pasted them on colored paper. They also labeled their pictures and gavae a brief report on their animal to the class. Now Bill gives each student a picture. Students can exchange pictures if they get one they don't like. Mai hands back the orangutan picture, explaining amid some laughter that she would rather have the picture of the kitten.

When each student has a picture, Bill says, "I want you to get together with everyone whose animal has the same outer covering. You're going to have to get up and walk around to do this. When you find the other people whose animals have the same outer covering, you should all stand together." For the next few minutes, there is a babble of voices. As students move around, words like *fur* and *feathers* are repeated many times. Soon students separate into groups. Students with pictures of the elephant and the walrus call José, who has a rhinoceros picture, over to their group away from the dolphin and shark group.

Once the groups have formed, Bill asks each group to hold up their pictures and say what kind of outer covering their animals have. Then he asks the other groups if they agree that all the people should be in that group. Elise, who has a picture of a collie, is told to move from the short hair group (tiger, deer) to the long hair group (goat, fox), and Veronica with a picture of a cow moves from the short hair group to animals with hides (camel, giraffe). Xia with her picture of a porcupine is all by herself.

When all the students agree that the groupings are right, the teacher gives a second category, "Now I want you to get together with all the others who live in the same environment." Later, students whose animals eat the same things form groups. In some cases, students who are together for one category have to regroup for the new category, and in other cases, they can stay where they are. For each new category, students decide if the groups are properly formed. Sometimes they aren't sure about where certain animals live or what they eat, and the teacher notes those questions on the board for later research. Throughout this activity there is a great deal of meaningful language use. Words like fur, moun*tains*, and *plants* are repeated many times as students hold up their pictures and walk around the room to find other students whose animals fall into the same category as their animal.

Next, Bill asks the students to sit with the others in the group they just formed. He splits the larger groups and students pull their desks together in groups of three or four. One student collects the pictures as Bill hands each group a copy of *Zoobooks*, a magazine published by the San Diego Zoo. Each issue of Zoobooks features a particular kind of animal. As with the pictures, Bill gives groups a choice of several books. After a quick perusal, one group exchanges their issue on birds of prey for one on pandas. The students begin to leaf through the magazines, looking at the many colorful pictures and drawings and reading the captions.

As soon as each group has a magazine, Bill announces, "We only have a few minutes left today. Tomorrow we're going to start some research projects on animals, but in the time we have left I want you to look through your magazine and find a fact about your animal or animal group that you think might be interesting for the class. Make up a question about the information. Be sure your question is clear and that the answer is in your book." For the next few minutes, the students look through their magazines and discuss possible questions.

Bill asks for the students' attention. "Who has a question for us?" Xia raises her hand—"How many hours a day does a panda eat?" she asks. The other students call out their guesses: "Two hours?" "Eight hours?"

"You better tell us, Xia" says the teacher.

"Sixteen hours a day!" says Xia.

"Boy, those pandas must get fat. What do they eat all day?" asks another student.

"Bamboo," says a student from Xia's group, making a face.

Other groups pose their questions. The bell is about to ring. A student collects the magazines and returns them to a stand in the front of the room. Bill reminds the students that they will start research on animals tomorrow, and they should be thinking about particular questions they would like to explore. They will become experts on certain animals or families of animals and have choices about how to share their knowledge: They might put together informational books or newsletters; decorate the room with charts, models, and drawings; and/or prepare a program to be shared with parents or others in the school. The bell rings and the students file out of the classroom joking with each other about the animals they had pictures of or had read about in the magazines.

Bill organized this lesson using the model of the Wonderfilled Lessons described in Chapter Five. The following list shows how this lesson on animals introduces a unit by following the steps of the Wonderfilled Lessons.

Animal Lesson and the Wonderfilled Lessons

1. What do you know about animals?
   a. Quickwrite in response to pictures: What vocabulary do you know?
   b. Categorization of list and comparison/contrast of two pictures
   c. Moving into groups with pictures: What concepts do you know?

2. What do you wonder about animals?

   Questions arise as students form groups: What food do they eat? Where do they live?

3. How can we find out?

   Research using Zoobooks and other resources.

4. Action Plan

   Students choose an animal and plan own research.

5. Celebration

   Students report on their research.

Bill's lesson is consistent with the principles outlined so far. It moved from whole to part. Rather than starting with the preteaching of vocabulary and facts about animals, Bill showed the students a picture and the students came up with all the descriptive words they knew. They looked at an entire magazine that had not been simplified to find information for questions of interest to them. These aspects of the lesson also made it learner-centered. Students had choices and could draw on what they knew as they participated. This helped them find a purpose in what they were studying. They learned language through meaningful content rather than focusing on the language itself. In addition, there was a good deal of social interaction. Students worked in pairs and small groups during most of the period.

Using All Four Modes

This lesson also followed a fifth important principle for successful practice. Bill involved his students with both written and oral language throughout the lesson. Rather than assuming that students must develop an oral language base before learning to read and write, Bill recognized that both oral and written language can develop together. He found ways to foster reading and writing in his classroom because he believes that reading and writing are important components of every lesson and that it is important to develop both oral and written language proficiency for all students.

In his lesson, Bill involved students in many different ways in order for them to learn both language and content. He realized that some of his students had difficulty with written English so he limited the time of the quickwrite and then had students share in pairs. Not only did students share ideas, but they also moved physically with their pictures as they formed groups corresponding to different categories. Using a language experience approach, Bill wrote words on the overhead transparency and the chalkboard for the students to see as they shared their ideas. The reading material was rich in context because there were pictures and drawings. The amount of print was not overwhelming, and students could make sense out of the print with the help of others in their groups. After researching different animals, students were offered the opportunity to share what they learned through artwork, group-made books, or oral presentations.

Collier (1989) showed that although second language students can develop oral proficiency in about two years, it takes at least five years for these students to develop academic proficiency as measured on standardized tests. Although Bill does not accept the value many place on the results of those standardized tests, he realizes that it is important to offer his students many ways to learn content. He knows that his junior high students cannot take the time to perfect their listening and speaking skills in English before starting to read and write. If they do, they will almost surely fail academically because they will fall far behind in the content area coursework they need. Bill's students don't have the five years that Collier's research suggests English language learners need to compete with native speakers of English. Like many second language students before them, they will drop (or be pushed) out of school well before that, if they are not given opportunities to develop proficiency in both oral language and academic written language.

Written Language in Traditional Second Language Teaching

Although Bill, an ELD teacher, is aware that written language actually can support the development of oral language, many methods of teaching a second or foreign language emphasize mastery of oral language before the introduction of reading and writing. These methods are based on insights from structural linguists who claimed that "Language is speech, not writing" (Diller 1978). The audiolingual method (ALM) even proclaims the primacy of speech in its title.

Although teachers may include written language in early lessons, they sometimes find it difficult to integrate the four modes the way Bill did. Materials for traditional second and foreign language teaching often separate the areas of listening, speaking, reading, and writing, and produce one book for each of the skill areas. In addition, many ESL programs, especially at the postsecondary level, provide separate classes for each of the skill areas. Students might take a class in listening followed by one in speaking or reading. In practice, teachers often ignore these distinctions, but if the class is called "reading" or "speaking," that is what is emphasized. In professional materials, the four skill areas also are treated separately. Textbooks discuss speaking, reading, writing, and listening in different chapters. When students in training to teach ESL or EFL are presented with professional texts and commercial materials such as these, they naturally come to regard listening, speaking, reading, and writing as distinct skills to be taught separately, and, as a result, that is the way they organize their own courses.

Research on Using the Four Modes

Even though some methods and materials emphasize oral language, researchers in second language acquisition have come to recognize the important contribution written language makes in the development of a new language. Krashen (1993) found that "reading exposure" or "reading for genuine interest with a focus on meaning" provides language learners with written "comprehensible input" similar to oral "comprehensible input." He argues that reading contributes to second language acquisition in the same way as listening to oral language does and proposes that reading contributes to competence in writing just as 'istening helps children develop the ability to speak.

Elley and Mangubhai (1983) also conducted research that supports the importance of reading for acquiring a second language. In one study, they found that fourth and fifth grade Fiji students learning English as a foreign language who had time for free voluntary reading in English or who were involved in a shared book program (teachers read big books in English to the class and then discussed them) outperformed similar students who received traditional audiolingual instruction on tests of reading comprehension, writing, and grammar. In a second study involving some 3,000 six-to nine-year-olds in Singapore, Elley (1991) found that students who were involved with free voluntary reading and shared book experiences outscored students in audiolingual classes in measures of reading comprehension, vocabulary, oral language, grammar, listening comprehension, and writing.

Hudelson's (1984, 1989) research provides additional support. Children who speak little or no English can read print in the environment and can write English, using it for various purposes. In fact, Hudelson found that some English language learners can write and read more easily than their oral performance in English might indicate. Along those same lines, Edelsky's (1986) research in bilingual classrooms indicates that written expression in English may precede formal reading instruction and that bilingual learners use knowledge of their first language and knowledge of the world as they write in a second language.

The research suggests, then, that functional reading and writing as well as speaking and listening should be integral parts of all language classroom activities because all these processes interact with one another. Harste, Woodward, and Burke (1984) explain that each time some-one reads, writes, speaks, or listens, this language encounter feeds into a common "data pool." In subsequent encounters with language, the person can then draw on this pool. Rather than assuming that speaking, listening, reading, and writing should be kept separate, they explain that all expressions of language "support growth and development in lit-eracy" (Harste, Woodward, and Burke 1984, p. 53). This data pool con-cept suggests that requiring bilingual students to master oral skills before they write and read actually can limit their learning potential by limiting the number and kinds of language encounters they have.

One of the problems of focusing first on oral language and delay-ing reading and writing, is that we are limiting choices and limiting the ways Effective teachers find a number of ways to support students' learning. They are aware that for many English language learners, long lectures or extensive textbook reading assignments may be particularly difficult. These teachers ensure that all students have chances to talk and listen, as well as read and write every day by embedding all learn-ing in a rich verbal and nonverbal context. In additon, they provide op-portunities for students to learn through drama, art, music, and dance.

In the section that follows, we provide three examples of lessons that are good illustrations of how all the modes can be used with En-glish learners of different ages. These examples illustrate the benefits of including music and art as well as speaking, listening, reading, and writ-ing to help students develop both concepts and ways of expressing those concepts.

Katie's Valentine Lesson

In Katie's first grade, students discuss ideas and class activities. They read, draw, sing, and write stories. They also write in their interactive journals daily.

Even when English is not their first language, children read and write from the start in Katie's classroom. This is demonstrated clearly by a story written by Dan Hue, a Hmong child. The children had talked and read about Valentine's Day. They made valentines and exchanged them, and they had their party. The next day, Dan chose to write and illustrate a story about the experience. His sophisticated illustrations and his story show that he is well on his way to literacy in his second language, English (see Figure 7-1).

Dan's writing shows his understanding of story sequence. He has a title page, tells the story, and then lets us know that he has reached "the nd." His spelling is not completely conventional, but his invented spell-ings show that he is using his knowledge of English phonology to write

Figure 7–1   *Valentine Story*

words the way they sound. For example, he leaves the *a* out of *prte* because of the effect of the *r* on the vowel. He uses the letter *k* for both /k/
sounds in *cake*. He also spells the plural of "cardz" the way it sounds. He
hypothesizes that vowels say their own name, as in *at*, *kak*, and *hom*.

Sometimes teachers of younger children feel that they should not
introduce reading and writing too soon. This is particularly true for
teachers of young English language learners. This example from Dan
shows the value of introducing reading and writing from the beginning.
There is no need to insist on perfect pronunciation and lots of vocabulary drill before allowing a student to read or write.

Miriam's Houses Lesson

Most of Miriam's adult students from different parts of Southeast Asia
had no previous schooling before they began attending adult school.
They spoke very little English and were extremely shy about sharing
orally in class. Miriam also felt their frustration when they tried to write

in their journals because most of the students were embarrassed about their limited writing skills.

During one discussion, the class began talking about the differences in houses and yards in the United States and their native countries. The students tried to explain to their teacher what their homes in Thailand and Laos were like, but neither the students nor the teacher felt that important points were being communicated. Because the topic was one that everyone seemed very interested in, the students decided to draw pictures of their homes in their native lands as a homework assignment and that the discussion of differences in houses would be continued during the next class.

The following class meeting began with Miriam asking for the drawings. There was silence in the room. At first Miriam thought that no one had done the drawing, but she soon realized that the students were all hiding their work and were hesitant about showing their pictures. "No good draw," "Very bad," and "So sorry, teacher" were phrases that filled the room. After much coaxing, Miriam was finally able to get the students to reluctantly pull out their pictures. What Miriam saw brought tears to her eyes. Her students had spent hours painstakingly drawing their homes and yards, often in colored pencil with great detail. One student labeled each part of the picture and added a descriptive paragraph (see Figure 7–2). Another student used a style similar to the pandau tapestry that is embroidered by Southeast Asian women (see Figure 7–3). Miriam decided that she would never again limit her students' communication to only listening, speaking, reading, and writing.

Karen's Fast-Food Lesson

Karen is a fifth grade teacher whose class of twenty-seven is comprised of twelve students whose English is limited and fifteen who speak English as their first language. Karen found that the techniques she uses to make lessons comprehensible for her English language learners are helpful for all her students. The lesson described here was an introduction to a unit on health and nutrition. Karen wanted her students to identify questions of interest that they would explore over the next few weeks. At the same time, she hoped to assess what they already knew about this topic. In particular, she wanted to find out what her immigrant students knew about American food customs.

Karen started the lesson by announcing, "Today we're going to talk about a special kind of food, fast-food. Do any of you know the names of some fast-food restaurants? As the students called out, "McDonald's," "Wendy's," Kentucky Fried," Karen wrote the names on the board. After a few minutes she had compiled a list of fourteen restaurants. Then she

Figure 7–2   House Drawing

asked, "What kinds of food can you buy in these restaurants?" She worked down the list with the class, writing the kinds of food each restaurant serves. The students knew that they could get hamburgers and fries at McDonald's, and that Domino's had pizza and salad.

When the students named all the foods they could think of for each restaurant, Karen asked them to do a quickwrite, "In the next two minutes, write down what you like and what you dislike about fast-food." The students worked busily for the next two minutes, often glancing up at the board where the names of the restaurants and foods were listed. At

Figure 7–3   Laos Story

the end of the time, Karen asked students to get together in groups of three and make one composite list. The students pushed their desks together and started on this activity. Karen circulated around the room, noting what the students were writing and answering questions. After a few minutes, she asked the students to stop. "I'm going to start with what you like about fast-food. I'll ask each group to give me one thing you wrote down, and I'll write it here on the overhead transparency."

Karen elicited first the likes and then the dislikes from the groups, writing their responses on a transparency on the overhead projector. Several of the likes and dislikes related to health matters. One group commented that they disliked fast-food because it was high in fat. Another group claimed that fast-food was too salty. Karen commented, "You've said that in some ways fast-food is not very healthy. Why don't you talk in your groups for a couple of minutes and try to decide what makes a healthy meal? Have somebody in your group write down your ideas, and I will ask you to report back." Again, as the students discussed this question, Karen circulated around the room.

The students came up with a list of factors that make a healthy meal. They mentioned low fat, low sugar, and a balance of all the food groups. Karen wrote their responses on another transparency. Then she handed out one pamphlet to each group. These were from the National Dairy Council (Fast 1989) and contained nutrition information. Such information is often provided by different organizations, restaurants, and companies. She asked the students not to open the pamphlets yet. On the colorful cover were pictures of a shake, a hamburger, and fries. At the top was written "Fast-Food" and below that title "Junk? Gems? or Just OK?" Karen asked, "Do you see some things on the cover that we have been talking about?" The students nodded in agreement. "Is there anything on the cover we didn't mention?" The students noted that they had forgotten shakes, so Karen added that word to their food list.

"What do you think 'Junk' and 'Gems' refers to?" asked Karen.

The students responded, "Bad things and good things."

"Something worthless and something valuable."

Karen listed the responses on the board in two columns. "Are there other ways to talk about good and bad things?" she asked. One student mentioned "pros" and "cons" while another called out "likes" and "dislikes." Karen added these pairs to the list.

"OK, now open the pamphlet once." Inside was a series of columns printed in different colors. The first listed fast-food items by restaurant. For example, under Burger King, the Whopper was listed and under Arby's came Ham 'n Cheese. Beside each food item was the number of calories it contained. The remaining five columns were color coded. They were labeled milk group (blue), meat group (red), fruit-vegetable group (green), grain group (yellow) and others (gray). For each food group, the chart listed the number of recommended daily servings according to the Dairy Council and the important nutrients. Then, across from each food item, such as the Whopper, the ingredients included in each food group were indicated. The Whopper had cheese for the milk group; hamburger for meat; onion and lettuce for fruit/vegetable; the bun for grain; and catsup, pickles, and mayonnaise under others.

Karen asked a few questions to be sure her students understood how to read the chart. "How many calories would I get if I ate a Long John Silver's Fish and More?"

Quickly, one student answered "978."

"How many food groups are included in Wendy's chili?"

Another student answered, "Two."

"Which ones are missing?" asked Karen, and the student explained that chili lacks the milk, grain, and others groups. After a few more questions, Karen was satisfied that the students could read the chart.

"There's lots of fast-food listed here, isn't there?" Karen asked. "I'd like you to imagine that this chart is really a menu for a super fast-food restaurant. I'm going to be the waitress, and you'll be the customers. You can order anything you like that's on the chart. I want everyone to write down what people order. Now who would like to go first?"

Abel raised his hand. "I'll have a Taco Bell beef taco and a Dairy Queen ice cream cone."

"Would you care for something to drink?" asked Karen.

"Sure, I'll have a glass of milk."

Karen took orders from three other students. Everyone wrote down what the students ordered, often reading the chart to get the spelling right. Then Karen asked, "We've been talking about what makes a healthy meal. Who do you think ordered the healthiest meal? I want you to talk about this in your groups. Then we'll vote. Each group gets one vote, and you have to be able to justify your choice."

The students talked animatedly. They discussed which meals covered all the food groups, which meals had the most calories, and which meals contained the most nutrients. When they decided, they voted and discussed their choices. Karen distributed additional pamphlets so each student had one. "If you open up the pamphlets completely, you'll see that there is information about the question we've been asking, 'Is fast-food good for you?' You'll also see some meals like the ones you just ordered, and each meal is analyzed. There's also a section called, 'So what should a fast-food eater do?' I want you to read this information tonight and decide whether or not you made a good choice when you voted on the healthiest meal. You might discuss this with your family. Then, we can talk more about it tomorrow."

The next day Karen and her students discussed the meals analyzed in the Dairy Council pamphlets. One student brought in a cereal box with the food pyramid on the back. Karen took out a food pyramid poster she had and then asked the students if the food pyramid was the same as or different from the basic food groups. Students talked about this together and noted that the food pyramid had fewer dairy products and more grains. To make this idea even more concrete, Karen gave out pictures of foods to the students. Then, the students physically formed themselves into a pyramid with the longer bottom made up of those with pictures of grains and the top with one person holding the picture of a rich dessert.

A discussion followed about the bias the National Dairy Council or cereal companies might have in putting together a nutrition chart for distribution. Other activities included visits to local fast-food restaurants, which included tours and free materials, interviews with parents and friends about their eating habits, and surveys of other students about how often they ate fast-food and which restaurants were their favorites. Perhaps the most important activity, however, was when students analyzed their own eating. Students kept track of their diet over several days in a journal and then analyzed the results. This gave Karen an excellent opportunity to discuss the wide variety of foods that students from different cultural groups ate. The students also talked about cultural differences in conceptions of healthy meals. For example, in some cultures, it is considered unhealthy to combine hot and cold food during a meal. Many cultures have very little meat in the diet. Some cultures use a lot of lard in cooking their food.

During these activities, students developed the vocabulary and concepts associated with food and health through reading, writing, speaking, and listening. They used this as a basis for investigating their own questions about food and health. Some students chose to look at the food customs of their own culture and contrast those with U.S. food. Others investigated whether or not immigrants to the United States retain their own eating habits or adopt U.S. customs. What was important was that as they explored these questions, Karen's students increased their content area knowledge and developed their oral and written language proficiency.

This unit on fast-food also follows the Wonderfilled Lesson model. The following list shows how the lessons in the unit correspond to the Wonderfilled Lessons.

Fast-Food and the Wonderfilled Lessons

1. What do you know about fast-food?

   a. Students brainstormed names of fast food restaurants and the food served in each restaurant.

   b. Students did a quickwrite about what they liked and disliked about fast-food. They shared their answers in small groups and then with the class.

2. What do you wonder about fast-food?

Based on student responses, Karen asked whether students thought that eating fast-food was healthy or not. (Note that the teacher can pose the question at this step so long as it emerges naturally from student comments.)

3. How can we find out?

a. Students read pamphlets, magazines, and other materials about healthy eating.

b. They compared materials from different groups as they looked at the four food groups and the food pyramid.

c. They toured fast-food restaurants and read the materials the restaurants provided.

d. They interviewed friends and family members.

4. Action plan

Groups of students chose specific questions related to health and fast food to investigate.

5. Celebration

Groups wrote and presented their reports.

Conclusion

English language learners find that reading, writing, music, drama, and art help them develop the language they are learning.

The same factors that help students develop oral language help them to develop written language. According to Cochrane and colleagues (1984), writing develops when students are immersed in a literate environment, when they find that written language is meaningful and purposeful, when they see people who are important to them using written language, when they get support in their attempts to read and write, and when they are given time to read and write daily.

Traditionally, oral language has been stressed over written language for students learning a second or foreign language. However, it is important that students have opportunities to read and write from the beginning as they learn a new language. Because oral language passes by rapidly, bilingual students have more control over written language. They can re-read passages, look at individual words, and take their time to express in writing what they want to say. In addition, teachers who follow the principles for success include reading and writing from the start and teach language through content because they know that their students need to develop academic competence as well as communicative competence.

EIGHT

Lessons Should Support Students' First Languages and Cultures, Part One

Well, I am born in Thailand, but I don't know how to speak Thai at all. You may find it amusing but I really don't know how to read or write, or speak Thai at all. Even though I'm Hmong, I don't even know how to read and write in Hmong. The only language I really know how to read and write is English. In my high school year, I'm planning to take French for my foreign language. (fourteen-year-old Hmong girl)

This writing sample comes from a journal exchange between Julie, a student teacher, and a Hmong junior high school student, but it could easily have come from any one of the many English language learners studying in ESL contexts. These students enter school as monolingual Spanish, Chinese, or Hmong speakers and leave as monolingual English speakers. They often lose their first language so completely that by the time they reach high school, they need to study a foreign language! This language loss is not only a loss to those who no longer speak their first languages, but it is also a loss to society as well. As Crawford (1997) points out, "Americans are finding out that monolingualism puts us at an increasing disadvantage not only in science, technology, and international business, but also in diplomacy, national security, and cultural exchange."

This girl is in danger of losing her first language, and she is also in danger of losing her cultural heritage. Her parents, like most Hmong, are from Laos, but she was born in a refugee camp in Thailand. As she enters high school, she will face increasing pressure to abandon her tenuous links to traditional Hmong culture in favor of popular American culture. It is ironic that she plans to study French, the language of the colonial power that ruled her native country for years. Without support, she may lose both her native language and culture.

Sometimes, as in the example of this Hmong teenager, children are not literate in their first language, and it is difficult to know how to support them. We find that when we show students the importance of their first language and culture, we provide empowering conditions. This empowerment helps them to see their own potential as learners in English, as well as in their first language. Effective programs for these students produce competent bilingual (or multilingual), biliterate (or multiliterate) and bicultural (multicultural) individuals.

The problem posed by this Hmong girl is not unique to the ESL context, but it is certainly more prevalent in countries like the United States. In EFL contexts, students learning English don't lose their native language or culture. It is possible, as we observed in parts of South America, for children to receive all their schooling in English and still speak and understand their native language. However, some students don't learn to read and write easily in English in these EFL contexts, and they may fail to fully acquire academic Spanish. Their Spanish literacy development may be limited by the early English immersion. For that reason, we feel that the principle that lessons should support students' first languages and cultures holds in any context. Nevertheless, we recognize that this principle is particularly crucial in ESL settings. Students like the Hmong girl are especially susceptible to losing their first language and culture, and teachers should make special efforts with students like her.

In this and the next chapter, we examine different aspects of bilingual education. We begin by describing how a bilingual Hmong teacher is making a difference for her Hmong students so they won't end up like the teen quoted above. Then, we examine several misconceptions about bilingual education and show how a teacher education class can help counter those misconceptions. Next, we describe a unit from a successful Spanish-English bilingual class. In the last part of this chapter, we review the history of bilingual education in the United States and we present the rationale for bilingual education. In the following chapter, we describe and analyze different kinds of bilingual programs. We also suggest how teachers who are not bilingual can support their students' first languages and cultures.

Bilingual Education for Hmong Children

In bilingual classes, teachers use two languages. They may start with the primary language and then introduce English little by little. Pa Houa, a credentialed Hmong bilingual teacher, tells how using her students' first language made a significant difference in their education:

It was August 6, 1997, our first day of kindergarten. When I said "Hello" to my students in English, they all sat in front of me silently as if no one was talking to them. Some of them asked me in Hmong, "What did you say?" I smiled at them and began to talk to them in Hmong. I pinned their name tags on them and called roll. "If you are here, please raise your hand for me, okay?" I asked in Hmong. Everyone quietly raised his or her hand as I called out their names. We went over the classroom rules. All instruction was done in Hmong because all of my sixteen students are Hmong and are extremely limited in English.

I wanted to see what my students knew and what they could do. I started by having them draw a picture of themselves and write their name on the paper. Some drew a person with missing body parts. Some drew pictures of unknown things, and a lot of them just made circles. None of the papers had names on them. When they were asked to put their names on their papers, many of them said that they didn't know how.

On the second day of school, during our opening time, we chose a star of the day, who would be the helper and the leader for the day. I was curious, so when the name was drawn, I said, "The star is a boy." in English. The students did not have any idea what a boy or a girl was. They did not know the words *shirt*, *pants*, or *shoes*. Right after that, I stopped speaking in English, and I started to give the clues in Hmong. I wanted to make sure they had the vocabulary in their first language, so I repeated in Hmong that the star was a boy. They understood and the boys stood up. One or two boys that were still sitting were quickly assisted by the other boys to stand. I started giving the students hints in Hmong every day, that the star was a boy or girl, wearing a red shirt, wearing a short or long sleeved shirt, wearing shorts or long pants, black pants, shoes with laces, etc. In the following weeks, we slowly switched to English, and they did very well.

By the end of the second week, students were well adjusted to school, classroom rules, and almost all were writing their names independently, compared to the little sguiggly circles and lines drawn on the first two days of school. I was noticing a great difference in how well this class behaved and how much they were involved in classroom discussion compared to classes in the past. I realized this was so because for the first time, I explained rules and regulations to them in a language that they could understand.

It was only September and we were doing interactive writing in English. My students were coming up to write words such as *a*, *the*, I, *star*, and their names in English. Some of them drew bears and wrote phrases such as "the 3 bears" to go with their pictures. By mid-September, all of my students could write their names clearly and independently with good letter formation. The students were getting really good at the star-of-the day-game also, even when I gave the clues in English. They all seemed to be enjoying school and seemed to be eager to learn. One other thing that struck me was that all of them came to class every day. I had never had a class with such good attendance before.

We are now entering our third month of school. In English my students can identify and write numbers up to at least five and letters that appear frequently in most of their names. Everyone can read independently with one-to-one match on most of the books we make in class and the star-of-the-day sentence on the board. I don't have to write the sentence on the board anymore because the students are volunteering to do the writing themselves. Instead of using clues like *boy* or *pants*, I tell the students the star has the letter *e* or *a* or *n* in his or her name. Students who do not have the letter sit down until everyone is eliminated except for the star. This is very exciting.

The way her students have responded has opened Pa Houa's eyes to the benefits of bilingual education. She concluded her reflections by writing:

The major difference, I know, has to do with the first language instruction I am doing this year. Everything I have learned about bilingual education is becoming clear to me now. I believe that bilingual education works because I see it in my classroom with my wonderful, intelligent, and capable Hmong students.

We began this chapter with a journal entry from the Hmong girl who couldn't read or write Hmong and who planned to take French as a foreign language in high school. Pa Houa's students are getting the base that girl lacked. They are learning to read and write in both Hmong and English. They are developing cognitive, academic, and linguistic proficiency in two languages. They will not have to explain in later years why they can't read or write their native language. Instead, they are developing a clear sense of their identities as competent bilingual and biliterate individuals. They are building a strong foundation for school success because they are receiving bilingual education.

Misconceptions About Bilingual Education

Anyone observing the group of inquisitive and engaged students in Pa Houa's bilingual class would conclude that they are having a successful school experience. In her reflections on her teaching, Pa Houa notes that her students have good attendance, good discipline, and a positive attitude toward learning. Why, then, is bilingual education so controversial?

Unfortunately, misconceptions surround bilingual education. Public acceptance or rejection of programs like bilingual education often is based more on politics or emotions than on what we know about learning and teaching. However, when we examine the research on bilingual education, it becomes clear that supporting first language development is critical because students learn concepts best in their primary language. The development of students' first languages leads to faster acquisition of English as well. Moreover, programs that support a student's first language and culture help the student gain self-confidence and a positive attitude toward school.

The sixth principle for successful practice is that lessons should support students' first languages and cultures so that teachers can draw on and develop student strengths. Probably no other principle that we propose for English language learners is more controversial than this one. The debate over bilingual education has continually confused both the public and educators. Since 1968, when the Bilingual Education Act was added as an amendment to the 1965 Elementary and Secondary Education Act, there has been misunderstanding about the purpose and effectiveness of bilingual education for language minority students. Opponents of bilingual education argue that students should be taught in English to become fluent in English and compete in our society. Bilingual education was attacked by former President Reagan (Crawford 1989) and former Secretary of Education Bennett (Bennett 1985) and continues to be attacked today by U.S. English advocates (Porter 1990, Imhoff 1990, Rossell and Baker 1996).

We can see an extreme example of opposition to bilingual education in California. In the fall of 1997, Unz and Tuchman, two politicians who had lost previous bids for state office, sponsored the "English as Required Language for Instruction Initiative" by collecting signatures for the 1998 electoral ballot. This initiative mandates schools to teach academic subjects only through English, using "structured English immersion," and makes it difficult for schools to offer any primary language support for students. Only students with a high level of English proficiency would have the choice to develop bilingual skills. Bills such as this one feed on anti-immigrant sentiment and ignore the research on effective education.

The effectiveness of bilingual programs has been carefully evaluated, but academic research is not widely disseminated. In one study, McQuillan and Tse (1997) found that between 1984 and 1994, 87 percent of the academic publications favored bilingual education, but only 45 percent of the opinion articles in newspapers and magazines supported it. Despite the media's anti-bilingual spin, many people still favor bilingual programs. Krashen (1996) reviewed a series of studies on attitudes of parents and the public toward bilingual education and found that "No matter how the question (about bilingual education) is asked, however, most respondents support bilingual education" (p.45).

Although newspapers often report on polls showing public opposition to bilingual education, it is important to understand that public response depends on how the questions are posed. McQuillan and Tse found that the public is not generally opposed to bilingual education when asked if the first language could be used as a teaching tool or when asked if a bilingual program using English and the first language is acceptable. On the other hand, when surveys ask parents whether they want their children to learn English, parents respond *yes*, and the papers report these responses as rejections of bilingual education. In part, this comes as the result of a basic misunderstanding. Often, people don't realize that *bilingual* means two languages. In the Unz and Tuchman initiative, bilingual education is defined as "a language acquisition process for students in which much or all instruction, textbooks, and teaching materials are in the child's native language" (Jones 1997, p. 2). What the public does not realize when presented with legislation like this initiative is that bilingual programs *do* provide both first language support *and* English and that extreme political measures will hurt both children and society as a whole.

Some educators who recognize the importance of the language and culture that native English-speaking students bring with them to school do not fully understand the importance of building on the language and cultural base that other students bring. This became clear to us over the past several years as we worked with experienced teachers who studied best practices in schools.

Bilingual Education Experience for Teachers

One of the courses teachers in our graduate program take is "Current Theories, Methods, and Materials for Bilingual Education." Yvonne decided to teach this course bilingually in Spanish and English even though only one-fourth to one-third of the students speak or have studied any Spanish. Yvonne felt it was critical to try to "practice" what she was "preaching." She wanted to make the course comprehensible to non-Spanish-speaking teachers, and she wanted the teachers to experience what it was like to have to learn in a second language. Yvonne employed strategies and techniques consistent with the principles for success. She demonstrated what a good bilingual classroom looked like to help her students understand the research and reading they were doing on bilingual education. Although some teachers resisted taking the class and began it with reservations or even fear, their weekly responses and self-evaluations show that their attitudes changed and that they realized the value of first language support for their own students. Responses from two of the teachers illustrate how they changed their attitudes toward bilingual education as a result of their reading and research and also because of their experience of being second language learners in this class. Rose Marie wrote:

> I know I've been a little obnoxious about this class (OK, a lot obnoxious). You were absolutely right about teaching this class in Spanish. I think I have a greater understanding about bilingual education because of the Spanish. As a person who believes in choice, I am conflicted about having to take this class. Yet, if there was a choice I would not have chosen this class.

Nancy reflected on her past experience and could see how her attitude had changed:

> When I was a student teacher in the teacher education program, almost every day I would walk by the office of bilingual education. I would think, "What is this program needed for? We don't need bilingual education. It is the parent's fault that the minority students are failing in school—not the teacher's fault!" Now it is embarrassing to me to realize how prejudiced I felt about the bilingual education program. Even worse my opinions were completely unfounded. I knew nothing about the bilingual education program. . . . I now realize that my prejudice arose from ignorance and fear.

Teachers like Rose Marie and Nancy came to understand bilingual education and joined us in our concern over the misunderstandings some educators and the public developed about bilingual education. Many bilingual teachers are empowered by the experience of taking the class. For Spanish speakers, a kind of role reversal occurs. Instead of being the ones who don't speak the language of prestige and power in the classroom, they are suddenly the *stars*. During the class, students often meet in family groups to discuss lectures or short articles read in class, and the Spanish speakers naturally take a leadership role at these times.

During the bilingual methods class, Yvonne often shares examples of successful teaching practices from bilingual classrooms. One of these comes from Francisco, a Spanish-English bilingual teacher who follows the principles for success.

Francisco's Ocean Unit

Francisco teaches in a Spanish immersion program where the Latino students in his rural farming community receive most of their daily content and literacy instruction in Spanish through third grade. Francisco feels a special responsibility as a third grade teacher, because although students continue receiving some first language support in the upper grades, after third grade, a major portion of their instruction is in English. In order to best serve his students, Francisco has worked hard at planning curriculum that will lead them to biliteracy (Freeman and Freeman 1997, 1998). Because he knows that literacy and content knowledge developed in the first language transfer to the second language (Cummins 1981), Francisco tries to integrate his daily ELD time with the content being studied in Spanish. Francisco has seen that once his students are empowered by their ability to read, write, and learn academic content in their native language, they can more confidently use English for academic purposes. His bilingual, biliterate students have more potential for long-term academic success than students who are not biliterate.

A good example of how Francisco follows the principles for success comes from an ocean unit he developed. Because his students come from a rural, agricultural area and have had little previous experience with the sea, Francisco wanted to start his unit by giving them time to think and talk about the ocean and its inhabitants. The activities he planned served as a primary language preview. (See Chapter Two for discussion of preview-view-review).

Francisco first brought out a globe and asked the students what part of the globe represented water. This led the students to talk about how most of our world is made up of water and how important the oceans are to all of us. He then read them the first of many books about the ocean, *Datos pescados* (*Fishy Facts*) (Chermayeff 1997), which gives many interesting facts about fish. (See Figure 8–1 for a complete bibliography of the literature in this ocean unit.) He also read two limited textbooks to his students, Un *cuento curiosos de colores* (A *Fish Color Story*) (Wylie and Wylie 1983) and Un *cuento de peces y sus formas* (A *Fishy Shape Story*) (Wylie and Wylie 1985), to give them ideas about the colors and forms of fish in the sea. Francisco invited students to use their imaginations to construct their own fish, using different colors and shapes. As they worked, students chatted in Spanish about their fish creations and what they knew about the fish. The finished, individual creations were then put together on the wall to form a multicolored fish kaleidoscope quilt. That day, during physical education time, Francisco and his students sang and played the traditional "A la víbora de la mar." ("The Sea Serpent") (Orozco 1994).

The next day Francisco continued with the preview activities by reading a content big book, En *aguas profundas* (*In the Depths*) (García-Moliner 1993). After a short discussion of the reading, Francisco wrote on the whiteboard, "Qué sabemos del mar?" ("What do we know about the sea?") Students responded by telling him about the water in the

Ocean Unit Bibliography

Aliki. 1993. "El celacanto perdido." In *En Aguas Profundas*. Boston: Houghton Mifflin.

Berger, Melvin. 1996. *The Mighty Ocean*. New York: Newbridge Communications Inc.

Bracho, Coral. 1993. *Jardín del mar, Reloj de versos*. México, D.F.: CIDCLI.

Craig, Janet. 1987. *Cómo son los Habitantes del mar, Cómo son*. México, D.F.: SITESA.

Chermayeff, Ivan. 1997. *Datos pescados*. Boston: Houghton Mifflin.

———. 1997. *Fishy Facts*. Boston: Houghton Mifflin.

DeSaix, Frank. 1991. *The Girl Who Danced with the Dolphins*. New York: Farrar Straus Giroux.

Dubovoy, Silvia. 1990. *Poncho, el cangrejo presumido*. México, D.F.: SITES.

———. 1991. *Turquesita, Colección Barril Sin Fondo*. Amecameca: C.E.L.T.A.

Fernández, Flora 1984. (Traductora). *A la orilla del mar, Biblioteca temática para niños: Coleccion naturaleza*. México, D. F.: Fernández Editores.

García-Moliner, Graciela, ed. 1993. *En Aguas Profundas*. Boston: Houghton Mifflin.

Garland, Peter. 1992. *La orilla del mar*. Crystal Lake, IL: Rigby.

Girón, Nicole. 1993. *El mar, Celebremos la literatura*. Boston: Houghton Mifflin.

Granrows, Alvin. 1986. *La ballena azul*. Lexington, MA: Schoolhouse Press.

Kovacs, Deborah. 1987. *A Day Under Water*. New York: Scholastic.

Lauber, Patricia. 1996. "An Octopus Is Amazing." In *Treasure*. Boston: Houghton Mifflin.

———. 1997. *El pulpo asombroso, Invitaciones*. Boston: Houghton Mifflin.

Orozco, José Luis. 1994. *De colores and Other Latin-American Folk Songs for Children*. New York: Dutton Children's Books.

Figure 8–1   *Ocean Unit Bibliography*

ocean, shells on the beach, the names of some fish, and some personal experiences. Then Francisco wrote, "¿Qué quieren saber del mar?" ("What do you want to know about the sea?") This led students into asking questions about different sea animals, especially *delfines*, (dolphins) *ballenas*, (whales) and *tiburones* (sharks).

The discussion and brainstorming in Spanish led Francisco nicely into ELD time. The instruction in English served as the "view" portion of the plan. He began by reading the English version of *Datos pescados* (*Fishy Facts*) (Chermayeff 1997). He then led his class in a picture walk through *The Mighty Ocean* (Berger 1996). For the picture walk, Francisco asked stu-

Pfister, Marcus. 1994. *El pez arco iris*. New York: Ediciones Norte-Sur.

Revello, Rosina. 1996. "Las canciones de mi isla." In *Observa la naturaleza*. Boston: Houghton Mifflin.

Sands, Stella. 1997. "Oceans."New York: Kids Discover.

Sheldon, Dyan. 1993. *El canto de las ballenas*. Translated by Nelson Rivera. Caracas, Venezuela: Ediciones Ekaré.

Wilson, Lucy Cruz. 1991. *El mar y la costa*. Edited by Rodolfo Fonseca, *Educación ambiental*. México, D.F.: CONAFE.

Wylie, Joanne, and David Wylie. 1985. *Un cuento de peces y sus formas*. New York: Childrens Press.

———. 1983. *Un cuento curioso de colores*. New York: Childrens Press.

Zoehfeld, Kathleen Weidner. 1994. *Dolphin's First Day*. New York: Scholastic.

———. 1996. "What Lives in a Shell?" In *Friends*. Boston: Houghton Mifflin.

———. 1997. "¿Qué vive en una concha?" In *Invitaciones*. Boston: Houghton Mifflin.

Figure 8–1 *continued*

dents to look at the pictures in the big book and comment quietly on what they saw. He also asked them what things they saw there that they could talk about in English. Once they finished looking at the book, students dictated, in English, words and phrases about the ocean that the book brought to mind. Then Francisco read the book to them, stopping to answer their questions and to discuss parts that especially caught their interest. Because *The Mighty Ocean* repeated many of the themes that the students had already read about in *En aguas profundas*, Francisco involved the students in a comparison of the two books in English using a Venn Diagram. In this way, both concepts and vocabulary about the ocean were reinforced. He concluded the lesson by having the students meet in small groups to discuss what they had learned. Students reviewed the lesson in their primary language.

In the next few days, Francisco and his students followed the same pattern of preview/view/review as they read many books and magazines in Spanish and English that reinforced the content in both languages. Students read from Kids Discover magazines on *Oceans* (Sands 1997) and found a chart of ocean animals and plants living at different depths that paralleled charts found in both E*n aguas profundas* and *The Mighty Ocean*. They pored over the charts in the magazines and big books, using vocabulary in both English and Spanish. Another section of "E*n aguas profundas"* explained how people have explored the depths of the ocean, so Francisco read the students *A Day Under Water* (Kovacs 1987) and the class talked about how scientists travel near the floor of the ocean to study the animals and plants there. A co-teacher working with Francisco had done some deep sea diving, so he talked with the students about his experiences and answered their questions.

Other books in Spanish about the animals in the ocean included limited text content books such as *Cómo son los habitantes del mar* (*What Are the Inhabitants in the Sea Like?*) (Craig 1987) and *La ballena azul* (*The Blue Whale*) (Granrows 1986). More challenging reading included *El Mar* (*The Sea*) (Girón 1993) and *El pulpo asombroso* (Lauber 1997). Later the students could read the English version of the latter, *An Octopus Is Amazing* (Lauber 1996), not only because they had read the story first in Spanish but also because the pictures and charts related clearly to the text.

Francisco and his students also were interested in shells and animals that live near the shore of the ocean. They read together *La orilla del mar* (*The Seashore*) (Garland 1992), *A la orilla del mar* (*On the Seashore*) (Fernández 1984), *El mar y la costa* (*The Sea and the Seashore*) (Wilson 1991), *Poncho, el cangrejo presumido* (*Poncho, the Stuck-up Crab*) (Dubovoy 1990), and *¿Quién vive en una concha?* (*What Lives in a Shell?*) (Zoehfeld 1997). During ELD time, students looked at shells Francisco and some students brought from home and identified the shells using the English versions of *¿Quién vive en una concha?* (*What Lives in a Shell?*) (Zoehfeld 1996).

Students also read poetry from *Jardin del mar* (*Garden of the Sea*) (Bracho, 1993) and fiction, including *El pez arcoiris* (*The Rainbow Fish*) (Pfister 1994), *El celancanto peridido* (*The Long-Lost Coelacanth*)(Aliki 1993), *Las canciones de mi isla* (*Songs of My Island*)(Revello 1996), *Turquesita* (*The Little Turquoise One*) (Dubovoy 1991), and *El canto de las ballenas* (*The Song of the Whales*) (Sheldon 1993).

When working in English, students drew on what they had learned in their first language. Francisco read them I*s This a House for a Hermit Crab?* (McDonald 1997) to reinforce what they had read in Spanish about shells and seashore animals, Using poems from *Jardin del mar* as models, they wrote poems in Spanish about the sea. Then they read and translated their poems into English for English-speaking visitors. The class read and discussed *The Girl Who Danced with the Dolphins* (DeSaix 1991), a story that reinforced ideas found in *El canto de las ballenas* (*The Song of the Whales*) (Sheldon 1993). This resulted in another Venn diagram activity in English, in which the students compared and contrasted the Spanish story about whales and the English story about dolphins. Another story about dolphins that the students especially enjoyed was *Dolphin's First Day* (Zoehfeld 1994). Dolphins were one of the students' favorite sea animals.

After learning so much about the ocean, the students engaged in several culminating activities. For one ELD lesson, they talked about some old posters that Francisco had found in a cupboard in his classroom. The posters, entitled "Fish that We Eat, Fish that Eat Us, Shells, Shellfish," and "Man Abuses the Sea," were put in a corner of the room for students to refer to. They used the posters when they made a huge ocean mural of the sea and the seacoast. In groups of four, children chose animals and plants they had learned about. They looked at the posters and looked through various books. Then, using construction paper, they made different sea animals and plants. The students worked together to place their creations on the mural. Finally, the students dictated to Francisco in English a description of their mural, which was typed on the computer, printed in large letters, and placed next to the mural.

The students were able to write rich stories in Spanish and English about the ocean. Their writing reflected the content learning they had done and the literature they had read. For example, Veronica wrote and illustrated an eight page story in Spanish entitled *El pez feliz* (The Happy Fish) that was similar to the story *El pez arcoiris*. Juan and Jackie wrote stories in English entitled, "The Dolphins Jumping," and "Dolphins Flipper," that showed what they had learned from reading about dolphins. The stories Francisco's students wrote in English reflected both their academic content knowledge and language development in English.

The final project that each student did was an individual poster, in English, about the ocean. The students could choose to draw and write anything they wanted on the posters, but most students chose to write about taking care of the ocean. The walls of Francisco's room were covered with posters including "Save the Whales," "Don't Throw Garbage in the Ocean," "We Need to Take Care of the Ocean or We Are Going to Die," and "Save the Ocean. It's the Home of the Fish."

Students in Francisco's class learned a great deal during their study of the ocean. The content knowledge they developed in Spanish transferred into English. By reading a variety of rich literature, organizing curriculum around a theme and using a variety of strategies, including preview-view-review, Francisco helped his students in their quest to become both bilingual and biliterate.

Francisco's class provides a clear example of bilingual education working well. Anyone visiting his class or Pa Houa's class would see the merits of starting with the students' first language. However, a brief historical review of bilingual education in the United States reveals that although teaching students some content in their native language has been a general practice, opposition to bilingual education has been a consistent factor and problem.

Historical Background of Bilingual Education

The perception of the general public is that English has been the official language of the United States since the early settlers arrived in the 1600s. Yet, in 1664 at least eighteen different languages were spoken on Manhattan Island (Crawford 1989). During the 1700s, bilingualism was quite common. In 1750, for example, when Benjamin Franklin tried to force schooling in English because he could not reach the German-speaking electorate, he was voted out of office. By the mid-1800s, bilingual schools in different languages were operating across the United States: German/English schools in twelve states, French/English schools in Louisiana, and Spanish/English schools in the Territory of New Mexico.

To give an idea of the extent of bilingual education, in 1900, more than four percent of the elementary school population was receiving instruction partly or exclusively in the German language. In the early 1900s, with the threat of war against Germany, Theodore Roosevelt led a campaign against bilingualism, giving immigrants five years to learn English or be deported. Letters to the editor in various newspapers today are similar to Roosevelt's sentiments:

> . . . any man who comes here must adopt the institutions of the United States, and therefore he must adopt the language which is now the native tongue of our people. It would be not merely a matter of misfortune but a crime to perpetuate differences of language in this country. (reported in Trueba and Barnett-Mizrahi 1979, p. 3)

This attitude toward immigrants led to the view that the United States should be a great melting pot and that the goal for all immigrants should be to melt into the rest of society. Some still hold this belief today: "The idea of teaching children in other languages is an affront to sacred traditions" (Crawford 1989, p. 18). The battle between the "English Only" advocates who oppose bilingual education and the pro-bilingual "English Plus" followers has never been merely a language issue. A review of the research supporting bilingual education suggests that there are other, more disturbing reasons why bilingual education elicits such intense opposition. A careful look at the historical roots of U.S. language policy also makes this clear (Crawford 1992). JoAnne, another graduate student, reflected on this phenomenon:

> I began this semester wondering why, when there seemed to be such a sound rationale for bilingual education, there could be such

controversy surrounding it. I did not realize that bilingual education is more than an educational issue, that it is part of a societal context involving the power struggle between ethnic and racial groups.

We will explore some of the concerns with the power struggles involved in bilingual education, but first we will consider the rationale for bilingual education.

Rationale for Bilingual Education

Recent research strongly supports bilingual education (Greene 1998, Collier 1995, Collier and Thomas 1996, Ovando and Collier 1998, Crawford 1989, Cummins 1996, Krashen 1996, Krashen and Biber 1988). When we support students' first languages, we are building on their strengths and validating them as individuals. Drawing on the work of Krashen (1996), we developed a list of six reasons for bilingual education:

Six Reasons for Bilingual Education

1. Students can learn academic content and develop the skills needed for problem solving and higher order thinking in their first language while they become proficient in English.
2. The academic concepts and skills learned through the first language transfer to English because there is a common underlying proficiency.
3. There are better home/school connections. Parents can help with homework and communicate with the school.
4. It is practical to learn two languages because there are more job opportunities for bilinguals.
5. Bilinguals are more cognitively flexible.
6. Competent bilinguals feel good about themselves and have pride in their cultures.

In the following sections we discuss each of these reasons by providing theoretical and research support.

Students Learn Academic Content and Skills

Considerable research shows that students who speak, read, and write their first language well are more apt to succeed academically in English (Collier 1995, Collier and Thomas 1996, Ovando and Collier 1998, Cummins 1996, Krashen 1996). Whether English language learners have always lived in the United States, have arrived recently as refugees, or have immigrated, if they are school-aged, they are faced with both learning English and learning the academic content of school subjects. Learning another language well enough to compete academically with native speakers takes a long time. While students are acquiring English and becoming accustomed to a new school in a new country, their native English-speaking classmates are continuing to learn and advance. In trying to catch up, students acquiring English are shooting at a moving target.

In good bilingual programs, students receive instruction in their first language and can keep up academically while they are learning English. In contrast, programs that focus exclusively on teaching English may do so at the expense of academic achievement. If students' school time is spent learning English, they fall behind in math, social studies, science, and other subjects. It is very difficult for students who lag two or three years behind in academic subjects ever to catch up with their English-speaking peers.

When concepts are taught in their first language, English language learners are able to grasp those ideas more easily. If they are receiving content instruction in comprehensible English at the same time, they also can learn the language associated with those same concepts in English and thus learn both concepts and language (Krashen 1985).

To make this process clearer, it might be helpful to provide an example. Imagine a kindergarten classroom at the beginning of the school year. Several children in the class speak only Spanish. Their teacher and the other students speak only English. The teacher has a camera. She explains to the class that they are all going to go on a tour of the school to take pictures of people and places around the school. The class visits the attendance office, the principal and vice-principal's offices, the school cafeteria, the school custodian's office, and the library. At each place, the teacher and the children take pictures and interview the school personnel. When they return to their classroom, the teacher explains that when the pictures are developed, the class will write stories together about the people in the pictures and make a big book about their school.

It is quite possible that the non-English speakers in the classroom might have been thoroughly confused by this activity. Although the teacher provided context by actually taking the children to see the places and talk to the people, the purpose of the activity was probably lost on the Spanish-speaking children. They might not have made the connections between the tour of the school, the pictures, and the class book until the pictures arrived and the class began to assemble the book. Even when the class started to make the book, the Spanish-speaking children might not have been able to fully participate because the brainstorming about what should be written in the book and the actual writing took place in a language they did not understand. The learning the teacher hoped would take place might have been minimal for the non-English speakers.

If we change the scenario, there is great potential for learning for both the native English speakers and the English language learners. Before introducing the activity to the class, the teacher has her Spanish-speaking aide, a Spanish-speaking parent, or an older bilingual child give her Spanish-speaking kindergartners a preview of what is going to happen. The non-English-speaking children understand the purpose of the tour, and as they move from place to place, they can predict what is being talked about in English. In some cases, the person being interviewed might also speak Spanish, so the interviews could be done in both languages. Then, the activity not only has a purpose for them, but, because the students understand what is happening, they can make more sense of the English being spoken and begin to pick up English words.

It is important, however, that the learning not be restricted to the learning of language. The teacher did the activity with her English-speaking students so that they would be comfortable in their school and understand their school community. The goals should be the same for the Spanish speakers. If these students understood the purpose of the tour and could make predictions, they would have much to say about what they saw and learned. Even though they could not yet explain their understanding to their teacher in English, the children could be encouraged to work with a Spanish-speaking classroom helper to brainstorm and make pages for a big book in Spanish. Thus, they would have the same kind of learning experience as their English-speaking peers. In addition, they would build more background, and they would be more likely to understand the big book when it is read in English.

Use of the primary language can help students develop academic concepts and can also help lead them into English. When students have a good understanding of a subject area, they can more easily comprehend a discussion in English about the subject. Their knowledge of the content helps them make predictions about the meaning of the English words.

It is also important that students develop one language fully in both oral and written form. Children come to school with a language that has served their needs up until that time. If the language is English, the school will continue its development. Although six-year-olds have good control of the phonology of their first language, their syntactic competence doesn't fully develop for at least another six years, and their vocabulary continues to develop throughout their lives. Some students have begun to develop reading and writing abilities when they enter school and others have not, but all native English speakers receive literacy instruction throughout their school years.

Children who come to school speaking a language other than English have not fully developed their oral language abilities in their primary language. Depending on the schooling they receive, they may not have opportunities to develop additional registers of the spoken language, and they may not learn to read and write in their first language. They may continue to develop their primary language at home, but their academic development may be entirely in English.

In some of her early research, Collier (1989) found that even when there was school support for first language, it took students five to seven years to catch up with their English-speaking peers in academic subjects as measured by tests in English. More recently, in a longitudinal study with over 700,000 students, Collier found that students with no schooling in their first language can take seven to ten years to reach grade level norms with native English-speaking peers (Collier 1995). Without first language support, students may never catch up. It's not that they lack language—they are not *alingual* or *semilingual*—they just don't speak the language that counts in school, and they fall behind academically while they are trying to learn it.

If, on the other hand, language minority students can develop their first language fully in both oral and written form, their knowledge of language forms and functions transfers to English in the same way as their knowledge of any other subject matter. In other words, the more students know about their native language, the more background they have to understand the English language.

Research on language universals shows that even unrelated languages share many common features of both structure and function. People who speak several languages often comment that the third language was easier to learn than the second, and the fourth easier than the third. These people have a rich linguistic repertoire that makes learning new languages easier. English language learners retain this same advantage if they are allowed to develop their first language fully.

Academic Concepts and Skills Transfer

Cummins (1996, 1984, 1981) argues that students acquire concepts most readily in their first language and then understand them in their second language. In other words, what we learn in one language transfers into the new language. Cummins compares the languages that bilinguals speak to two tips of a large iceberg. That's all we can see, but the main part of the iceberg, which is below the surface, contains all the concepts developed in the two languages. The languages are simply channels that allow bilinguals to take in or express the concepts.

Cummins argues that the concepts a bilingual person builds form a Common Underlying Proficiency (CUP), which is available for expression in any language the person speaks or writes. Once a child knows how to read in one language, for example, the child can transfer that knowledge about the reading process to another language. The child does not have to learn to read all over again any more than Einstein needed to learn physics all over again in English when he came to the United States with limited English proficiency. If high school students come to this country having studied algebra in their first language, they don't need to learn algebraic concepts a second time. What they need is the ability to express their mathematical understanding in English.

It is easier to learn something in one's first language. However, there may be other reasons for learning basic skills in the first language. Swain and colleagues (1990) report on an interesting study that compared bilingual students who had learned to read in their first language with other bilinguals who had learned to read in their second language. When both groups of students studied a third language in school, the bilinguals who had developed literacy in their first language learned to read the third language faster than the other bilinguals. This study suggests that there may be cognitive benefits from developing the first language as fully as possible.

The commonsense assumption for English language learners—that "more English equals more English"—does not hold true. Cummins explains that those who insist on using only English to teach English do not understand how building concepts in the first language supports second language learning. A person who insists that instruction be given in English only must believe that the different language systems are totally separate and that what one knows in one language cannot be transferred to a second language. This idea is what Cummins has labeled SUP or Separate Underlying Proficiency.

Both research and personal experience discredit the idea of SUP. For example, we have a close bilingual friend who lives in Mexico City. When we visit Lucy, she encourages conversation in English so she can practice. Lucy's husband, however, does not speak English. When he joins us, Lucy is able to recount the gist of our conversation in Spanish even though the conversation was in English. The ideas we discussed in English can be explained easily in Spanish. The things we learn are not restricted to one language or another and are not kept in separate parts of the brain.

Research by Kolers (1973) supports the claim for a common underlying proficiency. In one experiment, he asked English/French bilinguals to read passages that contained words in both English and French. He found that bilinguals could silently read passages that mixed the two languages as rapidly as they could read passages that were written entirely in either French or English. This led him to conclude that these bilinguals read directly for meaning. They did not have to convert words in a mixed passage to one language to understand them.

> If the readers had had to make all of the words of a mixed passage conform to a single language before they could understand them, they would have had less time to work out the meaning of a mixed passage than of a unilingual one; and having less time, their comprehension would have been poorer. But it was not (p. 47).

Kolers summarized his conclusion by explaining that "when a reader knows the words of a language, he perceives them directly in terms of their meanings" (p. 47).

Words are the surface-level elements of language. Meaning occurs at a deeper level, and it was this deeper level that the bilinguals in Kolers' experiments worked on when they perceived the meanings of the words. When people read for meaning, they access what Cummins describes as the common underlying proficiency they have developed. In the first experiment described, the bilinguals read silently. In another, they read the bilingual texts aloud, and when they did, they often substituted French words for English words or English words for French words. They might say *door* when *porte* was printed, or the reverse. These substitutions occurred at points in the text where there was a switch from one language to the other. The substitutions of the equivalent words were translations that showed again that the readers were focusing on the meaning of the passage and not on the surface elements, the words. In fact, although the bilingual readers could accurately retell the main ideas from what they had read, they could not remember whether particular words were in French or in English. They had focused on the deep level meaning, not on surface level aspects of the words in the text.

Proficient readers focus on meaning, not on the surface forms of the language. Proficient bilingual readers, as Kolers' experiments have shown, are not even concerned with the language the text is printed in because they have developed a proficiency common to the languages they speak or read. The language input is comprehensible for them in either language. However, for students beginning to read or beginning to cope with academic content, input in English may not be comprehensible. In Chapter One, we discussed Krashen's idea of the importance of teachers' providing second language learners with lots of comprehensible input. In his research and writing on bilingual education, Krashen explains that the best way to make input comprehensible is to use the students' first language (Krashen 1985).

Smith (1985) expresses the same idea when he argues that although learning is natural and happens all the time, we cannot learn what we do not understand. Learning involves demonstrations (we see people doing things), engagement (we decide we want to do those things), and sensitivity (nothing is done or said that convinces us we can't do those things). When the demonstration is given in English to nonnative speakers, they may not understand what they are seeing or hearing. If they don't understand the demonstration, they probably won't choose to engage in the activity. And if they don't understand what the teacher says, they may become convinced that they can't learn. At all three stages, instruction in English simply may not be comprehensible enough for learning to take place.

Better Home/School Connections

Too often parents of English learners are unconnected to the schools. Valdés (1996) has written powerfully about how little immigrant Mexican parents understand about the school system and the values that the system assumes all parents share. Valdés points out that while the parents in her study "believed that education was important, they did not put education first" (p. 189).

> For these families, prestige, intellectual achievement, and even wealth were less important than morality and family chances in this country. Education still played a small role in their understanding of life chances in this country (p. 189).

Valdés has serious concerns about the effectiveness of parent involvement programs. She suggests that programs for parents of Mexican-origin "must be based on an understanding of and an appreciation and respect for the internal dynamics" of the families and "for the legitimacy of their values and beliefs" (p. 203).

If teachers and school support staff cannot communicate with parents in the students' home languages, it is almost impossible for mutual understanding and respect to develop. Teachers must value students' home languages and cultures and help parents understand how to support their children by drawing on their strengths. Miramontes et al. (1997) explain what they see as important for parents of English language learners:

> Educators can make a significant contribution to students' engagement in learning by actively pursuing ways to support the primary language in the home, and by encouraging parents to actively participate in school learning experiences, regardless of their own level of schooling. Schools have a responsibility to actively support parents' use of their language with their children, and to provide them with the necessary encouragement and tools to do so (p. 41).

Bilingual education provides opportunities for all parents to be involved with their students' education. However, when schools do not support bilingualism, they may convey a negative message to parents. Lorna, a graduate student originally from the Philippines, describes the conflicts that her family experienced:

> My husband and I decided to bring up our first-born as bilingual. We were very proud of him when he first started to talk because he communicated with us in our native language. We thought he was very smart because he was fluent in Tagalog and learned also to speak some English. When he entered kindergarten, I filled out the form on the home language survey. I proudly wrote down that he speaks English and Tagalog. He was pretested and classified Limited English Proficient. My son, whom we thought was very smart before entering kindergarten, was not that smart anymore. Sometimes he would tell me that he was dumb. . . . I felt we were a failure as parents. I began blaming myself because I was the one who wanted to raise him as bilingual.

In contrast, when schools offer bilingual education, they affirm both parents and students. There are more opportunities for parents to communicate with teachers and to participate when the primary language is encouraged in classroom instruction. In studies of different models of bilingual education, Collier and Thomas (1996) found that one characteristic of effective bilingual programs was parental involvement. In those programs, non-English speaking parents were valued and were encouraged to participate. In turn, the parents felt able to contribute to their children's academic success. When students receive academic instruction in their primary languages, parents who do not speak English have more opportunities to help their children at home and to participate in classroom activities.

In their continuing long-term research on school effectiveness for language minority students, Collier and Thomas (1995) have come to specific conclusions about how parents of English learners can help their children's cognitive development in the primary language. The researchers have suggested that parents engage their children in daily, interactive problem-solving by asking questions, discussing daily activities, sharing values, giving moral support, and helping children make decisions and set goals. Parents can do this as they involve children in household responsibilities, including shopping, cooking, cleaning, and laundry. In addition, family activities such as telling stories, sharing family heritage, reading books together, going places together, celebrating together, and participating together in music, art, games, and sport activities are recommended. Bilingual educators can help non-English speaking parents do all of these things because they can communicate with parents and encourage them.

Bilinguals Have More Opportunities

Before we knew much about language acquisition and learning, we decided we wanted our children to become bilingual. We saw many bilingual and tri-lingual children in our travels, and we knew we wanted our children to ex-perience other ways of seeing the world. We knew this is only possible when one speaks and understands the language of another culture quite well.

When our children were small, there were very few bilingual pro-grams. We did not have the choice of sending our children to a bilingual school in the United States. We moved to Mexico and lived and worked there for two years. Our two daughters attended a bilingual school, and soon they were talking, playing, and learning in Spanish. Upon our re-turn to the United States, we were able to enroll our children in a bilin-gual program in Arizona so they could continue their development of Spanish. In addition, we became close to some political refugee teen-agers from El Salvador who were learning English.

Our children did experience different ways of seeing the world. Fur-ther, both of our daughters were offered several teaching jobs when they finished college because they were bilingual. In addition, they both have access to extended social groups. They are equally comfortable at a re-union of David's New England relatives or a Mexican wedding where few people speak any English. These personal experiences have helped re-inforce our belief that bilinguals have more opportunities.

When we went to Argentina and Venezuela recently, we were re-peatedly asked about the English Only movement in the United States. The educators in South America were mystified when they read that some people were opposed to bilingual education. In Latin America, all the best schools are bilingual, because parents realize that if their chil-dren are bilingual, they will have more choices in life. Middle class par-ents in these countries spend large portions of their income to enusre that their children become fluent in at least one other language. "How can anyone be against bilingual education?" they asked us.

Schools in the United States would benefit as well from effective bilingual programs. The United States is one of the few countries in the world where bilingualism is not highly valued. While people often think of Switzerland as the prototype of a bilingual country, people from other countries also value bilingualism. When we taught in Mexico, our stu-dents were adults who wished to learn English to advance in their work. They attended early morning or late night classes over a period of years to become bilingual. In Japan, ESL classes for adults are highly valued by students and businessmen, who realize the advantages of being bilingual. Good bilingual programs in the United States would allow all students to acquire a second language. Students who enter school with a language other than English could learn English, and students who come to school monolingual in English could learn a second language. They could also learn about a new culture. And they could learn how to deal with the diversity that exists in the larger communities they will be part of when they leave school.

Bilinguals Have Greater Cognitive Flexibility

In the first half of the twentieth century, bilingualism was considered a deficit. Because bilingual children often performed poorly in school and on standardized tests, some researchers concluded that trying to speak two languages was cognitively confusing. Students were said to have a language handicap, and schools worked hard to teach children English and get rid of their first languages.

However, Cummins (1996) has pointed out that "It appears more reasonable to attribute the academic difficulties of bilingual students to the treatment they received in schools rather than to their bilingualism" (p. 104). Cummins points out that "A large number of studies have reported that bilingual children exhibit a greater sensitivity to linguistic meaning and may be more flexible in their thinking than are monolingual children." Probably the most quoted research in this area has been done by Hakuta (1986) and Hakuta and Diaz (1985). These studies show that bilinguals are able to approach problems from more than one perspective. Although the evidence is not conclusive, it might be assumed that since bilinguals can express the same ideas in different ways, they are able to view tasks and problems from more than one perspective (Cummins 1996). As we enter the twenty-first century, there is no longer talk of bilinguals having deficits and being at a disadvantage. In fact, when students are in bilingual programs in which they become competent speakers, readers, and writers of two languages, the research is now showing that they achieve higher scores in English reading on standardized tests than monolingual English speakers do (Collier and Thomas 1996).

Competent Bilinguals Have Pride in Themselves and Their Cultures.

When students experience academic success and are affirmed in their cultural heritage, they naturally feel better about themselves. This sense of accomplishment and pride is particularly important for English language learners, because they recognize that they are not part of the mainstream. Even if their families have lived in the United States for generations, language minority students often view themselves as outsiders.

Students who are given no primary language support as they learn English are often lost in schools. The result is that they do not learn, and they feel frustrated. Later they may come to resent the schools or their families and experience both a language and culture loss. We opened this chapter with a journal entry from a Hmong teenager. This entry reveals her cultural ambivalence. She is a Hmong from Thailand who speaks, reads, and writes only English. She is obviously sensitive to this, because she reflects on it in her journal. Her schooling has not helped her develop pride in herself and her culture. Instead, she may be wondering just who she is.

As Skutnabb-Kangas (1983) points out, "A person who does not understand the language of instruction is bound to perform worse than the one who understands, and poor performance often leads to poor self-concept" (p. 118). Under those conditions, it is difficult for the student to learn either English or subject area content.

California Tomorrow is a non-profit, non-partisan organization built on the belief that the state's diverse population offers opportunities to create a fair multicultural society. This organization conducts studies to help citizens understand important issues related to living and working in a multi-racial, multicultural society. In *Crossing the Schoolhouse Border* Olsen (1988) interviewed a number of English language learners who expressed their frustration at not being able to understand instruction in English. An eleventh grade Cambodian boy commented, "My first school I didn't want to go, just to stay home. When I went I just sat there and didn't understand anything" (p. 62). The failure to understand can undermine a student's self-confidence. As a tenth grade Mexican girl put it:

> It's very frustrating. I didn't feel good. I couldn't really adjust to life here. I felt really dumb. I would sit in class and not understand anything. I went home and tried to read but had to look up every word in my dictionary. I spent hours reading each page. Sometimes I just gave up. The teacher didn't expect me to do anything. I was most fearful to get my report card (p. 64).

Often, we think that young children don't suffer the way these older students do because they learn language so easily. However, even young second language students experience frustration in an all English environment. Ger, a Hmong child, entered kindergarten in our community speaking no English. Now a third grader, she still remembers the experience vividly:

> I didn't know English until I learned in Kindergarten. When I was in Kindergarten, I didn't have any friends. I had one friend who was nice to me sometimes, but then she moved away and I had no one. I just sat quietly in my seat and did my work.

Ger was a case study subject chosen by Michelle, who was learning about language acquisition, bilingual education, and the complex factors that influence school performance for English language learners. Michelle observed:

> Kindergarten was hard for Ger because she did not understand much of what went on around her. On top of that, the kids in her class were not friendly to her because she could not speak English. Her kindergarten teacher was nice to her, but that did not keep her classmates from ignoring her. To further Ger's loneliness during her kindergarten year, none of her other classmates spoke Hmong, nor was there any type of primary language support to help her in her efforts to learn English.

If Ger had been in Pa Houa's class, her experience would have been different. Development of a positive self-image is a benefit of bilingual education. Since bilingual education values the languages and cultures of non-English speakers, it can help students value themselves. They are not put in a position where they have to choose between the culture and language of the school and the culture and language of the home. Lucas (1981) found that the students who dropped out of high school were not the least proficient students in English but the ones who rejected their native cultures and lacked confidence in themselves.

Michael teaches junior and senior English in a high school with a large Hispanic population. He asked his students to write about their bilingualism and what it meant to them. The following responses show how Michael's students struggle in a school where their language and culture are not valued. A twelfth grade Hispanic girl wrote:

> I have grown up in a Hispanic community since I can remember. But ironically the important thing in our classrooms was and is not how well you spoke your own language, unless that language was English. In fact the stress was on how "American" one was and is. But it wasn't until I got into the working force that I realized what people meant by the youth losing their culture. . . . It is extremely difficult for me to effectively communicate with my own people in Spanish. That is what I regret the most about "losing my culture" is losing my language.

An eleventh grade boy expressed his concerns:

> Our language at home is Spanish and English is our second. My youngest sister is only four. She speaks only Spanish. We want to teach

her all the Spanish she can get before entering the schools. If she doesn't learn the Spanish language now, we're afraid she never will.

Another twelfth grade Hispanic girl also shows the tension that results from being in a situation where one language is used at home and another in school.

In our household Spanish is a first language but is often overshadowed by English. My mom and dad only speak Spanish but are accustomed to hearing English from us . . . so while they speak Spanish to us, we speak English to them.

When schools value students' languages and cultures, English language learners experience greater school success. In his high school English classes, Michael is trying to show students that he values their language and culture. Michael himself has a Hispanic heritage that was lost in his schooling. He does not want that to happen to his students. Michael's encouragement and support helps his students develop pride in their backgrounds. One of his twelfth graders wrote:

Spanish is important to me because it is part of my history. To me being bilingual is an important part of my life because my parents have always influenced me to know Spanish and also to speak fluent Spanish and among all things never to be ashamed of my heritage. I believe that I should be proud of my heritage and I was taught to be proud and to let everyone know of my Hispanic background and my Spanish-speaking family and people.

By showing a respect for diverse cultures and by providing bilingual support, schools and teachers can help students take pride in themselves and realize their potential. This lessens the tension that many English language learners feel when the school culture and language differ from the home culture and language. An effective bilingual program allows students to succeed in both arenas. Their bilingualism is seen as a benefit, not a deficit.

Both home and school communities would profit if more students who come to school speaking a language other than English could become proficient bilinguals. When bilingualism is not valued in schools, many students who enter schools monolingual in a language other than English leave school monolingual in English. They look for success in their new culture rather than returning to enrich their home communities. The students who do return are often those who have not assimilated, who have rejected English and the culture of those who speak English. However, they return to their communities without the education they need to contribute positively to that community. If students' first language and culture were valued, there would be less tension between home and school, between parent and child. Bilingual graduates could return to their bilingual communites as contributing, educated members.

The biggest obstacle to establishing bilingual programs is the lack of bilingual teachers. For example, in 1997 there were more than 1.3 million students in California schools who were identified as limited English proficient (Education 1997). The state needed more than 34,000 bilingually credentialed teachers to serve those students. Because there were only 13,548 bilingual teachers, that left a shortage of 20,827 bilingual teachers. This follows annual trends. Since 1993, there has been a shortage each year of around 21,000 bilingually certified teachers. However, there is some good news. More new teachers are earning their bilingual credentials. California added about 1,400 bilingual teachers in 1997. As a result, in 1996–1997, the bilingual teacher shortage grew by only 96 teachers.

Unless schools develop proficient bilinguals who value education, the shortage of bilingual teachers will continue. When there are not enough bilingual teachers, schools can't fully implement bilingual programs. Schools that do not have effective bilingual programs do not produce students who become bilingual teachers. We must stop the cycle of eliminating students' first languages in schools and then needing bilingual teachers in the next generation.

Even when schools are able to hire bilingual teachers, they still must decide on the kind of bilingual program they wish to institute. In the next chapter, we review the types of bilingual programs that have been successful, and we also discuss ways teachers can support students' first languages and cultures even when they don't speak those languages.

Lessons Should Support Students' First Languages and Cultures, Part Two

Effective bilingual programs offer students a number of cognitive and affective advantages, as outlined in the last chapter. But not all bilingual programs are equally beneficial. We begin this chapter by reviewing the research on different bilingual program models. This research clearly indicates the kinds of programs in which students develop the highest levels of academic and linguistic proficiency. Since we are interested in the principles that underlie successful practice, we move beyond program models to examine the key features of the best programs. This review reveals that the features of successful bilingual programs match our principles for successful practice.

Even though we would like to see every student in a high quality bilingual program, we recognize the reality within which many teachers work. Often, students in classes speak a variety of primary languages. The teacher can't be expected to speak all of these languages. Even if the teacher could speak three or four languages, it is not clear how the teacher would organize multilingual instruction. For that reason, we also discuss ways that monolingual teachers or teachers who do not speak all of their students' primary languages can support their students' first languages and cultures.

Bilingual Education Programs and Models: What Really Works?

Bilingual education programs have received a great deal of negative press over the past two decades. The American Institutes for Research (Danoff et al. 1977, 1978) and Baker and de Kanter reports (1981) challenged the effectiveness of bilingual education. More recently, books and articles, such as Porter's *Forked Tongue* (1990) and Rossell and Baker's (1996) extensive review of the research on bilingual programs, have called for English immersion as the solution to working with English language learners. These publications have continued to stir the debate over bilingual education.

Critiques of these publications by Crawford (1989, 1992), Cummins (1996), and Krashen (1996), have shown the research base of opponents of bilingual education to be incomplete. Reviews of studies supporting English immersion raise questions about how programs were evaluated and how results were interpreted. For example, some bilingual programs cited in these studies did not have any bilingual teachers or materials.

In contrast, research into programs that provide first language instruction has shown consistently positive results (Cummins 1996, Dolson and Lindholm 1995, Krashen 1996, Krashen and Biber 1988, Ramírez 1991, Collier 1992, 1995, Collier and Thomas 1996, Ovando and Collier 1998).

The debate over bilingual education continues in academic circles, but, at the same time, the debate is also being carried out in the popular press. In Chapter Eight we cited the study by McQuillan and Tse (1997) that showed that while 87 percent of the academic articles in a ten-year span favored bilingual education, only 45 percent of the newspaper articles were favorable. Cummins (1996) calls the publicity against bilingual education "disinformation." He believes a deliberate attempt has been made to misinform the public about bilingual education:

> The psychoeducational concerns of policy-makers, educators and academics about bilingual education hindering the acquisition of English simply mask the more pressing concern that bilingual education programs have increased the status and power of the Spanish-speaking minority at a time when demographic changes are already posing a threat to the dominance of the Euro-American majority in several parts of the country. Thus, it becomes important to eliminate these programs in order to preserve the current power structure (p. 213).

In both academic and popular discussion, part of the controversy that surrounds bilingual education stems from confusion about programs that have been called "immersion" and those called "submersion."

Immersion versus Submersion

Advocates of the English Only movement and backers of ballot initiatives such as the Unz initiative," English as the Official Language of Instruction," propose an immersion program for language minority students. Often, they claim that their proposals are for programs similar to the successful French immersion programs in Canada. Their reasoning is that immersion worked in Canada, so why can't the same model work in the United States? In some school districts in the United States, immersion programs have been implemented. However, because of key differences between the United States and Canadian programs, the immersion education many language minority students in the United States have received really amounts to "sink-or-swim," or submersion education.

. The goals and results of the French immersion programs in Canada are very different from the immersion programs offered to language minority students in the United States (Hernández-Chávez 1984). In the original St. Lambert French Immersion program, middle-class, educated parents of English-speaking Canadian children requested French immersion so that their children would become bilingual and bicultural. In kindergarten, the children were put into an all-French classroom with other English-speakers. There were no native speakers of French to compete with. Teachers were bilingual and allowed the children to ask questions and give answers in English. The teachers received special training in using techniques to make the content of the classes comprehensible to the children. These techniques helped them teach the French language through academic content. As students progressed through school, their first language, English, was added to the curriculum, until in the sixth grade, when 40 percent of the curriculum was in French and 60 percent in English (Genesee 1984). At the end of fifteen years of study, it was clear that French immersion students achieved on a par with students in the regular English programs, except that the French immersion students achieved in both French and English.

The success of the Canadian programs can be attributed to several factors. Parents initiated and supported the programs. Bilingual teachers were carefully prepared to work with the children. They taught the new language through content. All the children in a class were at about the same level of French ability. They did not have to compete with native speakers of French. At the same time, there was no danger of students' losing their English, since that was the language spoken in the home, and it was the prestige language of the larger community. Further, more English was added to the curriculum each year so that by sixth grade, more teaching

time was given in English than in French. The goal was to produce students who were bilingual and bicultural in both French and English. As Lessow-Hurley explains, "immersion programs are most effective when they are linguistically and culturally additive" (Lessow-Hurley 1996, p. 17).

In the United States, English language learners face a very different situation when they are put into a structured immersion program. In the first place, they are minority, not majority, students, and they are in direct competition from the beginning with native English-speaking peers. Their teachers are not usually bilingual, so at the early stages, the teachers can't answer questions the students ask in their primary languages or respond when students speak in their first languages. There is no provision for the students' primary language to be added to the curriculum as they advance through school. Their parents have not chosen the immersion program to make them bilingual and bicultural. In fact, since their parents are often from a disempowered segment of society, they have little voice in what happens in the school program. The first language and culture of the language minority students is not valued by the larger community, and it is clear from the beginning that the goal is not to produce bilingual, bicultural students but to produce students who are monolingual English speakers.

Immersion programs in the United States are really submersion programs, where students are likely to "drown" in the English they receive. Since no first language support is given, and teachers are seldom prepared to be sensitive to the needs of English language learners, students do not receive comprehensible input and soon fall behind academically. Unlike the Canadian program, which is additive in that students come out of the programs with proficiency in two languages, immersion programs in the United States are subtractive because students lose their first language as they learn English. In fact, not only do these programs fail to develop students' primary languages, especially the written forms, but students rarely come out of immersion programs with a level of English proficiency that allows them to achieve at the same level as native English speakers.

Few educators who propose immersion for English learners understand the differences between the Canadian and U.S. versions of immersion education. This is doubly unfortunate because when students fail in immersion programs in the United States, the perception is that it is because something is wrong with the students whose first language is not English. The students or the students' background and culture is criticized because, "After all, immersion worked so well in Canada."

Immersion programs are one model that is used for English language learners, and each immersion program is slightly different. How-

ever, all the English immersion programs in the United States have one thing in common. Students are not offered academic instruction or other support in their primary languages. Bilingual education also has many models. Although the key component of any bilingual program is primary language instruction, successful bilingual programs, which we describe in the next section, always include effective English instruction as well. Often, people think that in bilingual programs, students spend the whole day receiving instruction in their first language. In fact, they also receive instruction in English. Effective English instruction is meaningful, functional, and context-rich so that it meets the needs of bilingual students. In other words, it contains large amounts of comprehensible input. Krashen (1985) has shown that it is comprehensible input that counts in language acquisition, not just exposure to a second language. That is the reason why students receiving only one or two hours of English a day may actually acquire English more rapidly than students who are in an English environment all day long. The students in the bilingual program with good English instruction are receiving greater amounts of comprehensible input.

Models of Bilingual Education

When administrators or teachers ask us, "What model of bilingual education is best for my school?" we have difficulty answering them. As mentioned earlier, one of the biggest obstacles to establishing bilingual programs is that schools lack bilingual teachers. When schools are able to hire bilingual teachers, they still must decide on the kind of bilingual program they wish to institute. Administrators, teachers, and parents must consider the many factors involved in establishing a successful program, and they must plan carefully and collaboratively as they develop a program. Everyone involved must understand the rationale for bilingual education and share common goals.

Almost as many models of bilingual programs exist as there are programs. Below, we describe five models that are widely in use. Four of these offer some kind of primary language instruction. These five models have very different success rates (Collier and Thomas 1996). We will describe each type of program briefly, beginning with the model Collier and Thomas have shown to be most successful and ending with the least successful approach. Within each model, many possible variations may be found. Nevertheless, the general description of these models should help readers evaluate the programs they are familiar with or are considering implementing. It should also be noted that in their study, Collier and Thomas only reviewed programs that had implemented each model very well.

Canada good 'cause didn't compete with native speakers
What?

Two-Way Developmental Bilingual Education

In two-way developmental models, each class contains both native English speakers and English language learners, all of whom speak the same primary language. "The strength of this approach is that it aims at additive bilingualism for all the students involved (Lessow-Hurley 1996, p. 15). All the students learn a second language because instruction is given in the two primary languages the students represent. In the United States in 1995 there were two way programs in English and Spanish, Korean, French, Navajo, Cantonese, Japanese, Russian, Portuguese, Chinese, and Arabic (Christian and Whitcher 1995). The popularity of this two-way model is growing so rapidly that new programs and new languages are being added each year.

The amount of time spent in English and in the other language varies in different two-way programs. Some programs have one half day in English and one half day in the other language. Others organize differently. For example, in one popular Spanish/English two-way model, kindergarten children spend 90 percent of their day in Spanish and 10 percent in English. In each grade, more time is added in English. By third or fourth grade, students spend one half the day in English and one half in Spanish.

Other differences exist as well. In some programs, all students are taught to read and write in the non-English language first and then English literacy is introduced at second or third grade. In other programs, students develop literacy in two languages simultaneously. Despite these differences, all the programs have certain features in common. They are either staffed with bilingual teachers, or a monolingual English teacher is paired with a bilingual teacher, and students spend part of the day with each teacher. Materials are available in both languages. As a result, teachers teach both languages through academic content. All the two-way programs extend at least through sixth grade.

Late-Exit-Bilingual Education Plus ESL
Taught Through Academic Content

In this bilingual model, students whose first language is not English receive instruction in their first language through at least sixth grade. In the early grades, they receive more primary language instruction, but by third or fourth grade, they spend a substantial part of each day studying subject matter and reading and writing in English as well as in their first language. Throughout this program, English is taught through academic content. At some schools, in the upper grades, bilingual students may be mixed in the same classrooms with monolingual English speakers. However, a late exit program is not two-way because the native speakers of English receive all their instruction in English while the bilingual students continue to receive some instruction in their primary language.

Early-Exit Bilingual Education Plus ESL Taught Through Academic Content

Early exit programs are the most widely implemented of all. They appeal to those who want to see children in all English classes as soon as possible. Since most children develop conversational proficiency in about two years, teachers and administrators use this as an indication that the children are ready for all English instruction.

In early-exit programs, students are prepared to transition into all English classrooms within three years of beginning school as non-English speakers. Theoretically, non-English speaking students who enter school in second grade (or later) should also receive three years of primary language support. However, in practice, older learners usually receive fewer than three years of first language instruction. There are fewer bilingual upper grade teachers, and often even those teachers are encouraged to get students into English as quickly as possible. As in the late exit program, students are taught English through academic content.

Early-Exit Bilingual Education Plus ESL Taught Traditionally

In this model students also receive primary language content instruction for about three years and then are transitioned into English. However, the early English instruction these students receive is different. English is not taught through meaningful content, but instead is taught more traditionally. Students study English by practicing dialogues and drills, studying grammar rules, and memorizing vocabulary lists organized around traditional themes such as food, clothing, or transportation.

ESL Pull-Out Taught Traditionally

In ESL pull-out programs, English language learners are taken out of their regular classroom for a portion of their day to concentrate on learning the English language. Students in ESL pull-out programs receive little or no primary language support. Occasionally, a few phrases or words are translated to help students with procedural matters, but instruction during pull-out time and in the mainstream classroom is given in English. ESL instruction centers on vocabulary acquisition, understanding grammatical structures, and practicing drills.

Least effective

As we explained when we introduced this section, these models are described in the order of their effectiveness from most to least effective, as measured by students' scores on standardized tests given in English.

Students in the first programs we described scored highest, and ESL pull-out was the least effective model for helping students succeed academically. In the following section, we review the Collier and Thomas research results as well as other bilingual research results. We also discuss the key characteristics of successful programs.

Features of Effective Programs for English Language Learners

Probably the most important recent research for bilingual education comes from the work of Thomas and Collier (1997). They have analyzed data for over 700,000 language minority students from five large school districts in various regions of the United States. In their analysis, Thomas and Collier looked at the types of services English language learners received and the academic results the students achieved over time. They contrasted their long-term analysis of students' progress from kindergarten through high school with many previous short-term studies comparing student progress in bilingual and English immersion or ESL programs. These earlier short-term studies had reported little difference in academic achievement when comparing students in ESL pull-out, structured immersion, early exit, and late exit bilingual program models. The short-term studies led critics to conclude that bilingual education was not really very effective. However, Thomas and Collier's long-term data, which included achievement in upper grades, revealed very different results.

> Only those students who have received strong cognitive and academic development through their first language for many years (at least through Grade 5 or 6) as well as through the second language (English) are doing well in school as they reach the last of the high school years (Young 1997, pp. 12–13).

Thomas and Collier's research is important because it clearly confirms the benefits of providing extensive first language support through bilingual education. Students in programs that provide primary language instruction at least through sixth grade score higher on standardized reading tests given in English than students in programs that offer limited or no primary language support.

In addition, Thomas and Collier were able to identify key predictors of student success (Thomas and Collier 1995). In their review of different bilingual programs, they found that all successful programs were characterized by similar features. These predictors provide guidelines for educators planning programs for English language learners at their school sites. The key features are listed here.

Key Predictors of Academic Success
Thomas and Collier 1995

These predictors are more important than program type or student background variables.

1. Cognitively complex academic instruction through students' first language for as long as possible and through the second language for part of the school day

2. Use of current approaches to teaching the academic curriculum through both L1 and L2 through active discovery, and cognitively complex learning

3. Changes in the sociocultural context of schooling such as:

   a. integration with English speakers in a supporting, affirming context for all

   b. an additive bilingual context in which bilingual education is perceived as the GATE program for all students

   c. transformation of majority and minority relations in school to a positive school climate for all students in a safe school environment

When language minority students are able to continue to learn in their primary language for at least six years and, at the same time, are taught English through cognitively complex and comprehensible content during part of each school day, they succeed in English and complete high school at higher rates than students in programs that lack these features. In fact, English language learners who receive adequate first language support reach the 50th percentile in English reading in four to seven years, while those who do not receive primary language support take seven to ten years to reach norms in English reading on standardized tests (Young 1997).

Simply teaching students acquiring English in their first language is not enough. The orientation to teaching and learning that Thomas and Collier recommend is the one we described in Chapter One as sociopsycholinguistic. According to Thomas and Collier, teachers in effective programs use strategies such as "discovery learning, interactive instruction, cooperative learning, thematic instruction, problem solving, and the incorporating of technology, fine arts, and other disciplines which tap the 'multiple intelligences'"(Young 1997, p. 13).

Thomas and Collier's third predictor of success deals with the important sociocultural context of schooling. They explain that schools need to integrate English learners and affirm them and their culture. The way to do this is to promote the bilingual program as an enrichment program, one in which all students would want to be involved. This is what happens in schools with two-way bilingual programs. When all students, including English learners, are perceived as talented and capable, relationships among different cultural groups are positive, and schools become true communities of learners.

Each year, more and more school districts are implementing two-way developmental bilingual programs to serve both their English language learners and the native English-speaking population. Five years ago, two-way programs were relatively few in number, but at the 1997 Two-Way Developmental Bilingual Education Conference, more than 650 participants from around the United States enthusiastically met to share ideas. Program directors and administrators of programs for native Spanish, Korean, French, Chinese, Portuguese, and Arabic students attended. The 1998 conference is expected to attract more than one thousand participants.

The goals of two-way developmental programs and Thomas and Collier's key predictors of school success are consistent with Cummins' (1996) ideas for education for the empowerment of diverse students. In his Intervention for Collaborative Empowerment, Cummins challenges schools to take an intercultural orientation rather than an assimilationist orientation to working with culturally diverse students. He says that students' cultures and languages must be welcomed and incorporated into the school curriculum, the school and parents must be included in a collaborative community, the approach to pedagogy must be transformative, and assessment must be viewed from an advocacy perspective. Cummins' suggestions parallel the key predictors of Thomas and Collier in the areas of support for first language and culture, approach to teaching and learning, and the need to create a positive and supportive school context.

For Cummins, the end result of an intercultural orientation is the transformation of power relations within the schools, and, eventually, in the greater society. This transformation occurs when two languages and cultures achieve equal prestige and power in a society. Two-way programs attempt to create this kind of balance. However, as some researchers point out, it is difficult for schools to create programs that upset the power relations among groups that exist in the wider society.

Valdés (1997), for example, raises some important questions. In a dual language program, is the quality of instruction in the minority language equal to the quality of instruction in English? Differences in quality could result from differences in preparation and expertise of the teachers or differences in availability of resources. A second question concerns intergroup relationships. Are teachers able to create equal status among language minority and majority students within a class when considerable status differences exist beyond the classroom, differences that both the students and their parents are aware of?

A final question concerns the effects of dual language programs on power relations among groups in the larger society. Will such programs level the playing field for language minority students, or will they continue to privilege the native English speakers? One concern, for example, is that English speakers receive praise and attention for learning another language, but language minority students are usually expected to learn English and are not singled out and praised for that accomplishment.

The questions Valdés raises are important. Dual language programs have great potential, but they are not a panacea. Teachers and administrators should be aware that providing instruction in two languages is only one step toward ensuring that all students receive the best possible education. Despite these cautions, two-way programs have proved successful, in part because they provide extended primary language instruction.

Another important longitudinal study on bilingual education was conducted by Ramírez and his colleagues (Ramírez 1991). This study was contracted by the United States Department of Education and was watched carefully over several years by both proponents and opponents of bilingual education. It included 750 classrooms with 2,000 students in three kinds of bilingual programs: Structured English Immersion, Early-exit, and Late-exit. Students in Structured English Immersion were taught only in English. In the Early-exit programs, students were supported in their first language for two to three years and then exited into all-English programs. In the late-exit programs, students received some support in their first language for up to six years, even after they had become proficient in English. The study offered seven important conclusions:

1. When second language students receive substantial primary language support, their English development is not delayed.

2. Developing proficiency in English takes more than six years, regardless of which of the three approaches is used.

3. When students receive primary language support, they also progress in content instruction. However, they fall behind when they are too quickly switched to all English instruction.

4. Students who receive either early-exit (three years) or late-exit (six years) primary language instruction show more growth in English language, reading, and math than students in all English programs.

5. When primary language instruction is part of a program, minority language parents are more involved in their children's schooling.

6. Minority language parents would like to see their children become bilingual.

7. There is a need for preparing teachers to work effectively with second language learners. This preparation should emphasize a more active learning environment for language and cognitive development.

Researchers consistently find that successful programs for English learners share similar characteristics. For example, Lucas and her colleagues (1990) conducted a comprehensive study of six high school programs that had achieved high rates of academic success with language minority students. The first of the eight features those schools had in common was "Value is placed on the students' languages and culture." The researchers listed eight specific ways that teachers and administrators in these schools showed they valued their students' language and culture:

1. Treating students as individuals, not as members of a group

2. Learning about students' cultures

3. Learning students' languages

4. Hiring bilingual staff with cultural backgrounds similar to that of the students

5. Encouraging students to develop their primary language skills

6. Allowing students to speak their primary languages except when English development is the focus of instruction or interactions

7. Offering advanced as well as lower division content courses in the students' primary languages

8. Instituting extracurricular activities that will attract students (p. 324)

In this study of secondary schools, Lucas and colleagues also identified seven other features that appear to be necessary for students' success.

1. There are high expectations for language minority students.

2. School leaders make the education of language minority students a priority.

3. Staff development is explicitly designed to help teachers and other staff serve language minority students more effectively.

4. A variety of courses and programs for language minority students is offered.

5. A counseling program that includes bilingual counselors gives special attention to language minority students.

6. Parents of language minority students are encouraged to become involved in their children's education.

7. School staff members share a strong commitment to empower language minority students through education.

Another California Tomorrow report "Embracing Diversity: Teachers' Voices from California Classrooms" (Olsen and Mullen 1990) offers additional evidence for the importance of this approach to teaching language minority students. This study summarizes the characteristics of thirty-six teachers working with diverse student populations. Through interviews and classroom visits, the authors of the report, Olsen and Mullen, identified the core elements of the classroom approaches these successful teachers use. They:

- Teach to and from the experiences of the students;
- Provide a strong academic context and basis for exploring and understanding issues students face in their own lives;
- Emphasize the development of language and communication including a rigorous integration of oral language and writing;
- Emphasize critical thinking;
- Validate the student's experiences and culture, including the use of language, dialect, literature, music, and the fine arts from the student's culture;
- Use curriculum to explore cultural and national differences, and also emphasize similarities and universals in human experience;
- Create a student-centered classroom in which students learn from each other, with group work and interactive techniques;
- Choose materials and design curriculum specifically to provide all students with exposure to the rich contributions of many cultures and peoples;
- Bring the world into the classroom and the classroom to the world;
- Actively use supplementary materials and teacher-created curriculum;
- Use visuals and emphasize concept development; and
- Integrate the curriculum.

The research studies conducted by Thomas and Collier, Ramírez, Lucas, and Olsen and Mullen, which examined program models and classroom characteristics, all point to similar conclusions. Students need extensive opportunities to learn in their primary language as they learn English. Classes should be cognitively demanding. Students should be involved in interactive, discovery learning.

Although individual teachers can make a real difference for students, the best results come when teachers work in programs that are carefully thought out and that are supported by all the people involved in the education of our multilingual, multicultural students. When schools make an effort to include the features that both research and practice have shown to be successful in the education of their English language learners, everyone benefits: the students, the teachers, the administrators, the parents, the community, and, ultimately, society as a whole.

Teachers Supporting Students in Non-bilingual Settings

Even though research shows the importance of teaching students through their primary languages, many teachers working with bilingual or multilingual students do not speak all their students' first languages. In some cases, students with different first languages are mixed in a classroom. In other cases, the teacher may be monolingual. Nevertheless, as the following examples show, all teachers can support the development of their students' first languages and cultures.

Marilyn, an ESL high school teacher explained how she, as a monolingual English-speaking teacher, has supported Southeast Asian students. She has Hmong and Laotian students for two periods a day, and although she doesn't speak their languages, she has an aide who does. Using a preview, view, review model, Marilyn's aide presents a lesson to students in their native languages first. The next day Marilyn gives a follow-up lesson on the same content in English. Afterwards, her aide leads a brief review session in the students' primary language. Marilyn testifies to the success of the program: "It is remarkable how much the students understand because it has been presented in their first language the day before. We use less English but I feel the students are learning more English."

Marilyn's Laotian and Hmong students are separated from other second language learners and from native English speakers for two hours each day to "help them feel their first language is important" and so they "can find comfort in a mostly uncomfortable environment." Marilyn and her colleagues recognize that the Laotian and Hmong cultures and languages are different. However, they are more alike than other non Asian cultures and languages. When these Southeast Asian students are with other language groups all the time, "they are very reserved and reluctant to participate in class." Her Hmong and Laotian class is "alive and animated." Marilyn lists three reasons for separating the Hmong and Laotian students for two periods each day:

> I feel their confidence comes from three things. First, the students know there is someone in class who can speak their L1 (first language) and if they have a *really* important message to get across, it will be understood. Second, these students are in a foreign environment. These students are only separated from other students for two hours. It's a much needed break for them. Third, I think they feel pride and self-esteem when they can use their first language to acquire L2 (second language).

Marilyn not only has tried this different approach, but she is also presently taking a class in Hmong. This adds to her ability to work with her students. "The students are so pleased when I attempt to speak to them in their native language, and they enjoy helping me acquire the language. I let them know English is easy for me but Hmong is very difficult."

Teachers like Marilyn make extra efforts to prepare themselves to meet the needs of all their students. They read current research, take college classes, talk with other professionals, and experiment with different techniques. As these teachers plan activities to expand the range of language uses for their students, they provide consistent opportunities for their bilingual students to develop listening, speaking, reading, and writing skills in two languages.

Vince provides another example of how important it is for bilingual children to be able to study in their first language. After reading and discussing research on the importance of first language support for second language learners, Vince shared an experience he had with one of his students:

> Chai came into my fourth grade classroom directly from the camps in Southeast Asia. She was the first second language student I was to come in contact with who felt good enough about her native language writing skills to employ them in class. I have to give the students in my class a lot of credit, too, as they strongly supported and encouraged Chai in all her efforts. When she was finished writing a piece, she would read it to other Laotian-speaking students in my class who would give suggestions on the content and share their ideas with her in Laotian.

Vince described his doubts about letting Chai work in Laotian because he somehow felt he wasn't "doing his job." She remained in his classroom for the rest of the year and seemed to be understanding some English, but she never spoke or wrote in English. The next year Vince met Chai's best friend, who proudly explained that Chai was now speaking English and writing it, too. Vince wrote his reaction to the news:

My first reaction was not one of achievement. It was rather a question as to what the fifth grade teacher had done that I hadn't done to get Chai to come this far along. Only later did it dawn on me that those early opportunities that empowered Chai were a big part of why she was comfortable speaking and writing English so soon after her arrival.

Vince had empowered Chai and allowed her to continue to develop her first language. He encouraged Chai to use her first language even though he didn't understand it. Often, teachers are not able to comprehend the first language of some of their students. However, if they allow the students to use their primary language, they may come to realize that the students are more competent than they may appear to be if they are limited to English.

Cross-age reading and pen pal letters, which we discussed in Chapter Seven, are excellent ways to encourage students to read, write, and interact in their first language even when the teacher only speaks English. When upper grade bilingual students prepare to read to younger children and are matched with younger children who speak the same first language, both age groups benefit. Urzúa (1990) has worked with teachers whose Southeast Asian sixth graders read to kindergartners who speak the same first language. Even when they read books in English, the sixth graders support the first language of the younger children by building background knowledge and then discussing the stories in their shared first language. As the children interact in two languages, both age groups improve their oral language and reading ability. Sometimes the sixth graders take notes on the lessons they prepare and evaluate their teaching, thus developing more reading and writing skills.

When it is impossible to arrange for children to go from one classroom to another, pen pal letters can support the development of the first language. A series of letters between Elena, a first grader, and Carolina, a college student, show that writing in a student's first language encourages real communication. In Chapter Five we discussed one of these letters (see Figure 5–2). In another letter Carolina asked Elena, "¿Qué vas a hacer para el día de San Valentín? ¿Van a tener una fiesta en tu salón de clase?" ("What are you going to do on Valentine's Day?" "Are you going to have a party in your classroom?") Elena's next letter responded directly to Carolina's questions: "Mi ma es tro si ba aser una fiesta en valentin y ba mos a comer pastel y stigurs tu a mi ga Elena" ("Yes, my teacher is going to have a party on Valentine's Day and we are going to eat cake and [have] stickers your friend Elena").

Creative teachers have found ways to support all of their students' first languages and cultures. We have drawn on these experiences to develop a list of "Seven Strategies for Supporting Students' Primary Languages and Cultures":

1. Ensure that environmental print reflects students' first languages.
2. Supply school and classroom libraries with books, magazines, and other resources in languages in addition to English.
3. Encourage bilingual students to publish books and share their stories in languages other than English.
4. Allow bilingual students to respond in their primary languages to demonstrate comprehension of content taught in English.
5. Have bilingual students read and write with aides, parents, siblings, or other students who speak their first language.
6. Use videotapes produced professionally or by the students to support academic learning and raise self-esteem.
7. Use reading, writing, and research activities to promote students' primary languages and cultures.

does Margaret do this?

Katie and Teresa provide us with two final stories of teachers who speak only English but have employed the principles for success to help their students by validating their first languages and cultures. They recognize that if they wish to teach the whole child and build on the strengths each child brings to school, they cannot ignore the language the child speaks or the culture in which the child has been reared.

In her pre-first classroom, Katie had several Hmong children who spoke little English and were often reluctant to participate. Katie learned a Hmong storyteller was available to come to classes to tell stories in Hmong; so she invited him to come to her class to tell "Three Billy Goats Gruff." Before the storyteller arrived, Katie read several versions of the folktale to her class. When the storyteller arrived, ready to take the Hmong students off to a corner to tell his tale, Katie insisted that he tell the story to the entire class in Hmong. She reasoned that the children knew the story so well that they would be able to follow along. She was right. When the storyteller arrived at the part of the story where the goats cross the bridge, the students shouted in delight at the "Trip trap, trip trap" spoken in Hmong. All the children, no matter what their language background, enjoyed the story.

The storytelling in Hmong was a positive experience for all Katie's students, but her support for her Hmong students' primary language paid added dividends. In the days that followed the storytelling, Va John, a quiet Hmong boy, proved that he could not only learn but also teach. First, Va John wrote and drew in his journal about his favorite story,

"Three Billy Goats Gruff" (see Figure 9–1). Then Va John became a "teacher" of Hmong to his own teacher. Figure 9–2 shows how Va John drew and labeled pictures to demonstrate what he had written. Below the pictures, he wrote in English "theys are mog log wich theys are the thine to me" (These are Hmong language. These are the thing to me.) Katie responded by telling him how much she liked reading his Hmong.

Figure 9–1   *Three Billy Goats Gruff*

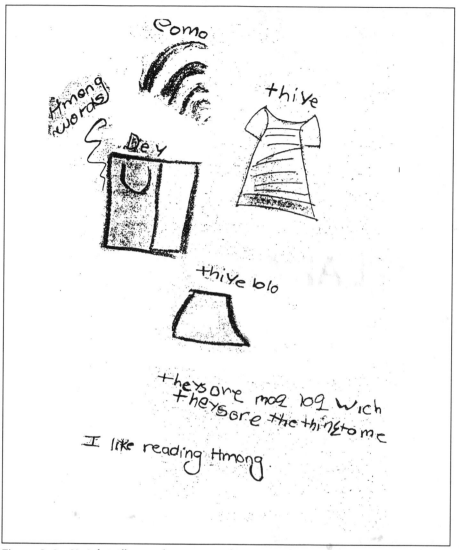

Figure 9–2 *Va John's Illustrated Hmong Words*

Katie reported that from the time of the visit from the Hmong storyteller, Va John showed not only a pride in his first language and culture but also an enthusiasm for school not evident before.

Teresa, a second grade teacher, also found a way to support the first language of her students. After a class discussion on the importance of being bilingual, Navy, a Khmer student, took recess and lunch time for several days to produce a book of letters, numbers, and words that would teach her classmates and the teacher Khmer. Teresa had the book laminated and put it in the class library, where it became a favorite. (See Figure 9–3.)

in love

mothers

nice

good

very good girl

Teacher: Teresa Calderón Parker
2nd grade

9 year old
Khmer lang.

Figure 9–3   *Page from Navy's Book in Khmer*

Neither Katie nor Teresa is a bilingual teacher, and their students are not in bilingual programs, but both teachers have found ways for their students to use their first language as they are acquiring English. Although neither Katie nor Teresa can provide primary language instruction themselves, they understand the importance of celebrating and expanding the language and culture of all of their students. Still, even under these good conditions, Va John and Navy may not be able to develop their first languages fully and may exit school as monolinguals in English. For students like them, the best education would come through a bilingual program that follows the principles for successful practice.

Conclusion

In the previous chapter we gave an example of ways Francisco, a Spanish-speaking bilingual teacher, has found to support his students' first language and, at the same time, help them develop English. Teachers who support their students' bilingualism are using an important principle in their practice. They know that their students are future bilingual citizens who can contribute positively to a world where more bilingual people will be needed in the work force. Perhaps even more important, however, is the fact that English language learners need to develop a positive self-image to share with their own children in the future. Nancy, a teacher of Portuguese descent who did not maintain her first language and culture, writes painfully of her loss. She does not want her Southeast Asian and Hispanic students to feel as she does when they are adults:

> My grandmother went into a coma last week. She came to this country as a young bride and in all the years here, she never became a fluent English speaker. When my parents were in the school environment they were made to feel inferior to their English-speaking peers (They both dropped out early on in high school). These feelings of inferiority are carried with them today. When I entered school, I was encouraged by both the people at school and parents at home to act "more American" and stop using Portuguese (Pride in my culture was likewise discouraged).

> I just came home from the hospital. As I stroked my grandmother's arm and forehead, I spoke to her (I really believe she could hear me), but I spoke to her in a language she doesn't really understand. She might know who was speaking, but she won't ever know what I really wanted to say to her. I don't ever want this situation to happen to my students. Yes, I do want them to become fluent in English and be able to compete with other students academically, but it is imperative to me that they retain pride in their culture and their bilingual abilities.

Nancy's story has been repeated too often in this country. We began our discussion of the sixth principle with an example of a Southeast Asian girl who, like Nancy, has lost her language. We hope to have success for English language learners in schools, but we must not repeat these mistakes of the past. It is important to look at the assumptions we have made about bilingual learners and turn to alternatives based on our best knowledge of current research. Teachers who follow the principles for success, including the principle of developing students' first languages and cultures, offer a chance for all students to achieve academically and to become contributing members of our complex, multilingual, multicultural society.

Faith in the Learner Expands Student Potential

◆

I had a teacher who knew I was in a gang. He would say, "Chola Margie, I can't believe how smart you are." He was one of my favorite teachers for English, creative writing. He really helped motivate me. He totally had faith in me and said, "I know you're going to be a writer one of these days. Your poetry is beautiful." That would make me feel good (Atkin 1996, p. 75).

These words come from Margarita (Margie) Ledezma, a former gang member, who graduated from high school, entered college, and now works in a teen center helping other young people who are or have been in gangs. Her parents immigrated from Mexico to San José, California, and shortly afterwards, Margarita was born. Margie's father returned to Mexico when she was four, leaving her mother to raise her alone. Margie, like many teens, joined a gang because in her words, "If you can't find something at home or if you don't get appreciated, or love, then you get it in the gang, because they give you respect"(p. 72).

Often it only takes one or two people in young people's lives to make a difference for them. Margie was lucky enough to have a teacher who believed in her and trusted her. Margie also found a mentor in a neighborhood youth center, where she took a job after being arrested several times. Margie realized she wanted a real future rather than time in prison, and she found the extra support she needed at that center.

The guy who helps run it, Tony, he used to be in a gang. And he was like a dad 'cause he took care of me. He'd say, Margie, you need to do this and that. He knew I lived around here and these are my people, and I was gonna hang out with them. But he saw in me that I was good in school and that I shouldn't be in a gang (Atkin 1996, p.75).

Margie was fortunate enough to have interested adults who gave her the attention she needed. They helped her develop pride in herself. Rather than rejecting her culture or language, she now wants to maintain it.

> If I have kids, . . . I'd want them to know about their culture and speak Spanish. I think it has more meaning than the English language, like when there's a real strong meaning in Spanish that you can't explain in English (Atkin 1996, p. 78).

Francisco, the bilingual teacher whose unit we shared in Chapter Eight, had different struggles from Margie's when he came to the United States as a teenager speaking almost no English. Teenagers often feel insecure, and those insecurities are stronger when the student worries about being different and speaking a different language. Francisco wrote:

> I remember going to school and feeling like an outcast. I felt like I didn't belong here and that I was taking away something from someone else. I felt the negative attitude that some people have towards people from other countries. Before walking into a classroom, I would pray that the teacher or anyone wouldn't talk to me so I wouldn't have to say anything. I was afraid that I would say something wrong and everyone would laugh at me. Every time I remember those experiences, I feel nervous and insecure.

Francisco, like Margie, found mentors who had faith in him. He was an excellent soccer player, and his high school soccer coach encouraged him to work hard in school and eventually got him a scholarship for college. Once in college, Francisco was overwhelmed by the heavy reading and writing load in English and considered dropping out.

However, the soccer coach helped again. The coach went to his home and talked to Francisco and his mother, encouraging him not to give up on college. Francisco tried another semester. That semester he became friends with a Spanish speaking Anglo who supported him and helped him edit papers. In addition, his bilingual advisor began to take an active interest in him and encouraged him to continue to study hard. By the time he graduated, Francisco had raised his grade point average to the B level required for entry to teacher education.

Many bilingual students never have the opportunities that Margie and Francisco had to work with people who believe in them. Teachers, especially those working in large, inner-city schools, want to support their students, but they may be locked into a teaching system that prevents them from providing that support. Unfortunately, in many of our schools, the full potential of bilingual students is not realized. These students may come to believe that they cannot learn, that their first culture and language are not valuable, and that there is no place for them in American society. This may occur if the curriculum centers on content that is presented part to whole, rather than on students. It may also result from a simplified curriculum that contains little real content. In either case, the message that many English language learners get is that they cannot learn or that there is nothing worthwhile to learn in school. To use Ken Goodman's terms (1991), these students need to "revalue" themselves as learners, and they need to revalue school as a place where important things can be learned.

Often students new to this country drop out of school. Others, like Margie, who do not fit easily into mainstream society take on negative behavior patterns in school or join gangs in desperate attempts to belong. Rather than labeling such students as Limited English Proficient (LEP) or learning disabled, teachers need to help students develop their potential by showing unwavering faith in their ability to succeed, as Margie's teacher and Francisco's coach did. Instead of subjecting these students to standardized tests that confirm they are below the norm, teachers need to become kid watchers and document the amazing progress these students can make. Even when students appear to be confused or seem slow to catch on or respond, teachers need to continue to engage them in meaningful activities; teachers need to keep issuing invitations to be part of a community of learners. We're convinced that if teachers can show students that they can learn and that there are things in school worth learning, there is no limit to their potential.

In the EFL context, students also need extra support. In the first place, some students may not value learning English. In addition, in bilingual schools, students are expected to learn the same academic content as any other student, and they are expected to learn English as well. For some students, the additional requirement of learning English can be overwhelming, especially if the teacher is not sensitive to the difficulties of learning a foreign language. For example, in some cases, native speakers of English, who themselves have not learned a foreign language, may be teaching in a bilingual school. These teachers may not empathize with children trying to learn English and also trying to learn other content areas in English. Parents may not be sympathetic either. In their desire to have their children learn English, they may insist that they work harder, and they may imply that the students are either lazy or not smart enough. For these reasons, EFL students need strong support from teachers and others who demonstrate faith in their potential.

In ESL contexts, ELD or SDAIE teachers often serve the role of mentors or advocates for their students because they recognize the strengths of English language learners. Mary, who teaches ELD classes at the high school level, describes how she helped the mainstream teacher come to value one student:

> When Jorge was in my ELD 4 class, he was a top student. He worked hard on all of his assignments and did a good job. This year I had him put into regular English 12. A few weeks into the school year, I asked the 12th grade English teacher how he was doing. She told me that from what she could see of his performance, he was a student who did not care about school because he did not even try in class.
>
> I expressed my surprise at her evaluation and explained that he had been one of my top students who worked hard on every assignment. The English 12 teacher had a talk with Jorge and asked why he was not doing any work. Jorge explained that he was confused about what was going on because he had entered the class about a week late. He had never received a textbook and was having a hard time sharing with others.
>
> This gave the teacher a whole new perspective on Jorge. She spent time helping him catch up, made sure he got a textbook, and showed more faith in him overall. Because of this, Jorge's performance has begun to improve.

Mary's talk with the English 12 teacher prompted her to take a new look at Jorge. Once she realized that he wasn't clear on the assignments and that he didn't have the textbook, she was able to get him involved in class. Then Jorge began to work up to his potential.

Another good example of how teachers can tap into student potential comes from Jason. One of his Hmong students, Aina, had come to America at age six. At age thirteen, Aina was extremely shy and quiet. "When called on in class, he would not say anything and only shake his head from side to side, the mute 'no'." Jason has his students write an I-Search paper instead of the traditional research report. Students research a topic of their choice and write about it. Jason gives this assignment to all of his students, including his English language learners, because he wants to demonstrate his belief that all his students can succeed. For his I-Search, Aina chose to write about the Hmong New Year. Jason commented:

> When it came time for him to present orally to the class his research, I was surprised when he pulled authentic celebration clothing, complete with intricate sewing, from his backpack. He also pulled a number of hand-drawn pictures of Laos from his backpack. I had expected him to again decline talking in public, and although his English was not perfect, he gave an excellent oral report.

Jason had given students choices in their project, and this allowed Aina to choose a topic that related to his own background and interests. The usually shy student spoke up confidently when describing things he really knew about.

At times, it is not just individual students but whole groups that need to feel a teacher's faith. Connie worked with a class that had been labeled "out of control." Connie recognized that their problem was a lack of self confidence. "The feeling of not being good enough is seen in their actions. In the beginning, many of my students were afraid to take risks. They would give up before they even started. This made it difficult to do group activities because they were afraid to work as a group." As Connie worked with the students to build their confidence, the atmosphere changed. "As the trust grew and they felt more comfortable, this barrier was taken down." The class was no longer "out of control" once they had a teacher who helped them develop confidence in their ability to complete their work successfully. As Connie concluded, "This tells me that beyond the curriculum, building self concept is essential to learning."

In *Lives on the Boundary*, Mike Rose (1989) tells the stories of a number of students who struggled academically, often because they believed the school's negative evaluation of their potential. One of these students, Lilia, came to the Los Angeles area from Mexico. She failed first grade and then was put in classes for slow learners. As Lilia puts it, "I guess there was a pattern where they put me in those really basic classes and then decided I would go through my elementary school years in those classes. I didn't learn to read or write" (p. 39). Fortunately, Lilia's parents were able to break this cycle. They moved to another community where "the schools were good." As Lilia recalls, "The teachers really liked me and I did very well" (p. 39).

Lilia attended a six-week summer program on the UCLA campus after finishing eighth grade. This program, designed for children of migrant workers, opened Lilia's eyes to new possibilities. "I made it my goal to come here." Later Lilia did attend UCLA. The new school her parents enrolled her in and her visit to the college campus had helped her build faith in her own potential. She was supported by teachers who "really liked me."

What is exciting is that Lilia and a number of other freshmen at UCLA, who began in a remedial writing course, were shifted to a special composition course. In this new course, Lilia and the other students tutored low-achievers in Los Angeles area schools and then wrote papers about their tutorial work and about issues of schooling. Lilia and her UCLA classmates are creating a new cycle. They are expanding their own potential and, at the same time, are creating possibilities for success for younger students who have had similar experiences in schools.

Most students are like Lilia or Jorge. They need some extra support to succeed. On occasion, a student has enough self confidence to rise above the negative expectations of the school system. Zilda, now a high school teacher, relates her early experiences:

> While I attended grammar school, I was enrolled in some pull-out ESL classes. As the years progressed, I learned English and was mainstreamed. By the time I graduated [from eighth grade], I had acquired the language. I was at the top of the class, graduating with high honors. Although I had "mastered" the language, I was a very shy, quiet person. When I met with the high school counselor to make my ninth grade schedule, my personality overtook my language ability, thus giving the impression that I wasn't very proficient in English. The result of this conference was devastating. I was placed in the lowest level of English in high school. Once I started school I realized the class was not appropriate for me. Therefore, with much hesitance I went to see my counselor and convinced her to place me in a higher class. The counselor was very hesitant to acknowledge my request. Yet, she made the change. Eventually, I progressed throughout my high school years ending up with AP (Advanced Placement) English my senior year.

Students like Zilda are the exception. Most students need support from a teacher or other mentor to reach their potential. Stories of students have convinced us that of all the seven principles for success, this "faith in the learner" principle is the most critical. When teachers show they believe in their students, the other principles follow naturally. When teachers have faith in the learner, they show students the big picture, not just bits and pieces of information. They understand that students learn when they are engaged in meaningful activities that relate to their own experiences. They realize that all four modes can provide important sources for learning, and it is not necessary to limit learners to one mode at a time. They recognize that during social interaction, students learn from each other, from teachers, and from the community. They know that building on students' strengths, including their first languages and cultures, expands their potential. In short, teachers who show faith in their students organize teaching and learning in ways that are consistent with all the principles for success.

As we work with students who are just entering the teaching profession, we find people who may have doubts about their ability to teach, but they seldom have doubts about students' ability to learn. They start out with faith in the learner and with a strong desire to develop the full potential of every student. Their experiences in schools, though, may dim their enthusiasm and their belief in students. We will look at some of the factors that may lead teachers to question the potential of their English language learners. First, we consider how the attitudes toward culturally diverse people can affect instruction. Then we raise some concerns with assessment and evaluation and suggest alternatives for evaluating bilingual students. Next, we discuss the importance of providing solid academic content for all students by teaching language through content. We conclude by describing several teachers whose students have developed faith in themselves. We highlight key features of classrooms and programs that have expanded the potential of bilingual students.

Attitudes Toward English Language Learners

The following journal entry comes from Irene, the only ESL/bilingual teacher in a school where 80 percent of the students are from Hispanic migrant families.

> It has disturbed me greatly to sit in the teachers' lounge and be approached by other teachers with the proposition that I take some of their "below grade level" Hispanic students for reading because they "just don't know how to motivate them." Furthermore, I have actually seen teachers look at their class lists, count the Hispanic, Portuguese, and Hmong surnames and begin to formulate the high, middle, and low reading groups.

The teachers Irene observed may simply be reacting in frustration. Many mainstream teachers have never had courses in language acquisition, cross-cultural education, or methods of teaching a second language. They probably are not sure what to do with their English language learners. They may lack faith in their own ability to teach these students. Or they may simply decide that these students can't learn, so they put them in the low groups. Whatever the case, their attitudes will not help them create classrooms where students develop faith in themselves. We believe that the attitudes expressed in the teachers' lounge toward language minority students are at least partially responsible for the failure of English language learners in many schools.

Crossing the Schoolhouse Border (Olsen 1988), the extensive statewide report from California that includes interviews with immigrant students, immigrant parents, educators, and politicians, brings out beliefs of teachers and concerns of students. A quote from Rosario Anaya, a member of the San Francisco School Board, highlights a key question about working with the state's diversity:

> Immigrant children in our schools enter an educational system that
> is foreign, where the language is incomprehensible, where the faces

of classmates are of many colors, and where parents feel unconnected and frustrated. It is alarming but not surprising that so many fail and drop out of school. While we talk democracy and equal opportunity, in reality many of our students are barely given a chance to get out of the gate. The basic question is not how can we teach these students, but whether we really want to. (Olsen 1988, p. 40)

This idea was brought home to Andrea, a student teacher in high school science, who was taking classes to prepare herself to work with English language learners. In her student teaching experiences, she was shocked at how some teachers responded to immigrant students. At the end of one period, the teacher glanced at the papers students had just turned in and said, "Half of the class doesn't speak English anyway, they don't understand the material so most of these papers will be Fs." In her journal, Andrea reflected:

> How is that for compassion? This example clearly shows some of the negative attitudes that these kids have to endure inside their own school grounds, the place where they are supposed to be protected and encouraged.

It is critical that attitudes toward bilingual students change, so that these students will be given the kind of instruction that will help them to learn. One problematic practice is labeling students. Labels applied to English language learners such as LEP (Limited English Proficient) focus on students' weaknesses and deny the value of what students know and can do in their first language. Labels, established by narrowly designed tests, lump together people who vary considerably from each other and suggest that there is something basically wrong with all of them. "They [labels] deny the notion that diversity is a major quality of American society and suggest that diversity in and of itself is something to be expunged from American classrooms" (Freeman and Goodman 1993).

Sofía, a Hispanic teacher education candidate, wrote of her own painful experiences with the false assumptions conveyed by the school's labeling process:

> In fourth grade, I could not read, write or multiply. My teacher asked my parents to come in for a meeting to discuss my progress. I accompanied my mother so that I could translate into Spanish for her. My teacher told my mother that I was a very slow learner and that perhaps I needed professional help. She suggested several tests so that I may be transferred to a "special class." My teacher said I was mentally retarded. At that age I understood well what my teacher thought of me. I hated school with a passion. The next year I had a different teacher. He recognized my shyness and insecurity. By the end of fifth grade I discovered that I could multiply, read, dance, and sing.

Often this kind of labeling occurs because a lack of fluency in English is interpreted as lack of understanding. In reality, although Sofía may not have been fully proficient in English, she was an interpreter for her family. Because she understood a great deal about this and other social situations, she was able to bridge the gap between cultures. Sofía's knowledge of her first language and culture was a real strength, but if her fifth grade teacher had not found her strengths and shown his faith in her, she might never have developed the self-confidence that resulted in her becoming a bilingual teacher.

If school psychologists, teachers, and others who evaluate students do not recognize that knowledge of a language other than English is valuable and that acquiring a second language takes time, they may underestimate the potential of bilingual learners (Cummins 1984). School officials often are unaware of how long it takes English language learners, even those from well-educated families, to compete academically with native English speakers (Collier 1989). Susan, a graduate student, took a survey of community attitudes toward bilingualism. She was dismayed at responses such as the one from an administrator who expressed a common view that students need to get to English as quickly as possible:

> They [bilingual students] need to learn to speak English as fast as they can. They should not have to be in a bilingual program for more than three years, at the maximum. Any child having to stay in a bilingual program longer than three probably has some type of learning disability.

Rather than seeing bilingualism as a special ability and valuing both the language and the culture of bilingual students, this educator views bilingualism as a hindrance. This type of attitude leads to the belief that students in bilingual classrooms are remedial. The goal is to mainstream students as quickly as possible into all-English classrooms. Children in countries all over the rest of the world learn two or three languages as a matter of course, but students in the United States who are bilingual are encouraged to suppress their first language in favor of English.

Susan was very disturbed at other responses she got from the survey of her community: "Mexicans are taking over the country as it is now, they don't need any special programs" and "Those Hmongs are taking over the country. We give them houses, welfare, they keep having kids, and then we want to hire Hmong teachers to teach them in Hmong. What kind of programs are these? They just let these people take over the country!"

Although less outspoken, there are also teachers who say it is unfair that they have to work with immigrant students. They insist that ESL pull-out teachers take students out of their classrooms or that they need paraprofessionals and special materials. These teachers claim they have enough problems to deal with already and that having to deal with a diverse student population demands too much of them. They believe they are neglecting their English-speaking students by giving too much attention to students needing special help.

Second language students are aware of the negative attitudes toward languages and cultures other than English, and they struggle to fit into American culture. Immigrant parents encourage their children to "speak English" and to "act American" because they see those goals as keys to success. It is often not until it is too late that their children realize they want to be bilingual and bicultural. Gina, an elementary school teacher, took a required second language acquisition course. After learning about bilingual education and social influences on learning, she wrote the following response:

> I have had a chance to speak to my mother about bilingual education and social attitudes. I was amazed at what I heard. When my mother was in school as a young child, her English was bad, and she was deprived of an education. She was in school but, because of the language barrier, she was not taught content in a way she could understand. So she just got further behind, and it affected her self-image. She did not see herself as a successful student. My mother is very bright, but she was not given the education she deserved so she married young and dropped out of high school. She went to beauty school and found a place there. Her experiences were so negative as a child speaking Spanish that I believe that she chose to only teach English to my brother and me. She did not want us to go through anything remotely similar to her school days. She had assimilated, and we were raised as "Good English-speaking Americans." The result has been that I have had to learn (and I am still learning) a second language in school and by picking up conversations that my mom and grandmother wanted to keep from me. I could have been truly bilingual, and I will never know what my mom could have achieved in her life if she had been valued and educated.

Gina's story clearly demonstrates that when teachers lack faith in their students, they limit their potential. Negative attitudes toward bilingual students are often created and justified by test results. In the next section, we look at the effects of testing on English language learners.

Assessment for English Language Learners

It is extremely difficult for teachers and administrators to change their view of bilingual learners and for bilingual learners to value themselves when they are labeled by inappropriate evaluation instruments. Standardized tests of all kinds tell educators what students cannot do but give very little indication of what they can do. Standardized testing is especially harmful to language minority students. When they are required to take nationally normed exams, they are at a disadvantage because they are competing with native English speakers.

In addition to standardized tests, English language learners take tests to determine their ability to use English. A review of three widely used tests of language proficiency gives an idea of the problems inherent in these instruments.

The Bilingual Syntax Measure (BSM) asks students to look at cartoon pictures and answer questions such as "What's he doing?" Responses are rated for grammatical correctness, based on conversational norms. Students are not expected to produce complete sentences, and pronunciation is not rated. This test is widely used to place students, but since it does not measure the ability to read and write English, it is not a good predictor of academic success.

Two other tests commonly used to measure English proficiency are the Language Assessment Scales (LAS) and the Idea Oral Language Proficiency Test (IPT). The LAS assesses pronunciation, vocabulary, syntax, and pragmatics, or functional language use. The IPT measures the same four areas. These tests include activities such as having students distinguish between minimal pairs (*pot* and *dot*), naming objects in pictures, and having them listen to a (very short) story and then answer questions about it. In the IPT, the questions are arranged in sequential order, and the tester stops as soon as the student reaches a level where he or she can't answer. Thus, for many students, this test is quite short. The LAS and IPT claim to measure both conversational and academic proficiency.

All three tests give only rough measures of what students can do. Generally, tests are first administered when students enter a new school system. The students may be confused. They are often undergoing some degree of culture shock, and they may not understand the purpose of the test. The test tasks they are asked to complete are not meaningful, and students may not see their purpose. Furthermore, these language proficiency tests are fairly expensive, and they are directly tied to specific instructional materials. The tests serve as placement measures for the ESL programs the test makers have also published.

In some schools, limited English proficient students are also tested for literacy development. These tests are used to supplement language proficiency tests. This helps compensate for the emphasis in the language tests on oral language. However, the literacy tests for second language students are the same tests used for native English speakers, so English language learners tend to score low by comparison.

Language proficiency tests such as the BSM, LAS, and IPT are not consistent with the principles for success. They test parts of language; they test language out of context; they have no meaning or function for the students; they are individual and competitive; they fail to draw on background knowledge and strengths of the students; and they are used to label students. The tests don't provide the kind of information that effective teachers need to make decisions about how to integrate English language learners into their classrooms.

Current testing practices may simply serve to reinforce negative impressions of English language learners. However, this is nothing new. In the next section, we put assessment of bilinguals in its historical context.

Bilingualism: A History of Misunderstanding

When teachers believe in the learning potential of all students and see bilingualism as an asset, the curriculum is enriched. Unfortunately, the general assumption has been that students who do not speak English fluently have some kind of learning disability. This is not a new phenomenon. Since the 1800s, immigrants have been labeled as deficient. Early immigrants were given I.Q. tests as they got off the boat at Ellis Island. When they did poorly on those tests, they were often labeled "feeble-minded" (Hakuta 1986). In 1910, Goddard, director of the Vineland School for Feeble-Minded Girls and Boys, gave the Binet intelligence test to thirty adult Jews through an interpreter and assessed twenty-five of them as "feeble-minded." He described the results of that testing:

> What shall we say of the fact that only 45 percent can give sixty words in three minutes, when normal children of eleven years sometimes give 200 words in that time! It is hard to find an explanation except lack of intelligence or lack of vocabulary and such a lack of vocabulary in an adult would probably mean lack of intelligence. How could a person live even fifteen years in any environment without learning hundreds of names of which he could certainly think of sixty in three minutes? (Hakuta 1986, p. 19)

In this and similar experiments, the validity of the tests was never questioned, despite the circumstances under which the tests were administered, the problems of translation, or the improbability of the results.

Over the years, educators opposed to bilingualism have debated whether bilingualism leads to language delay or even retardation and whether learning two languages confuses the child. Flores (1982) identified several kinds of deficits educators and the general public have used to explain the academic failure of Hispanic students in the United States:

1920s—Spanish-speaking children were considered mentally retarded due to language difficulty.

1930s—Bilingualism and its effects upon the reading aspects of language were considered a problem.

1940s—Because of their "language problem," it was thought that Mexican children should be segregated.

1950s—Schools were called upon to make up for deficiencies by providing "a rich and satisfying program."

1960s—The child's home and language were viewed as the primary cause of school failure.

1970s—It was thought that when bilingual children *code switch*, mix their languages, it was an indication that they knew neither well.

1980s—Students not fluent in English are limited. Intolerance of languages other than English mounts.

1990s—"Immigrant bashing" and demands for "English only" instruction increases.

As Brisk (1998) points out, "In the 1980s opposition toward use of languages other than English in education and other services for language minority students swept the country" (p. 10). She points out that growing immigration in the United States in that period caused "xenophobic intolerance." English language learners were officially labeled "Limited English Proficient," giving students and those who worked with them the impression that they were deficient.

The 1980s was a time of concern about the growing number of immigrants coming into the United States. By the 1990s "immigrant bashing" entered the political arena. Politicians could win votes by calling for an end to bilingual education and for limits on instructional support for students who did not speak English. Immigrants have been blamed for unemployment, faltering economies, rising crime and, of course, failed schools.

The United States has long been considered a "melting pot," where the advertised goal to be achieved by all diverse peoples is to blend in and be homogenized into the mainstream. Melting, however, is not easy. Mary Ellen, a graduate student, began reading about attitudes towards immigrants in her classes. When she attended an Italian-American social function, she was seated between her daughter's boyfriend's mother and grandmother who had immigrated to the United States. Mary Ellen asked them about their memories concerning immigrating to America.

Camille, the mother, said she was 12 at the time and could only read and write in Italian, yet she was placed in a regular classroom. I asked her how it went. She said, "Not good. The Americans, you know, are not very nice to newcomers." I was shocked. Her mother, Leonarda, agreed. "It was very, very hard," she said. I really felt bad that our corporate personality exhibits this cruel attitude toward newcomers.

The students who experience the most difficulty are those who stand out physically, who traditionally have been exploited by the Anglo populations in power, and who have formed communities within the larger American society. Those groups include African Americans, Hispanics, and Native Americans (Cummins 1996). In the last ten years, Southeast Asian immigrant students, especially those most recently arrived from refugee camps, have also begun to experience problems because they do not fit into the expected norm.

It is made clear to students, even those who speak little or no English, that it is very important to "melt," that being different is not good. Stories from immigrant students support this perception. An eighth grade Vietnamese girl new to schools in the United States explained how the other students responded to her: "The day I started school all the kids stared at me like I was from a different planet" (Olsen 1988, p. 71). A Chinese immigrant student is much more graphic as she describes her introduction to life in the United States.

Before I came to America I had a beautiful dream about this country. At that time, I didn't know that the first word I learned in this country would be a dirty word. American students always picked on us, frighted us, made fun of us and laughed at our English. They broke our lockers, threw food on us in the cafeteria, said dirty words to us, pushed us on campus. Many times they shouted at me, "Get out of here, you chink, go back to your country" (p. 34).

History shows that adjusting to a new country and a new language is always difficult. When the school atmosphere is negative, immigrant children face special difficulties in building the faith in themselves they need to succeed. In some schools, however, immigrants are welcomed. When teachers view English language learners positively, they expand their students' potential.

Diversity Is Enriching

Embracing Diversity (Olsen and Mullen 1990) is a report that highlights thirty-six teachers who have worked successfully with immigrant students. A key to the success of many of these teachers, according to the report, is an emphasis on international and multicultural studies in the curriculum, which "provides a backdrop for exploration of basic human experience and human rights" (p. 28). As one of the teachers, Amelia Ramirez, explained, "The world is becoming smaller and smaller, and we need to understand each other, or we'll be in big trouble" (p. 29). In Amelia's classroom and the classrooms of the other teachers described in *Embracing Diversity*, this positive approach toward diversity allows students who represent cultures, languages, abilities, ages, or socioeconomic status different from the dominant culture to contribute to a true democratization of American society.

When teachers get to know their immigrant students, they are able to see their incredible accomplishments. In a letter to the editor of our local newspaper, Wayland Jackson, a middle school teacher, shared how much progress the Hmong immigrants in our community have made in ten short years:

> Recently I attended a party at the home of some Hmong friends. As the evening progressed, I recalled the first Hmong party I went to ten years ago. At that time there was only one person present who could speak enough English to explain to me some of the rituals and the customs being observed. I knew that every person in my view was on welfare and would need help for years to enter American society.
>
> At the recent party I reflected that the host had had a job for years as repairman at a large apartment complex and now works on weekends at a second job. The hostess is a substitute custodian for the local school district. Their daughter works for the welfare department and her husband works for the school district translating materials to and from Southeast Asian languages. Her husband's family pooled their resources so that now they also own and operate a small farm. . . . The occasion for the party was to say good-bye to the host's son. He was moving . . . to Wisconsin, where he has been accepted for doctoral studies at the University of Wisconsin . . . when the son was in high school I read his account of his family's escape from Communism. What a change from fleeing for one's life to flying off to a major university for advanced study. I feel privileged to have witnessed this remarkable progress (Jackson 1991).

Mr. Jackson knows what immigrants can do, and in his own middle school class, he has helped his students reflect on their experiences. Each year students publish their writing in books that are used as a reading resource in school and in the community.

Teachers who show faith in their students produce amazing individual results. Rhoda, whose class we described earlier, was concerned about one of her students, Surjit, a Punjabi from India. He was twelve years old with no literacy in his first language. Surjit had only been in the United States for five months and had attended school in this country only the last two months of the previous school year. He was entering Rhoda's classroom having already established a reputation for disturbing classmates and having little potential. The previous teacher had recommended that Surjit be tested for a learning disability.

The first month with Surjit was discouraging. His lack of previous schooling and English kept him from participating. Because he could not understand, he often wandered around the room disturbing the other students as they worked together on projects. Rhoda, however, decided she would not give up. Each time he wandered, she involved him in some kind of activity. She tried to find activities that provided enough nonlinguistic context so that he could participate at least minimally. She set a goal for herself and Surjit: She wanted to get him to participate with other students in their group work by the end of the year.

Because Rhoda stressed the importance of community, the students in her classroom also took responsibility for Surjit. In October, two girls asked if they could be Surjit's ESL teachers during writers' workshop. This was the beginning of Surjit's real integration into the classroom. He was encouraged by his peer teachers and the entire class. By Christmas he was speaking enough English for the students to communicate with him. When he wrote his first coherent story, the whole class applauded. By the end of the year, Surjit participated in a simulation Oregon Trail project and even made a travel brochure for a state report.

Rather than being singled out as a student with learning disabilities, Surjit was viewed by his teacher and his classmates as having learning potential, and he showed incredible growth. Rhoda, in fact, concluded at the end of the year that he not only had potential and could participate and achieve if encouraged, but that he succeeded beyond her wildest dreams: "I think I could have expected even *more* of him!" The most important lesson we can learn as teachers is that our students have unlimited potential and that we must show our faith in them to allow them to reach their potential.

Bilingual teachers face many challenges as they work with immigrant students because bilingual education is "controversial, stigmatized, and complex" (Lemberger 1997, p. 1). In her book, Lemberger inspires readers through her narratives of eight bilingual teachers representing various language and cultural backgrounds who are each unique but who are "all fighters, persistent, with a strong sense of self and of their missions as bilingual teachers"(p. 137). Because these bilingual teachers have such a strong sense of commitment to students and families, and because they have been creative in their approaches to the many problems that confront them, they have been able to help their students succeed, despite the strong negativity that exists against those who do not speak English.

Many classrooms in the United States are not true democracies. Children who are put in the low reading group in first grade are still there when they finish elementary school. However, in the classrooms of teachers who follow principles for success, there is both democracy and the hope of redemption. In these classrooms, teachers look at ethnicity positively. Instead of subscribing to the melting pot image, they see their students as a great patchwork quilt. Each piece of the quilt is unique and adds beauty to the entire effect. The diverse languages and cultures that bilingual students bring to the classroom can provide that beauty in classes where teachers celebrate diversity. Manouchka, the Haitian bilingual teacher featured in Lemberger's book, does a lot of storytelling with her students because it reinforces their language and their cultural identity:

> As I tell a particular story, children excitedly exclaim, "Oh, I remember my grandmother told me the same one!" Sometimes versions of the stories differ across regions, so we explore those differences. I often chart the differences using a Venn diagram. I also use those stories for writing topics . . . That's why the bilingual program is so important. Children learn to appreciate their culture, as they learn English and the American ways (p. 47).

Manouchka supports her students and leads them to success in two languages. Teachers like Manouchka realize that standardized tests as well as tests of language proficiency often can lead to a negative view of their bilingual students. These teachers support their students by finding alternative means of measuring their achievements.

Portfolios: An Alternative to Traditional Assessment

One alternative assessment tool is a portfolio. In the professional world, portfolios are often used: artists gather a variety of their work to display; financial counselors make up a portfolio of information to suggest investments to clients. In schools, portfolios give more complete views of students. Although portfolios are most commonly thought of as a selection of students' writing, they may also contain information about students' reading, science and math projects, social studies reports, and interests outside of school.

Because portfolios contain work done as part of the regular curriculum, they do not take the time from the teaching and learning process that traditional testing does. Instead, they become part of the process itself. A major difference between traditional testing and portfolios is that portfolios involve students in their own evaluation. In portfolio assessments, students can evaluate the products of their classroom work with their teachers and set immediate goals for further study.

Portfolio assessment can provide school administrators, teachers, and students with a new view of achievement. Since portfolios contain information over a period of time, a more complete picture of student capabilities emerges. Those involved with bilingual students know that these students learn much more than standardized tests show. Their learning is often phenomenal; yet teachers, administrators, and students become discouraged when this is not reflected by traditional tests. In addition, whereas standardized tests are usually in English, portfolios can contain work students do in their first language as well as in English. For example, writing samples of non-English-speaking students at the beginning of the year show their ability to express themselves in their first language. As the year progresses, a selection of writing in both English and in their first language shows how their ability to express themselves in both languages develops.

A helpful resource for teachers wishing to implement portfolio assessment is the California Learning Record (1995, 1994). Two handbooks have been developed, one for K-6 teachers and another for middle and high school teachers. The handbooks contain observation scales and forms for recording student progress in the areas of reading, writing, speaking, and listening. The California Learning Record was modeled on the Primary Language Record (Barrs 1990), a handbook for elementary teachers in England (where "primary" refers to elementary students, not to their first language).

The California handbook includes forms for recording interviews with parents and students. The first interview is held in the fall, when teachers fill out a short set of forms that indicate students' strengths, needs, and interests as well as their proficiencies in the languages they speak. A longer form, completed at mid-year, summarizes student progress to date and also sets out plans for working with the student for the rest of the year. A third set of forms is filled out near the end of the year. This summary assessment is passed on to the student's next teacher.

The California Learning Record is available in both English and Spanish. The observation scales and other forms are helpful for teachers wishing to evaluate their students' progress in developing their speaking, listening, reading, and writing skills in one or more languages. The handbooks are valuable for any teacher who is willing to use a portfolio approach to take a thoughtful and critical look at assessment.

Portfolios in Dos Palos

In Dos Palos, California, teachers worked for two years on developing a system of portfolio assessment (Freeman and Freeman 1991). They studied language development and then created their own model for portfolio assessment. These teachers collected writing samples, conducted interviews, and recorded observations of bilingual students.

In addition, the teachers in Dos Palos decided they might find out more about their students if they listened to the parents during the parent-teacher interview, rather than telling the parents about their own child. Although there was some concern that bilingual parents might not want to or be able to answer, the teachers decided to give the interview a try. They devised a simple, short list of questions including the following:

What does your child like to read at home?

What does your child write at home?

Whom does your child read and write with?

What does your child like to do at home?

What does he/she like to play with?

How does he/she spend a lot of time?

The results of the interviews were exciting. The teachers could not believe how much more they enjoyed the parent-teacher conference time and how much they had learned about their students. The enthusiasm of the parents moved the teachers and helped them understand the parents' commitment to their children. The interviews were so successful that the teachers continued them in the second parent-teacher conference, altering the questions only slightly to further probe the same areas:

What has your child read at home since our last conference?

What has your child written at home?

Does your child read and write more this year?

Whom does your child read and write with?

What does your child like to do at home?

What does he/she like to play with?

How does he/she spend a lot of time?

Have any of these changed this year?

For the portfolios, the teachers collected writing samples, tape recordings, and lists of books the students read. They created and revised Spanish/English writing and observation checksheets. Using portfolios helped these teachers see their bilingual students' strengths and growth and also informed their teaching by showing them the kinds of activities that were most effective with their bilingual learners. At the end of the 1991 school year, Linda, a first grade teacher, gave the following recommendation in the summary of her case study on seven-year-old Francisco:

Francisco is the type of child that it would be easy to overlook. It is important that Francisco be encouraged to continue writing and reading and that his work be praised. Because of observations of his responses to different activities, it is recommended that he be looked at seriously for a bilingual placement next year. Strong support in his first language would give Frankie the support he needs to progress even more quickly in English.

Portfolios made a difference in how Dos Palos teachers viewed their students, especially their English language learners. In going through the portfolios, Linda and the other teachers involved in the portfolio project found that they had more complete information on their students than they had had in the past, using report cards and standardized test scores. They felt confident about making recommendations and were amazed at how much they had learned about their own teaching.

Portfolio assessment is a valuable tool for all students but especially for bilingual students. The following guidelines for portfolios for English language learners might be helpful to teachers considering portfolio assessment.

Portfolio Assessment for English Language Learners

1. *What is a portfolio?* A portfolio is a box, folder, or other container with various kinds of information that has been gathered over time about one student. Some teachers have worked with students to create multimedia, electronic portfolios on CD-ROMs. This approach opens up exciting possibilities and also overcomes some of the storage problems associated with traditional portfolios.

2. *What goes into a portfolio?* Items for portfolios should be carefully selected, not just randomly collected. A portfolio is most commonly considered a selection of students' formal and informal writing. However, portfolios might also contain photographs or audio or videotaped recordings of students' projects, including science and math projects, art projects, programs from music and drama events, or social studies reports. In addition, teacher/parent observation notes, lists of books read with dates and notes, and lists of activities the students are involved in outside of school can be included. For second language students, samples are selected in the students' first as well as second languages.

3. *Who is a portfolio for?* A portfolio is for teachers, all support personnel who work with the students, the students themselves, parents, and administrators.

4. *Why is portfolio assessment important for second language students?* Research shows that it takes four to nine years for second language

learners to achieve on a par with native speakers of English when growth is measured by norm-referenced standardized tests (Collier 1989). However, bilingual students learn much more than standardized tests show. Portfolios provide examples of students' abilities and growth over time in their first language, as well as their second language.

5. *Who decides what goes into a portfolio?* Students, their parents, and all teachers working with the students make choices.

6. *How often do things get put into a portfolio?* This varies, but at least once a month. Some teachers and students put things into a portfolio weekly and then, at the end of each month, choose things to be left in.

7. *What does a portfolio show teachers and administrators?* It shows student growth over time, student interests, student strengths in the first as well as second language, and the effectiveness of the present curriculum for the student.

8. *What does a portfolio show students?* It shows them what they have learned, what they spend time and energy on, and what they need to work on more.

9. *What does a portfolio show parents?* It shows parents what their children are learning, what they are doing in school, what kinds of activities are valued in school, and what kinds of activities parents can do at home to support learning.

10. *What are the advantages of a portfolio over other types of evaluation?* Portfolios involve students and allow them to both show and see progress over time. Instead of highlighting what students cannot do, portfolios allow students to show what they can do without time restraints. Portfolios enable students to evaluate what they have learned, to set goals for future learning, and to monitor their progress toward their own goals.

Portfolio assessment has benefits for everyone. In Dos Palos, for example, portfolios helped the teachers see their bilingual students' strengths and growth and also helped them to improve their teaching by revealing the activities most effective with their English language learners.

Portfolio assessment not only informs teachers about their students, but also helps them as they plan curriculum. In their research, Garcia and colleagues (1994) gave two different groups of teachers information about students they did not know. To the first group, the researchers gave traditional assessment information, including standardized test scores, the results of the BSM, a writing assessment, a report on a reading conference, and anecdotal records from the previous teacher. To the second group of teachers, the researchers gave all the materials just mentioned as well as each student's portfolio. The portfolios included a miscue analysis of oral reading, story retellings, entries from a personal reading journal, and interactive written journals. The results showed how important portfolio assessment can be.

Teachers receiving the portfolio data were able to design specific instructional strategies for the students: strategies that, in fact, matched the plans made by the teachers of these students who had worked with them for a year. Teachers receiving only the traditional assessment data requested additional information and were unable to recommend specific instructional plans (p. 431).

Portfolio assessment can help both teachers and students decide which classroom activities are worthwhile and lead to both language development and academic development. In classes where teachers apply the principles for success and teach language through academic content, there are many items to put in a portfolio. As they reflect on their portfolios, students develop greater faith in themselves. The portfolios show the world what these students can do.

Applying Principles of Success for English Learners

In the following sections, we provide additional examples of teachers applying the principles for success and showing faith in their English language learners.

Rhoda

Rhoda, the fifth grade teacher who worked successfully with Surjit, taught in a school with a majority of students from Hispanic and Punjabi backgrounds. She was sensitive to the needs of her English language learners as she planned her curriculum. Of her twenty-six students, only eight were native English speakers. Ten of her Hispanic and Punjabi students were labeled as Limited or Non-English Proficient, and four others were considered to have learning disabilities. Rhoda knew she would need to involve all of her students in meaningful activities to help them understand academic subjects and learn English at the same time. Rhoda understood the principles for success, and she used specific techniques to make academic content comprehensible.

The social studies content for fifth grade is U.S. history. In order to give meaning to the many isolated facts presented in the U. S. history textbook, Rhoda reasoned that her students needed to understand the big picture first. To teach from whole to part, Rhoda organized the year around big questions. She knew that theme study would be especially helpful to her English language learners, because there would be a natural repetition of vocabulary as concepts developed. Rhoda proposed projects centered on different themes, including the people of the United States, the geography, and historical incidents.

The class began the year by reading and discussing literature about different Native American groups across the United States and Canada, such as *Annie and the Old One* (Miles 1971), *The Sign of the Beaver* (Speare 1983), I *Heard the Owl Call My Name* (Craven 1973), *Ishi: Last of His Tribe* (Kroeber 1964),*Between Earth and Sky* (Bruchac 1996), *The Windigo's Return* (Wood 1996), *Old Turtle* (Wood 1992), and *Calico Captive* (Speare 1957). This led to comparing and contrasting the lifestyles of the different Native American groups, including discovering how the geography of where they lived influenced how they lived. Figure 10–1 lists the books Rhoda used.

Another major topic during the year was slavery. Again students read literature books, including the stories of famous slaves. Then the class followed the escape route of one slave from Louisiana to Canada. A final major project was an Oregon Trail simulation, in which groups of students formed wagon trains, took on pioneer personalities, and solved problems as they moved across the United States. Students planned the supplies they needed, calculated costs, and wrote about and discussed their feelings as they encountered simulated obstacles similar to those that the original pioneers had faced.

Throughout the year, students worked collaboratively as they read, wrote, and discussed. Groups produced reports for each major project. For the first project, students drew a web, or semantic map, that included the different ideas they had developed about Native Americans and the effects of the environment on their life-styles. In the second

Bruchac, J. 1996. *Between Earth and Sky*. San Diego: Harcourt Brace & Company.

Craven, L. 1973. I *Heard the Owl Call My Name*. New York: Dell.

Kroeber, T. 1964. *Ishi: Last of his Tribe*. New York: Bantam.

Miles, M. 1971. *Annie and the Old One*. Boston, MA: Joy Street Books.

Speare, E. 1957. *Calico Captive*. New York: Dell.

Speare, E. G. 1983. *The Sign of the Beaver*. New York: Dell.

Wood, D. 1992. *Old Turtle*. Duluth: Pfeifer-Hamilton.

Wood, D. 1996. *The Windigo's return*. New York: Simon & Schuster.

Figure 10–1   *Rhoda's Native American Bibliography*

major report of the year, Rhoda encouraged students to create a table of contents for their reports on slavery and to divide their work into chapters. The final report centered on one of the states in the United States. The students chose a state and were encouraged to organize their report by themselves in any way they wished. Many of the reports contained not only a table of contents and chapters but also a bibliography. Students who felt less confident about their command of English made travel brochures. Rhoda was pleased and excited about the development of content and language that these reports revealed.

Rhoda taught language through content. Students focused on one topic at a time. They read and discussed works of fiction that helped provide context for the nonfiction textbook. Their projects were done in heterogeneous, collaborative groups. Rhoda used many visuals and engaged students in hands-on activities. Because of the community spirit that Rhoda created, students less fluent in English were supported by peers in both their first and second languages. Rhoda had high expectations for her students and showed them that she had faith that they could and would learn the content. By the end of the year, all the students in Rhoda's class were proud that they had learned so much about U.S. history. They felt good about themselves as learners. Rhoda's faith in her students helped them develop their potential and develop faith in themselves.

Rhoda is an exceptional teacher, but she is not really an exception. As we have worked with teachers, we have become increasingly aware of how many of them expand the potential of their bilingual students by showing faith in their abilities and engaging them in learning meaningful content.

Michael

Michael, a high school and community college English teacher who works with many English language learners, recently shared how his growing understanding of principles for success is affecting the way he views curriculum:

> As I am growing more and more into the understanding of [the principles], I am better able to see methods I can easily apply to my high school English classes at all levels and with much interest and enthusiasm gained. This coming fall, with both Honors English and English Proficiency, the high and the low, I have great plans. For one thing, I plan on taking similar attitudes with both classes—that all of my students can learn equally well if given the chance (faith in the learner) and that all of my students can accomplish critical tasks which ask them to think on their own. I would especially like to begin with both an autobiographical collection of student writings and

a newsletter. I have also made plans with another teacher to team-teach units that incorporate local history with student writing, very much like the Foxfire series (Wigginton 1985), but with the addition of audiovisual documentaries done by the students about their families. I thought it would be a great idea to videotape interviews my students have with the elders of their rural community, many of whom are Mexican immigrants who contain within them ancient stories and folklore which would be wonderful to save both in writing and on tape.

Michael is applying all of the principles of successful practice as he plans for next year, but, most of all, Michael has faith in his students. Instead of limiting what he would plan for students in the "low" group, he is offering the same rich curriculum to all his students, because he has faith in their potential.

Catherine

Catherine is an EFL teacher in Venezuela who works with a variety of students from the community and the university in the university English extension program. She had already worked as an EFL teacher for some years when she was introduced to the idea of teaching language through content, giving students choices, making curriculum student-centered and meaningful, using all four modes, and believing in all students, despite varied backgrounds and experiences.

Catherine realized that there were several obstacles to overcome to successfully reach her EFL students. In the first place, there were teenagers, university students, and college professors in her class. In addition, her students were taking her class for different reasons. Some needed to fulfill English requirements, a few wanted to read and comprehend English textbooks, and still others wished to communicate with English speakers as they traveled abroad. Her students were used to learning English traditionally and expected her to teach grammar and vocabulary. The designated textbook consisted of grammar and vocabulary exercises based on notions and functions that were not necessarily related to student needs or interests.

Since the textbook was her students' only resource, and Catherine knew her students would feel they needed to use it, she always began with the book and the functions and notions featured in each lesson. However, she involved students in investigations, reports, and presentations to extend their use of English while they learned more about different topics.

For example, when a lesson centered on finding travel information, Catherine brought in some travel brochures from different parts of the world. Students got into groups according to the countries they were interested in and planned a trip to that country. The students used a variety of resources: interviews with local community people, magazines in Spanish and English, videos, encyclopedias, textbooks, and travel agencies. They drew maps and made brochures, wrote out itineraries, and gave presentations to the class, all in English. Catherine's classes at the university soon became the first to fill up, and she became one of the most popular teachers. Her students told everyone how much English they were learning and how much they enjoyed studying English!

Conclusion

As we have worked with teachers in our graduate classes and visited classrooms in schools in the United States and abroad, we have become even more convinced of the importance of the faith in the learner principle for teaching all students, especially English language learners. It has become clear to us that when educators have faith in their students, they are more likely to apply the other principles. Teachers who have faith that their students can and will learn more naturally start with the whole, rather than feed students small parts. They organize curriculum around big questions and teach language through content. They develop learner-centered lessons, drawing on the interests and needs of their students, rather than imposing their own agenda.

They ensure that classroom activities are meaningful to students and serve some purpose in the students' lives rather than teaching solely to meet school, district, state, or country curriculum mandates. In these classrooms, one hears the productive buzz of students interacting in groups. These teachers provide opportunities for students to express themselves through reading, writing, drama, art, music, dance, exercise, and other mediums, rather than insisting that students master oral language first. They find ways to provide primary language support, because they understand that bilingual students learn more English when they can first develop concepts in their native language, rather than accepting the commonsense assumption that "more English equals more English." They have faith in the infinite possibilities of all students rather than holding a limiting view of their students' potential.

These teachers organize collaboration at their school sites as they encourage their colleagues to read and talk about the latest research and share personal writing with one another. They are excellent teachers in their own classrooms, and they are willing to extend their efforts beyond their classrooms to the school community. Their goal is to create a positive atmosphere where there are high expectations for all students, and particularly for English language learners.

Epilogue

◆

Elaine—Putting All Seven Principles into Action

Elaine is an outstanding teacher working in a multilingual, multicultural classroom. She understands all the principles we have described in this book and applies them daily. Elaine puts all seven principles into action. She is one of many outstanding teachers we have had the opportunity to work with, and when we evaluate her activities using the Principles for Success Checklist, we can answer an emphatic "yes" to each question.

Elaine, an inner city fourth grade teacher, has Hispanic, Hmong, Cambodian, Laotian, and African American students. The students were, for the most part, born in this country and many have little understanding of or appreciation for their own roots or those of their classmates. The different groups of students in Elaine's classroom do not always appreciate each other or value one another's cultures, and some of their older brothers and sisters are members of rival ethnic gangs. Elaine wants to help her students value their own culture and the cultures of their classmates. To achieve this she and her students begin the year with a unit based on the big question, "Who am I and what are my roots?"

Elaine believes that building a strong classroom community is critical, and her students can only do this if they have a strong sense of themselves and respect for each other. Early in the year, Elaine uses several different strategies to build community. During the first week of school, students are asked to do a heritage investigation. They interview family members to find out about their own birthplace and those of their ancestors. Then the students find these locations on a map. They put a card with their name on the map and connect their name to their birthplace with one color of yarn and to their ancestors' birthplace with another color yarn. When the entire class has finished, they have created a colorful representation of the multiple origins of their class (see Figure E–1). Elaine believes this activity validates each child's cultural heritage, provides opportunities for parents to communicate with their children

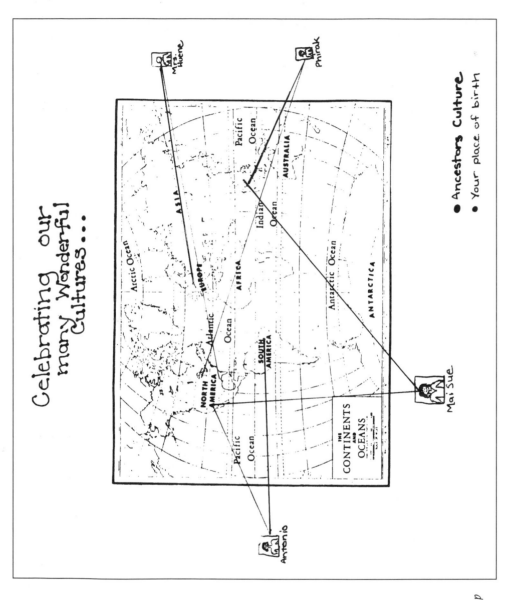

Figure E–1
Elaine's heritage map

about their family history, ignites students' curiosity about their own cultural heritage and that of their classmates, and visibly shows students that together they have a rich cultural heritage.

Another strategy Elaine developed to encourage students to think about who they are is a culture share. For this activity students bring something from home that represents their culture. It could be an object, a picture, a piece of clothing, a recipe, or a piece of writing. Before and after students choose their own item to share, Elaine reads stories which tell of objects like those the students might bring to class or talk about. She reads books such as *The Whispering Cloth* (Shea 1995) the story of a young Hmong girl learning to make a Hmong story cloth, *Angel Child, Dragon Child*, (Surat 1983) which tells of a Vietnamese child who keeps her mother's picture in a match box so as not to forget her, or *Saturday Sancocho* (Torres 1995), the tale of a girl and her grandmother bargaining to get the ingredients for a delicious chicken soup, *sancocho*. Reading these books helps students think about the importance of cultural objects in their own lives.

Students share the objects they bring to school in small groups and, if they are willing, with the whole class. Elaine found that this activity validates students' cultures, communicates the teacher's acceptance and celebration of multiculturalism to parents and students, and provides a casual environment which encourages oral language development.

These early activities lead to reading many pieces of literature that feature immigrants and celebrate cultural diversity. Some of Elaine's favorites include, *Talking Walls* (Knight 1992), *Who Belongs Here?*(Knight 1993), *Grandfather's Journey* (Say 1993), *Amelia's Road* (Altman 1993), and *My Name is María Isabel* (Ada 1993). Because students have already seen the importance of appreciating the diversity in their classroom, they welcome these stories and eagerly discuss them and write about them, relating them to their own experiences.

Elaine also encourages her students to study their own cultures. One activity is making cultural alphabet books. Students are divided into groups by their primary culture. In Elaine's class, this includes a Hmong group, a Cambodian group, and an African-American group. Each group works with a paraprofessional from the same cultural background. In their groups, students brainstorm the things from their culture whose English names start with each letter of the alphabet. The Hmong group, for example, chose objects (A is for apron), places (L is for Laos), activities (D is for dance), characteristics (I is for invite because Hmong people always invite others to their homes), and even family names (V is for Vang). Each page is carefully written and illustrated. The pages are bound, and the book for each culture is put into the class library.

These alphabet culture books are very popular. Students constantly check them out. As they read them, they realize that the various cultural groups have many things in common. Figures E-2, E-3, and E-4 show pages from the Hmong, Cambodian, and African-American culture books.

Besides supporting the cultures of her students, Elaine has found a way to develop literacy in their first languages even when few resources are available. First, Elaine reads to her students predictable books in English with fairly limited texts. She chooses books that were students' favorites when they were younger, stories such as *The Very Hungry Caterpillar* (Carl 1969) or *Ten, Nine, Eight* (Bang 1993).

Next, primary language tutors translate the texts of these stories into Khmer, Hmong, and Spanish and write or type the text for each page on blank sheets of paper. Then, after a discussion of how text and illustrations should match, students work in cross-cultural teams to illustrate the books. Students often have to go back to the familiar English stories to be sure they understand the text for each page. Even the native speakers of each language may have trouble reading stories in those languages, and one of Elaine's goals is to move them toward primary language literacy. Once the books are illustrated, they are laminated, bound, and put into the classroom library. Figure E–5 shows a page from *Ten, Nine, Eight* in Hmong and Figure E–6 shows a page from *The Very Hun-*

Figure E–2 H *is for house*

Figure E–3   D *is for Dance*

A is for Africa

African American people come from Africa.

Figure E–4   A *is for Africa*

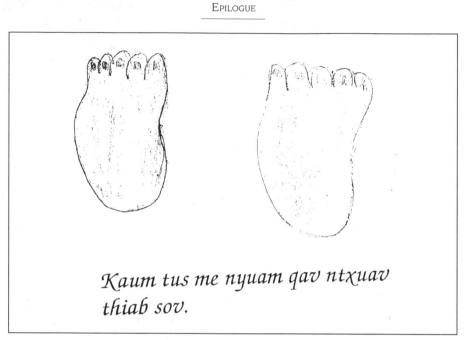

Kaum tus me nyuam qav ntxuav thiab sov.

Figure E–5   *Page from* Ten, Nine, Eight *in Hmong*

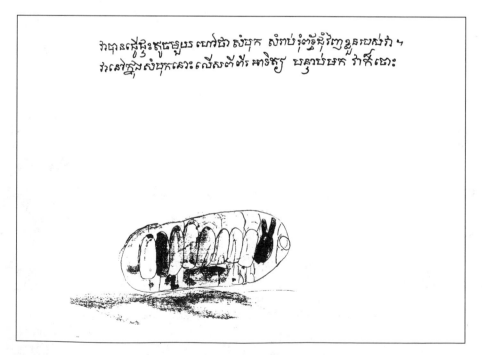

Figure E–6   *Page from* The Very Hungry Caterpillar

Ada, Alma Flor. 1993. *My Name is María Isabel*. New York: Atheneum Books.

Altman, Linda Jacobs. 1993. *Amelia's Road*. Ney York: Lee & Low Books Inc.

Bang, Molly. 1993. *Ten, Nine, Eight*. New York: Mulberry Books.

Carl, Eric. 1969. *The Very Hungry Caterpillar*. Clevland: The World Publishing Company.

Knight, Margie. 1992. *Talking Walls*. Gardner, ME: Tilbury House.

————. 1993. *Who Belongs Here? An American Story*. Gardiner, Maine: Tilbury House.

Say, Allen. 1993. *Grandfather's Journey*. Boston: Houghton Mifflin.

Shea, Pegi. 1995. *The Whispering Cloth: A Refugee's Story*. Honesdale, PA: Boyds Mills Press.

Surat, M.M. 1983. *Angel Child, Dragon Child*. New York: Scholastic, Inc.

Torres, Leyla. 1995. *Saturday Sancocho*. New York: Farrar Straus Giroux.

Figure E–7   *Books from Elaine's Unit*

gry Caterpillar in Khmer. Figure E–7 lists some of the books Elaine used in teaching this unit on "Who am I, and what are my roots?"

Another activity that Elaine organizes for her class is a "Cultural Potluck." These potlucks are designed to help students appreciate each others' cultures through food. Twice a year, students write invitations for their families for this event. The families are asked to bring some food that is representative of their culture to the school. The day before the potluck, primary language tutors call home to remind the family about the potluck and to answer any questions. Meanwhile, students discuss what is polite to do if you do not like something from another culture. Elaine explains that she will bring soup and pickled okra, something that not everyone will like. Everyone is encouraged to at least try a little of everything. If they do not like something, they should just leave the rest on their plates without saying anything.

The day of the potluck, parents bring food to the classroom around lunch time. The cafeteria provides drinks, plates, silverware, and napkins. Parents and children organize the food on tables according to culture and make signs that name each dish. Students describe the food their parents bring and the ingredients. Discussion of similarities always takes place. After the meal, students perform cultural dances and sing. Elaine found that these student performances, which celebrate yet another aspect of the cultures represented in her classroom, help ensure that parents will not just bring in their food and leave quickly.

Elaine always uses these experiences to promote student writing. The following day, the students write their response to the potluck. Figure E–8 shows a writing sample in which the student raises an interest-

Our (cultural) pot luck
For our pot luck on Friday I
brought eggroll that my mom
made. My mom put in meat, carrot,
peas, and some egg to make it
stay. I sure did have fun and
the food tasted very good. I
wish that I know how to
make it to eat every day when
I grow up. I really the food
that Chana brought because
it tasted very good. the food that
every body brought was also good.
I wonder why do Hmong people
food are almost the same as
Cambodia culter. I really have
fun and I wonder when will
we gonna have a pot luck again
lick this. I wish we could have
more of Mrs Huene and Miss Martens
soup and that theng that Mrs Huene
brought and I forgot what it
call

Figure E–8   *Cultural Pot Luck Writing Response*

ing question, "I wonder why do Hmong people food are almost the same as Cambodia culture?" Later, Elaine can discuss with the class how foods are similar or different across cultures. This student also comments that she wishes "that I know how to make it to eat everyday when I grow up." She is starting to be aware of the importance of retaining some of her heritage, one goal of an activity like this.

If Elaine evaluated these lessons using the "Principles for Success Checklist", she could answer "yes" to all seven questions. She organized activities around an important question, "Who am I, and what are my roots?" Every activity drew upon the students' backgrounds and provided them with choices in what they shared. As students collaborated on different projects, it was clear that the content was meaningful for them. They did lots of reading and writing as well as oral sharing. The primary language books helped them value and develop their first languages and cultures. Perhaps most importantly, however, is that students felt good about themselves and could see the results of projects completed successfully.

In her diverse classroom, Elaine has implemented the seven principles for success in ways that both support and challenge her students. She teaches language through meaningful, academic content. As a result, Elaine's students come to see themselves for what they are—creative and competent—ready for citizenship in a multicultural world.

Literature References

◆

Ada, Alma Flor. 1993. *Canción de todos los niños del mundo*. Boston: Houghton Mifflin Company.

———. 1993. *My Name is María Isabel*. New York: Atheneum Books.

Aliki. 1993. "El Celacanto Perdido." In *En aguas profundas*. Boston: Houghton Mifflin.

Almada, Patricia. 1997. *From Father to Son*. Crystal Lake, IL: Rigby.

Altman, Linda Jacobs. 1993. *Amelia's Road*. New York: Lee & Low Books Inc.

———. 1993. *El camino de Amelia*. Translated by Daniel Santacruz. New York: Lee & Low Books.

Atkin, Beth. 1996. *Voices from the Streets*. New York: Little, Brown and Co.

Atkin, S. Beth. 1993. *Voices from the Fields: Children of migrant farmworkers tell their stories*. Boston: Little, Brown and Company.

Avila, Edward, Sharon Duncan, and Celia Navarette. 1987. *Finding Out/Descubrimiento*. Northvale, NJ: Santillana.

Badt, Karin. 1994. *Good Morning, Let's Eat*. Chicago: Children's Press.

Bang, Molly. 1993. *Ten, Nine, Eight*. New York: Mulberry Books.

Berger, Melvin. 1996. *The Mighty Ocean*. New York: Newbridge Communications Inc.

Bracho, Coral. 1993. *Jardín del mar, Reloj de versos*. México, D.F.: CIDCLI.

Brimmer, L.D. 1992. *A Migrant Family*. Minneapolis: Lerner Publications Company.

Bruchac, Joseph. 1996. *Between Earth and Sky*. San Diego: Harcourt Brace & Company.

Buirski, Nancy. 1994. *Earth Angels*. San Francisco: Pomegranate Artbooks.

Carl, Eric. 1969. *The Very Hungry Caterpillar*. Cleveland: The World Publishing Company.

Cheltenham, Elementary School. 1991. *We Are All Alike . . . We Are All Different*. New York: Scholastic.

———. 1994. *Todos somos iguales.. . . Todos somos diferentes*. New York: Scholastic.

Chermayeff, Ivan. 1997a. *Datos pescados, Invitaciones*. Boston: Houghton Mifflin.

———. 1997b. *Fishy Facts, Invitaciones*. Boston: Houghton Mifflin.

Cisneros, Sandra. 1984. *The House on Mango Street*. New York: Vintage Contemporaries.

———. 1991. *Woman Hollering Creek*. New York: Vintage Press.

Coerr, E. 1979. *The Thousand Paper Cranes*. New York: Dell Publishing Company.

Craig, Janet. 1987. *Cómo son los habitantes del mar*. México, D.F.: SITESA.

Craven, L. 1973. *I Heard the Owl Call My Name*. New York: Dell.

Day, Frances Ann. 1997. *Latina and Latino Voices in Literature*. Portsmouth: Heinemann.

DeSaix, Frank. 1991. *The Girl Who Danced with the Dolphins*. New York: Farrar Straus Giroux.

Dooley, Norah. 1991. *Everyone Cooks Rice*. New York: Carolrhoda Books, Inc.

———. 1993. *Todo el mundo cocina arroz*. New York: Scholastic.

Dubovoy, Silvia. 1990. *Poncho, el cangrejo presumido*. México, D.F.: SITESA.

———. 1991. *Turquesita, Colección Barril Sin Fondo*. Amecameca: C.E.L.T.A.

◆

Fernández, Flora (Traductora). 1984. *A la orilla del mar, Biblioteca temática para niños: Coleccion naturaleza.* México, D. F.: Fernández Editores.

Fritz, Jean. 1987. *The Double Life of Pocahontas.* New York: Putnam's Sons.

García-Moliner, Graciela, ed. 1993. *En aguas profundas.* Boston: Houghton Mifflin.

Garland, Peter. 1992. *La orilla del mar.* Crystal Lake, IL: Rigby.

Girón, Nicole. 1993. *El Mar, Celebremos la literatura.* Boston: Houghton Mifflin.

Goldstein, Bobbye S., ed. 1995. *What's on the Menu?* New York: Puffin Book.

Gonzalez-Jensen, Margarita. 1997. *Judge for a Day.* Crystal Lake, IL: Rigby.

Grande Tabor, Nancy María. 1995. *Somos un arco iris: We Are a Rainbow.* Watertown, MA: Charlesbridge Publishing.

Granrows, Alvin. 1986. *La ballena azul.* Lexington, MA: Schoolhouse Press.

Herrera, Juan Felipe. 1995. *Calling the Doves: El canto de las palomas.* Emeryville, CA: Children's Book Press.

Klein, Ann. 1994. Sandwiches From Around the World. *Crayola Kids.*

Knight, Margie. 1992. *Talking Walls.* Gardiner, ME: Tilbury House.

————. 1993. *Who Belongs Here? An American Story.* Gardiner, Maine: Tilbury House.

Kovacs, Deborah. 1987. *A Day Under Water.* New York: Scholastic.

Kroeber, T. 1964. *Ishi: Last of his tribe.* New York: Bantam.

Lauber, Patricia. 1996. "An Octopus is Amazing." In *Treasure.* Boston: Houghton Mifflin.

————. 1997. *El pulpo asombroso, Invitaciones.* Boston: Houghton Mifflin.

Lord, B. Bao. 1984. *In the Year of the Boar and Jackie Robinson.* New York: The Trumpet Club.

McDonald, Megan. 1997. *Is This a House for a Hermit Crab?, Invitaciones.* Boston: Houghton Mifflin.

Miles, M. 1971. *Annie and the Old One.* Boston, MA: Joy Street Books.

Morris, Ann. 1989. *Bread, Bread, Bread.* New York: Mulberry Books.

————. 1989. *Hats, Hats, Hats.* New York: Lothrop, Lee & Shepard Books.

————. 1990. *Loving.* New York: William Morrow.

————. 1992. *Houses and Homes.* New York: Lothrop, Lee and Shepard Books.

————. 1996. *On the Go, Invitations to Literacy.* Boston: Houghton Mifflin.

Nikola-Lisa, W. 1997. *America: My land, your land, our land.* New York: Lee and Low Books.

Orozco, José-Luis. 1994. *De Colores and Other Latin-American Folk Songs for Children.* New York: Dutton Children's Books.

Pascal, Francine. *Sweet Valley High series.* New York: Bantam Books.

Pfister, Marcus. 1994. *El pez arco iris.* New York: Ediciones Norte-Sur.

Prelutsky, Jack. 1996. "Spaghetti! Spaghetti!" In *Celebrate,* edited by J. David Cooper and John J. Pikulski. Boston: Houghton Mifflin.

Revello, Rosina. 1996. "Las canciones de mi isla." In *Observa la naturaleza.* Boston: Houghton Mifflin.

Rotner, Shelley, and Ken Kreisler. 1997. *Faces, Invitations to Literacy.* Boston: Houghton Mifflin.

Rotner, Shelley, and Ken Kreisler. 1997. *Rostros.* Boston: Houghton Mifflin.

Sands, Stella. 1997. "Oceans" New York: Kids Discover.

Say, Allen. 1993. *Grandfather's Journey.* Boston: Houghton Mifflin.

Scholastic News. 1995. "¿Qué paso aquí?" April.

Shea, Pegi. 1995. *The Whispering Cloth: A refugee's story.* Honesdale, PA: Boyds Mills Press.

Sheldon, Dyan. 1993. *El canto de las ballenas.* Translated by Nelson Rivera. Caracas, Venezuela: Ediciones Ekaré.

Simmons, Herrera. *Calling the Doves: El canto de las palomos*.

Soto, Gary. 1990. *Baseball in April and Other Stories*. San Diego: Harcourt Brace Jovanovich.

———. 1992. *Living up the Street*. New York: Dell Publications.

———. 1994. *Crazy Weekend*. New York: Scholastic.

———. 1995. *Chato's Kitchen*. New York: Scholastic.

———. 1996. *Neighborhood Odes*. New York: Harcourt Brace.

Speare, E. 1957. *Calico Captive*. New York: Dell.

Speare, E. G. 1983. *The Sign of the Beaver*. New York: Dell.

Spier, Peter. 1980. *People*. New York, NY: The Trumpet Club.

Staples, Suzanne. 1989. *Shabanu*. New York: Alfred A. Knopf.

———. 1993. *Haveli*. New York: Knopf.

Steinbeck, John. 1967. *The Grapes of Wrath*. New York: Penguin Books.

Stine, R.L. *Goosebumps Series*. New York: Scholastic.

Surat, M.M. 1983. *Angel Child, Dragon Child*. New York: Scholastic, Inc.

Thomas, Jane Resh. 1994. *Lights on the River*. New York: Hyperion Books for Children.

Tillotson, Katherine. 1997. *On Top of Spaghetti*. Boston: Houghton Mifflin.

Torres, Leyla. 1995. *El sancocho del sábado*. New York: Farrar Straus Giroux.

———. 1995. *Saturday Sancocho*. New York: Farrar Straus Giroux.

Tsuchiya, Yukio. 1988. *Faithful Elephants*. Boston: Houghton Mifflin.

Williams, Sherley. 1992. *Working Cotton*. Orlando: Harcourt Brace Jovanovich.

Wilson, Lucy Cruz. 1991. *El mar y la costa*. Edited by Rodolfo Fonseca, *Educación ambiental*. México, D.F.: CONAFE.

Wood, Audrey. 1997. *Quick as a Cricket, Invitaciones*. Boston: Houghton Mifflin.

Wood, Douglas. 1992. *Old Turtle*. Duluth: Pfeifer-Hamilton.

———. 1996. *The Windigo's Return*. New York: Simon & Schuster.

Wylie, Joanne, and David Wylie. 1983. *Un cuento curioso de colores*. New York: Childrens Press.

———. 1985. *Un cuento de peces y sus formas*. New York: Childrens Press.

Zoehfeld, Kathleen Weidner. 1994. *Dolphin's First Day*. New York: Scholastic.

———. 1996. "What Lives in a Shell?" In *Friends*. Boston: Houghton Mifflin.

———. 1997. "¿Qué vive en una concha?" In *Invitaciones*. Boston: Houghton Mifflin.

Professional References

◆

Adamson, H.D. 1993. *Academic Competence: Theory and classroom practice: preparing* ESL *students for content courses.* New York: Longman.

Asher, James. 1977. *Learning Another Language through Actions: The complete teacher's guide.* Los Gatos, CA: Sky Oaks Publications.

Baker, K.A., and A.A. de Kanter. 1981."Effectiveness of Bilingual Education: A review of the literature.": Office of Planning and Budget, U.S. Department of Education.

Barrs, M. 1990. "The Primary Language Record: Reflection of issues in evaluation." *Language Arts* 67, 3: 244–253.

Benedict, Susan, and Lenore Carlisle, eds. 1992. *Beyond Words: Picture books for older readers and writers.* Portsmouth, NH: Heinemann.

Bennett, William. 1985. Paper presented at the press release of address to Association for a Better New York, New York.

Brinton, Donna, and Peter Master, eds. 1997. *New Ways in Content-based Instruction.* Alexandria, Virginia: TESOL.

Brinton, Donna, Marguerite Snow, and Marjorie Wesche. 1989. *Content-Based Second Language Instruction.* Boston: Heinle and Heinle.

Brisk, María. 1988. *Bilingual Education: From compensatory to quality schooling.* Mahwah, NJ: Lawrence Erlbaum Associates.

Brumfit, C.J. 1979. "'Communicative' Language Teaching: An educational perspective." In *The Communicative Approach to Language Teaching,* C. J. Brumfit and K. Johnson, eds. 183–191. Oxford: Oxford University Press.

Bullock, Alan, ed. 1975. "A Language for Life." London: Her Majesty's Stationery Office.

The California Learning Record: Handbook for Teachers 6–12. 1995. San Diego: Center for Language in Learning.

The California Learning Record: Handbook for Teachers K–6. 1994. San Diego: Center for Language in Learning.

Calkins, Lucy. 1994.*The Art of Teaching Writing.* 2nd ed. Portsmouth: Heinemann.

Calkins, L.M. 1991. *Living Between the Lines.* Portsmouth, NH: Heinemann.

Cambourne, Brian and Jan Turbill. 1988. *Coping with Chaos.* Portsmouth, New Hampshire: Heinemann.

Chamot, A., and M. O'Malley. 1989. "The Cognitive Academic Language Learning Approach." In *When They Don't All Speak English: Integrating the ESL student into the regular classroom*, edited by P. Rigg and V. Allen. Urbana, Illinois: NCTE.

Chomsky, Noam. 1965. *Aspects of the Theory of Syntax.* Cambridge, MA: M.I.T. Press.

Chomsky, Noam. 1959. "Review of Verbal Learning." *Language* 35: 26–58.

Christian, D., and A. Whitcher. 1995. *Directory of Two Way Bilingual Programs in the United States*. Santa Cruz, CA: National Center for Research on Cultural Diversity and Second Language Learning.

Clark, Edward. 1988. "The Search for a New Educational Paradigm: Implications of new assumptions about thinking and learning." *Holistic Education Review* 1:1:18–30.

Cochrane, Orin, Donna Cochrane, Sharen Scalena, and Ethel Buchanan. 1984. *Reading, Writing, and Caring*. Winnipeg: Whole Language Consultants Ltd.

Collier, Virginia. 1989. "How long? A Synthesis of Research on Academic Achievement in a Second Language." *TESOL Quarterly* 23, no. 3: 509–532.

Collier, V. 1992. "A Synthesis of Studies Examining Long-term Language-minority Student Data on Academic Achievement." *Bilingual Research Journal* 16:1 & 2: 187–212.

Collier, Virgina P. 1995. "Acquiring a Second Language for School." *Directions in Language and Education* 1:4.

Collier, Virginia P. and Wayne P. Thomas. 1996. "Effectiveness in Bilingual Education." Paper presented at the National Association of Bilingual Education, Orlando, Florida.

Cox, Carole and Paul Boyd-Batstone. 1997. *Crossroads: Literature and language in culturally and linguistically diverse classrooms*. Upper Saddle River, NJ: Merrill.

Crawford, Alan. 1994. "Communicative Approaches to Second Language Acquisition: From oral language development into the core curriculum for L2 literacy." In *Schooling and Language Minority Students: A Theoretical Framework*. C. Leyba, ed. Sacramento: Evaluation, Dissemination and Assessment Center.

Crawford, James. 1989. *Bilingual Education: History, politics, theory and practice*. Trenton, NJ: Crane.

Crawford, James, ed. 1992. *Language Loyalties: A source book on the official English controversy*. Chicago: The University of Chicago Press.

Crawford, James. 1997. "Unz Initiative." http://ourworld. compuserve.com/homepages/jwcrawford/unz.htm.

Cummins, Jim. 1981. "The Role of Primary Language Development in Promoting Educational Success for Language Minority Students." In *Schooling and Language Minority Students: A theoretical framework*, 3–49. Los Angeles: Evaluation, Dissemination and Assessment Center, California State University, Los Angeles.

———. 1984. *Bilingualism and Special Education: Issues in assessment and pedagogy*. Clevedon, England: Multilingual Matters.

———. 1984. "Language Proficiency and Academic Achievement Revisited: A response." In *Language Proficiency and Academic Achievement*. C. Rivera, ed. 71–76. Clevedon, England: Multilingual Matters Ltd.

———. 1989. *Empowering Minority Students*. Sacramento: CABE.

———. 1989. "The Sanitized Curriculum: Educational disempowerment in a nation at risk." In *Richness in Writing: Empowering ESL students*. D. Johnson and D. Roen, eds. 19–38. New York: Longman.

———. 1996. *Negotiating Identities: Education for empowerment in a diverse society*. Ontario, CA: California Association of Bilingual Education.

Cummins, Jim, and Dennis Sayers. 1997. *Brave New Schools: Changing cultural illiteracy through global learning networks*. 2nd edition. New York: Saint Martin's Press.

Danoff, M.V., G.J. Coles, D.H. McLaughlin, and D.J. Reynolds. 1978, 1988. "Evaluation of the Impact of ESEA Title VII Spanish/ English Bilingual Education Program": American Institutes for Research.

Darling-Hammond, Jacqueline Ancess, and Beverly Falk. 1995. "Collaborative Learning and Assessment at International High School." In *Authentic Assessment in Action:*

Studies of schools and students at work, 115–167. New York: Teacher's College Press.

Day, Frances Ann. 1997. *Latina and Latino Voices in Literature.* Portsmouth: Heinemann.

Dewey, John. 1929. *My Pedagogic Creed.* Washington, D.C.: The Progressive Education Association.

Diller, K. 1978. The *Language Teaching Controversy.* Rowley, MA: Newbury House.

Dolson, D., and K Lindholm. 1955. "World Class Education for Children in California: A comparison of the two-way bilingual immersion and European Schools model." In *Multilingualism for All.* T. Skutnabb-Kangas, ed. Lisse: Swets & Zeitlinger.

Doorn, D. 1991. "The Seed Pod Travelers: A literacy exchange program for second language learners." TESOL *Matters* 1, 2 : 2.

Edelsky, C.1986. *Writing in a Bilingual Program: Había una vez.* Norwood, NJ: Ablex.

———. 1989. "Bilingual Children's Writing: Fact and fiction." In *Richness in Writing: Empowering ESL students.* D. Johnson and D. Roen, eds. 165–176. New York: Longman.

Edelsky, Carole, Bess Altwerger, and Barbara Flores. 1991. *Whole Language: What's the difference?* Portsmouth, NH: Heinemann.

Education, California Department of. 1997. "1997 LEP Counts for Top Five Languages." Sacramento: California Department of Education.

Elley, Warwick. 1991. "Acquiring Literacy in a Second Language: The effect of book-based programs." *Language Learning* 41:2; 403–439.

Elley, W., and F. Mangubhai. 1983. "The Impact of Reading on Second Language Learning." *Reading Research Quarterly* 19: 53–67.

Enright, D. Scott & Mary Lou McCloskey. 1988. *Integrating English: Developing English language and literacy in the multilingual classroom.* Reading, MA.: Addison-Wesley Publishing Co.

Fast-Food. 1989. Rosemont, IL: National Dairy Council.

Ferreiro, Emilia, and Anna Teberosky. 1982. *Literacy before Schooling.* Translated by Karen Goodman Castro. Portsmouth, NH: Heinemann.

Flores, Barbara. 1982. "Language Interference or Influence: Toward a theory of Hispanic bilingualism." Unpublished doctoral dissertation, University of Arizona: Tucson, AZ.

Freeman, David E., and Yvonne S. Freeman. 1994. *Between Worlds: Access to second language acquisition.* Portsmouth, NH: Heinemann.

Freeman, David E., Yvonne S. Freeman, and Roseann Gonzalez. 1987. "Success for LEP Students: The Sunnyside immersion program." TESOL *Quarterly* 21:2: 361–367.

Freeman, Yvonne S., and David Freeman. 1989. "Evaluation of Second Language Junior and Senior High School Students in the Whole Language Content Classroom." In The *whole language evaluation book.* K. Goodman, Y. Goodman and W. Hood, eds. 141–151. Portsmouth, NH: Heinemann.

———. 1989. "Bilingual Learners: How our assumptions limit their world." *Holistic Education Review* 2:4: 33–39.

———. 1991. "Doing Social Studies: Whole language lessons to promote social action." *Social Education* 55:1: 29–32, 66.

———. 1991. "Portfolio Assessment: An exciting view of what bilingual children can do." BEOutreach 2:1: 6–7.

———. 1991. "Using Sheltered English to Teach Second Language Learners." *California English* 27:1: 6–7, 26.

———. 1997. *Teaching Reading and Writing in Spanish in the Bilingual Classroom.* Portsmouth, NH: Heinemann.

———.1998. *La enseñanza de la lectura y la escritura en español en el aula bilingüe.* Portsmouth, NH: Heinemann.

Freeman, Yvonne S. and Yetta Goodman. 1993. "Revaluing the Bilingual Learner Through a Literature Reading Program." *Reading and Writing Quarterly: Overcoming learning difficulties.* 9: 163–182.

Freeman, Yvonne S., and Roberta Mason. 1991. "Organizing Units around Powerful Contrasts, Concepts, and Content." In *The Whole Language Catalog.* K. Goodman, L. Bird and Y. Goodman, eds. Santa Rosa, CA: American School Publishers.

Freeman, Yvonne S., and Sam Nofziger. 1991. "WalkuM to RnM 33: Vien Vinidos al cualTo 33." In *Organizing for Whole Language.* K. Goodman, Y. Goodman and W. Hood, eds. 65–83. Portsmouth, NH: Heinemann.

Freire, Paulo. 1970. *Pedagogy of the Oppressed.* Translated by Myra Ramos. New York: Continuum.

Fries, Charles. 1945. *Teaching and Learning English as a Foreign Language.* Ann Arbor: University of Michigan Press.

Fu, Danling. 1995. *"My Trouble is my English": Asian students and the American dream.* Portsmouth, NH: Boynton/Cook.

Gamberg, R., W. Kwak, M. Hutchings, J. Altheim. 1988. *Learning and Loving it: Theme studies in the classroom.* Portsmouth, N.H.: Heinemann.

García, Georgia. 1994. "Assessing the Literacy Development of Second-Language Students: A focus on authentic assessment." In *Kids Come in All Languages: Reading instruction for ESL students.* Spangenberg-Urbschat and R. Pritchard, eds. 180–205. Newark: DE: International Reading Association.

Gardner, Howard. 1984. *Frames of Mind.* New York: Basic Books.

Genesee, F. 1984. "Historical and Theoretical Foundations of Immersion Education." In *Studies on Immersion Education.* D. Dolson, ed. Sacramento: California State Department of Education.

Goodman, Kenneth. 1967. "Reading: A psycholinguistic guessing game." *Journal of the Reading Specialist* May, 126–135.

———. 1986. *What's Whole in Whole Language.* Portsmouth, NH: Heinemann.

———. 1991. "Revaluing Readers and Reading." In *With Promise: Redefining reading and writing for "special" students.* S. Stires, ed. 127–133. Portsmouth, NH: Heinemann.Goodman, Kenneth. 1993. *Phonics Phacts.* Portsmouth, NH: Heinemann Educational Books.

Goodman, Kenneth, and David Freeman. 1993. "What's Simple in Simplified Language?" In *Simplification: Theory and application.* M. L. Tickoo, ed. 69–81. Singapore: SEAMEO Regional Language Center.

Goodman, Kenneth, E. B. Smith, R. Meredith, and Yetta Goodman. 1987. *Language and Thinking in School: A whole language curriculum.* 3rd ed. New York: Richard C. Owen.

Goodman, Kenneth S. 1996. *On Reading.* Portsmouth, NH: Heinemann.

Graves, Donald. 1994. *A Fresh Look at Writing.* Portsmouth, NH: Heinemann.

Graves, D. 1983. *Writing: Teachers and Children at Work.* Portsmouth, NH: Heinemann.

Greene, Jay. 1998. "A Meta-Analysis of the Effectiveness of Bilingual Education." Claremont, CA: Tomas Rivera Policy Institute.

Hakuta, Kenji. 1986. *Mirror of Language: The debate on bilingualism.* New York: Basic Books.

Hakuta, K., and R.M. Diaz. 1985. "The Relationship Between Degree of Bilingualism and Cognitive Ability: A critical discussion and some new longitudinal data." In *Children's language.* K.E. Nelson, ed. Hillsdale, NJ: Erlbaum.

Halliday, M.A.K. 1975. *Learning How to Mean.* London: Edward Arnold..

———. 1977. *Explorations in the Functions of Langauge.* New York: Elsvier North-Holland.

———. 1984. "Three Aspects of Children's Language Development: Learning language, learning through language, and learning about language." In *Oral and Written Lan-*

guage Development Research: Impact on the schools. Y. Goodman, M. Haussler and D. Strickland, eds. Urbana, IL: National Council of Teachers of English.

Harste, J., V. Woodward, and C. Burke. 1984. *Language Stories and Literacy Lessons*. Portsmouth, NH: Heinemann.

Heath, Shirley B. 1983. *Ways with Words: Language, life, and work in communities and classrooms*. Cambridge, England: Cambridge University Press.

Heath, Shirley Brice, and Leslie Mangiola. 1991. *Children of Promise: Literate activity in linguistically and culturally diverse classrooms*. National Education Association: Washington, D.C.

Hernández-Chávez, E. 1984. "The Inadequacy of English Immersion Education as an Educational Approach for Language Minority Students in the United States." In *Studies on Immersion Education*. D. Dolson, ed. 144–183. Sacramento: California State Department of Education

Holt, Daniel, ed. 1993. *Cooperative Learning: A response to linguistic and cultural diversity*. Washington, D.C.: Center for Applied Linguistics.

Howard, K. K. 1990. *Passages: An anthology of the Southeast Asian refugee experience*. Fresno, CA: Southeast Asian Student Services California State University, Fresno.

Hudelson, Sarah. 1984. "Kan yu ret an rayt en ingles: Children become literate in English as a second language." TESOL *Quarterly* 18:2: 221–-237.

————. 1989. *Write On: Children writing in ESL*. Englewood Cliffs, NJ: Prentice Hall Regents.

Hymes, Del. 1970. "On Communicative Competence." In *Directions in Sociolinguistics*, edited by J. Gumperz and D. Hymes, 35–71. New York: Holt, Rinehart and Winston.

Imhoff, G. 1990. "The Position of U.S. English on Bilingual Education." In *Annals of the American academy of political science*. C. Cazden and C. Snow, eds. 48–61. Newbury Park, CA: Sage Publications.

"Interact." 1997. 1825 Gillespie Way #101, El Cajon, CA..

Jackson, Wayland. 1991. *Fresno Bee*, Feb. 4, B 5.

Jones, Bill. 1997. "Jones Announces Circulation of New Initiative." Sacramento.

Kagan, Spencer. 1986. "Cooperative Learning and Sociocultural Factors in Schooling." In *Beyond Language: Social and cultural factors in schooling language minority students*, 231–298. Los Angeles: Evaluation, Dissemination and Assessment Center.

Kolers, P.A. 1973. "Three Stages of Reading." In *Psycholinguistics and Reading*, edited by F. Smith. New York: Holt, Rhinehart, and Winston.

Krashen, Stephen. 1982. *Principles and Practice in Second Language Acquisition*. New York: Pergamon Press.

————. 1985. *Inquiries and Insights*. Haywood, CA: Alemany Press.

————. 1993. *The Power of Reading*. Englewood, CO: Libraries Unlimited.

————. 1996. *Under Attack: The case against bilingual education*. Culver City: Language Education Associates.

Krashen, Stephen, and Tracy Terrell. 1983. *The Natural Approach: Language acquisition in the classroom*. Hayward, CA: Alemany Press.

Krashen, S., and D. Biber. 1988. *On Course: Bilingual education's success in California*. Sacramento, CA: California Association of Bilingual Education.

Kucer, Stephen B., Cecilia Silva and Esther L. Delgado-Larocco. 1995. *Curricular Conversations: Themes in multilingual and monolingual classrooms*. York, ME: Stenhouse.

Labbo, L. and W. Teale. 1990. "Cross-age Reading: A strategy for helping poor readers." *The Reading Teacher* 43: 6: 362–369.

Larsen-Freeman, Diane. 1986. *Techniques and Principles in Language Teaching*. Edited by W. Rutherford. Oxford: Oxford University Press.

Law, Barbara, and Mary Eckes. 1990. *The More than Just Surviving Handbook*. Winnipeg: Peguis.

Lemberger, Nancy. 1997. *Bilingual Education: Teachers' narratives*. Mahwah, NJ: Lawrence Erlbaum Associates.

Lessow-Hurley, Judith. 1996. *The Foundations of Dual Language Instruction*. White Plains, NY: Longman Publishers USA.

Lindfors, Judith. 1987. *Children's Language and Learning*, second edition. Englewood Cliffs, New Jersey: Prentice Hall.

Long, M. and P. Porter. 1985. "Group Work, Interlanguage Talk, and Second Language Acquisition." *TESOL Quarterly* 19:1: 207–228.

Lozanov, G. 1982. "Suggestology and Suggestopedy." In *Innovative Approaches to Language Teaching*, R. Blair. ed. Rowley, MA: Newbury House.

Lucas, I. 1981. "Bilingual Education and the Melting Pot: Getting burned." In *The Illinois Issues Humanities Essays*: 5. Champaigne, IL: Illinois Humanities Council.

Lucas, Tamara, R. Henze and R. Donato. 1990. "Promoting the Success of Latino Language-minority Students: An exploratory study of six high schools." *Harvard Educational Review* 60:3: 315–340.

Manning, Maryann, Gary Manning, and Roberta Long. 1994.*Theme Immersion: Inquiry-based curriculum in elementary and middle schools*. Portsmouth, NH: Heinemann.

McConnell, Francis, ed. 1984.*We Came to America*. Fresno, CA: Fresno County Migrant Education.

McQuillan, Jeff, and Lucy Tse. 1997. "Does Research Matter? An analysis of media opinion of bilingual education, 1984–1994." *Bilingual Research Journal* 20:1: 1–27.

Mills, Heidi, Timothy O'Keefe and Diane Stephens. 1992. *Looking Closely: The role of phonics in one whole language classroom*. Urbana, IL: National Council of Teachers of English.

Miramontes, Ofelia B., Adel Nadeau and Nancy Commins. 1997. *Restructuring Schools for Linguistic Diversity: Linking decision making to effective programs*. D. Strickland and C. Genishi, eds. *Language and Literacy Series*. New York: Teachers College Press..

Morrice, C. and M. Simmons. 1991. "Beyond Reading Buddies: A whole language cross-age program." *The Reading Teacher* 44: 572–577.

Morrissey, M. 1988. "When "shut up!" is a Sign of Growth." In *The Whole Language Evaluation Book*. K. Goodman, Y. Goodman and W. Hood, eds. Portsmouth, NH: Heinemann.

Nelson, Gayle L. 1995. "Cultural Differences in Learning Styles." In *Learning styles in the ESL/EFL Classroom*. Joy M. Reid. New York: Heinle & Heinle Publishers.

Olsen, L., ed. 1988. *Crossing the Schoolhouse Border: Immigrant students and the California public schools*. San Francisco: California Tomorrow.

Olsen, L. and N. Mullen. 1990. *Embracing Diversity: Teacher's voices from California classrooms*. San Francisco: California Tomorrow.

Ovando, C. and Collier, V. 1998. *Bilingual and ESL Classrooms: Teaching in multicultural contexts*, 2nd. ed. New York: McGraw Hill.

Peregoy, Suzanne F., and Owen F. Boyle. 1993. *Reading, Writing, & Learning in ESL*. New York: Longman.

Peterson, Ralph and Mary Ann, eds. 1990. *Grand Conversations*. New York: Scholastic.

Piaget, Jean. 1955. *The Language and Thought of the Child*. New York: Meridian Publishers.

Porter, R. 1990. *Forked Tongue: The politics of bilingual education*. New York: Basic Books.

Ramírez, J. David. 1991. "Final Report: Longitudinal study of structured English immersion strategy, early-exit and late-exit bilingual education programs." U.S. Department of Education.

Richard-Amato, Patricia, and Marguerite Snow, eds. 1992. *The Multicultural Classroom*:

Readings for content area teachers. White Plains, NY: Longman.

Richards, Jack and Theodore Rodgers. 1986. *Approaches and Methods in Language Teaching: A description and analysis.* New York: Cambridge University Press.

Rigg, P. and V. Allen. 1989. "Introduction." In *When They Don't All Speak English.* P. Rigg and V. Allen, eds. vii–xx. Urbana, IL: National Council of Teachers of English.

Rigg, Pat and Sarah Hudelson. 1986. "One Child Doesn't Speak English." *Australian Journal of Reading* 9, no. 3 (1986): 116–125.

Rios, Gabriel. 1997. "Body Language." *The Fresno Bee,* May 22. E6.

Rogers, Carl. 1951. *Client-centered Therapy.* Boston: Houghton Mifflin.

Romijn, E., and C. Seely. 1979. *Live Action English.* San Francisco: Alemany Press.

Rose, M. 1989. *Lives on the Boundary.* New York: Penguin.

Rosenblatt, L. 1978. *The Reader, the Text, the Poem: The transactional theory of the literary work.* Carbondale, IL: Southern Illinois University Press.

Rossell, C. and K. Baker. 1996. "The Educational Effectiveness of Bilingual Education." *Research in the Teaching of English* 30: 7–74.

Samway, Katherine, Gail Whang and Mary Pippitt. 1995. *Buddy Reading: Cross-age tutoring in a multicultural school.* Portsmouth, NH: Heinemann.

Scarcella, Robin. 1990. *Teaching Language Minority Students in the Multicultural Classroom.* Englewood Cliffs, NJ: Prentice Hall Regents.

Scarcella, Robin, and Rebeccah Oxford. 1992. *The Tapestry of Language Learning: The individual in the communicative classroom.* Boston: Heinle & Heinle.

Seely, Contee, and Elizabeth Romijn. 1995. *TPR Is More than Commands: At all levels.* Berkeley, CA: Command Performance Language Institute.

Segal, B. 1983. *Teaching English through Action.* Brea, CA: Berty Segal, Inc.

Short, Kathy, Jerome Harste and Carolyn Burke. 1996. *Creating Classrooms for Authors and Inquirers.* Portsmouth, NH: Heinemann.

Short, K. and K. Pierce, eds. 1990. *Talking about Books: Creating literate communities.* Portsmouth, NH: Heinemann.

Sizer, Theodore. 1990. "Student as Worker, Teacher as Coach." Paper presented at the Viewer's Guide to Teleconference.

Skinner, B.F. 1957. *Verbal Behavior.* New York: Appleton.

Skutnabb-Kangas, Tove. 1983. *Bilingualism or not: The education of minorities.* Clevedon, England: Multilingual Matters.

Smith, F. 1982. *Writing and the Writer.* New York: Holt, Rhinehart, and Winston.

———. 1983. *Essays into Literacy: Selected papers and some afterthoughts.* Portsmouth, NH: Heinemann.

———. 1985. *Reading without Nonsense,* second ed. New York: Teachers College Press.

———. 1990. *To Think.* New York: Teachers College Press.

Snow, Marguerite, and Donna Brinton, eds. 1997. *The Content-Based Classroom: Perspectives on integrating language and content.* White Plains, NY: Longman.

Stevick, E.W. 1976. *Memory, Meaning and Method.* Rowley, MA: Newbury House.

Stryker, Stephen, and Betty Lou Leaver, eds. 1997. *Content-Based Instruction in Foreign Language Education.* Baltimore: Georgetown University Press.

Swain, M. 1985. "Communicative Competence: Some roles of comprehensible output in its development." In *Input in Second Language Acquisition.* S. Gass and C. Madden, eds. 235–253. Rowley, MA: Newbury House.

Swain, M., S. Lapkin, S. Rowen and D. Hart. 1990. "The Role of Mother Tongue Literacy in Third Language Learning." *Language, Culture, and Curriculum* 3: 65–81.

TESOL. 1997. "ESL standards for Pre-K–12 students." Alexandria, VA.

Thomas, Wayne and Virginia Collier. 1997. "School Effectiveness for Language Minority Students." Paper presented at the CABE Conference, San Diego.

Thomas, Wayne P., and Virigina P. Collier. 1995. "Acquiring a Second Language for School." In *Language Minority Student Achievement and Program Effectiveness*. Washington, D.C.: NCBE.

Thomas, Wayne and Virginia Collier. 1995. "Language Minority Student Achievement and Program Effectiveness: Research summary of study in progress." CABE *Newsletter* 17:5: 19, 24.

Trueba, H. and Barnett-Mizrahi, eds. 1979. *Bilingual Multicultural Education and the Professional*. Rowley, MA: Newbury House Publishers.

Urzúa, C. 1990. "Read to Me! Tutoring at its best." Paper presented at the TESOL conference, San Francisco, CA.

Valdés, Guadalupe. 1996. *Con Respeto: Bridging the distances between culturally diverse families and schools*. New York: Teachers College Press.

———. 1997. "Dual-Language Immersion Programs: A cautionary note concerning the education of language-minority students." *Harvard Educational Review* 67:3, 391–429.

Vygotsky, L. 1962. *Thought and Language*. Translated by Eugenia Hanfmann Gertrude Vakar. Cambridge, MA: MIT Press.

———. 1978. *Mind in Society: The development of higher psychological processes*. Cambridge, MA: Harvard University Press.

Wallerstein, Nina. 1987. "Problem Posing Education: Freire's method for transformation." In *Freire for the Classroom*, Ira Shor, ed., 33–44. Portsmouth, NH: Heinemann.

Watson, D., C. Burke and J. Harste. 1989. *Whole Language: Inquiring voices*. New York: Scholastic.

Weaver, Constance. 1996. *Teaching Grammar in Context*. Portsmouth, NH: Boynton/Cook.

———. 1997. *Lessons to Share on Teaching Grammar in Context*. Portsmouth, NH: Heinemann.

Wells, Gordon and Gen Chang-Wells. 1992. *Constructing Knowledge Together*. Portsmouth, NH: Heinemann.

Whitmore, Kathryn F. and Caryl G. Crowel. 1994. *Inventing a Classroom: Life in a bilingual, whole language learning community*. York, Maine: Stenhouse Publishers.

Widdowson, Henry. 1978. *Teaching Language as Communication*. Oxford: Oxford University Press.

Wigginton, E. 1985. *Sometimes a Shining Moment: The foxfire experience*. New York: Doubleday.

Wilde, Sandra. 1989. "Looking at Invented Spelling: A kidwatcher's guide to spelling, part 1 and 2." In *The Whole Language Evaluation Book*, K. Goodman, Goodman, Y., and Hood, W., eds.213–237. Portsmouth, NH: Heinemann.

———. 1992. *You Kan Red This! Spelling and punctuation for whole language classrooms*, K–6. Portsmouth, NH: Heinemann.

Wilkins, D.A. 1976. *Notional Syllabuses*. Oxford: Oxford University Press.

Willis, J.D. 1983. "The Implications of Discourse Analysis for Teaching Oral Communication." Unpublished M.A. thesis, University of Birmingham.

Wink, Joan. 1997. *Critical Pedagogy: Notes from the real world*. Los Angeles: California Association of Bilingual Education.

Young, Margaret. 1997. "School Effectiveness for Language Minority Students." CABE *Newsletter* 20:6: 12–14.

Index